LING

LING

*The Rise, Fall, and Return
of a Texas Titan*

STANLEY H. BROWN

New York   Atheneum   1972

This book is for **Brenda, Hannah,** *and* **Matthew**

Acknowledgments

I HAVE MET and observed, at some time, almost every person in this book. Where I have put exact words into their mouths, I heard them spoken or read them in minutes, notes, or other documents made available to me by many people (though I have at times not identified my sources). If I have misread their motives, that is my own doing.

As for my understanding of the workings of business in general and corporate finance in particular, I am indebted to many people over the years. My former colleagues at *Fortune* magazine—especially Lucie Adam, Evelyn Benjamin, Nancy Bryan Faircloth, Angela Rabbia Haines, Marjorie Jack, Wyndham Robertson, Karin Cocuzzi Tetlow, and Ann Tyler —helped me learn much of what I know about the people, the places, and the financial dynamics that I have dealt with. David S. Brown, a distinguished lawyer who is my brother, endured countless phone calls at odd hours and patiently explained much that had been beyond my understanding.

A lot of people let me get close enough to their business lives to know that the gratifications extend far beyond the bottom line of a financial statement. Two among these many come to mind now: Frank A. Armstrong and Mike Epstein.

In Texas, I received invaluable help and guidance from M. Harvey Earp, Jerry Finger, Malinda Gowan, John W. Johnson, Richard L. Thomas, and the late Leonard Coe

Scruggs among others. Pamela Susskind and Kenneth Laptook worked with me on difficult transcripts, and Mary Ann Brussat and Barbara Dixon performed the indispensable function of producing a readable manuscript.

Many other people may see their influence upon me in this book. I regret the late Robert A. Colborn, a brilliant editor and a remarkable man, will not.

LING

I

THE big Alouette helicopter swept across the arid, steep hills of south central Texas, its own shadow the only trace of men visible to its passengers. Then suddenly the view changed. High on the west bank of the Nueces River stood what might have been a roadside motel or a country club.

At Corpus Christi, where it flows into the sea, the Nueces River once formed what the Mexicans thought was the southern boundary of Texas. But the Texans thought otherwise, so the Nueces is just a river running through south Texas. Upstream it flows through Zavala County not far from Crystal City, the spinach capital of the world, distinguished for its statue of Popeye and its ferocious relations between the Anglo landowners and the Mexican farm laborers. Farther north the river cuts through Uvalde County, burial place of Cactus Jack Garner, pecan farmer, Speaker of the House of Representatives, and thirty-second Vice President of the United States. The river forks west into Kinney and Edwards counties and east up into Real County.

The helicopter passed over this east fork of the Nueces and nestled down on a pad a few yards south of the cluster of low buildings. When the engine stopped and the dust of the pad settled, men in ranch clothes stepped forward from their waiting vehicles to gather up the tagged traveling bags and gun cases and drive the alighting passengers to their quarters. Drive to where? asked one of the passengers, who had noticed how close they already were to the buildings. Let's walk, replied James Joseph Ling. His fellow passengers, for whom walking was a rare activity even when golfing or hunting, clearly would have preferred driving even the thirty yards to their destination. But the decision had been made by the leader; they walked.

On this last day of September, 1969, Ling's empire was troubled, but empires always are. Besides, it was as large and important as it had ever been. And in the mind of Jim Ling, its architect, creator, and ruler, there were plans, projects, deals, hopes to solve everything and send it hurtling onward again. Ling was confident, supremely so, even a little oppressively so in public, and he seemed quite able to manage his small private doubts. After all, there were back-up alternatives for all those plans, projects, and deals that would inevitably, even in the normal course of events, fall through. For the next four days, he would be the model host, guide, moderator, and running commentator on the affairs of his state among the members of his court, his general staff, and his satellites, who would soon assemble around him.

They would represent segments, divisions, subsidiaries of an enterprise that had come out of nowhere a decade before, headed by a man on this day not yet forty-seven years old, and become one of the largest assemblages of business in the world. The term most used for this corporation and others bearing it a superficial resemblance is "conglomerate." And men like Ling are known as "conglomerators." To say that such terms have no meaning is inaccurate; to say that they are imprecise and only serve to make complex people and entities more manageable by shoving them into categories is more to the point. Though they have shared a context, how Ling built his corporation into the fourteenth largest industrial enterprise in the United States, according to the 1969 ranking of the largest 500 compiled by *Fortune* magazine, has little to do with what other so-called conglomerators have done. Why he did it has even less to do with them and more to do with his feelings about such impersonal standards as *Fortune*'s list and the fact that his company's $3,750,264,000 in sales put him ahead of du Pont, Shell, and

Westinghouse. That he was able to get control of—and combine—the sixth largest steel company, the eighth largest airline, the eighth largest defense contractor, the third largest
meat packer, the largest sporting-goods maker, and a string
of other companies in an almost random group of industries
may well be the most significant thing to be said about him.
Or maybe it is the fact that he performed all this from a base
of little education, no connections, no money, no status, no
leverage of any kind, but solely on the strength of what he
discovered and created.

Jim Ling walked fast from the Alouette. The heavy men
with him pumped to keep up. The regulars were used to
the pace, and mostly they loved it. After all, they were moving with the fastest mover on the American business scene.
They strode along the path toward the dormitories, past the
tennis court, the putting green (but no golf course), the
swimming pool, past a sporting-goods shop packed with
equipment from one of their own companies, the top name
in the business, Wilson. Ahead, down a steep dirt road, were
trap- and skeet-shooting ranges surrounded by banks of night
lights, and scattered all over the rough terrain were more
than a score of hunting blinds and towers.

Ling knew this place, the Eagle Ranch, well, even the remote areas reached in bumpy rides over dusty roads. He
knew it well because he and a group of his associates had
owned it until a year before, when they sold it to LTV. The
corporation, according to a proxy statement, had paid them
$1,046,000 in cash and notes, "no more than the price for
which the sellers could have sold the property to a non-
affiliated person." Since the corporation would now maintain
and improve it without depriving its former owners of access
to it (though it would charge them for personal use), the
sale was hardly a sacrifice for them despite Ling's belief that
he and his partners could have got $200,000 more from a
stranger. "The property has been and is expected to be used
by the Company and its subsidiaries for management meetings and business entertainment."

The event the Alouette's passengers were arriving for was

a combination of work and play characteristic of modern business life—the Ling-Temco-Vought Annual Offsite Five-year Planning Meeting. Its very name is an example of the curiously imprecise language that business has lately evolved to talk to itself and the outside world.

Consider first of all the word "offsite." It is not a dictionary word but rather an LTV coinage with a military flavor. Its purpose is to indicate that the meeting takes place not at corporate headquarters in Dallas (too many people for the LTV Communications Center or the board room) or in a nearby hotel ballroom or motel conference room. But if it were called the Eagle Ranch meeting, despite its unquestioned earnest purpose, that might create a somewhat frivolous impression. "Offsite," whatever it fails to convey, certainly sounds more businesslike. "Five-year Planning" unquestionably rings of attention to business. In reality, though, it often turns out to mean nothing at all. Men of LTV who would be describing the results of their operations for the next five years had already made egregious errors in predicting their sales and profits in the very shortest range, the period during which they were attending the meeting, though they had done well in previous years. Long-range forecasting, however hedged, is at best a kind of crap game, though it isn't faithful to any set of odds. Usually it becomes nothing more than a kind of corporate auto-eroticism. If it sometimes works, so do wishing wells. In some corporations, the title "Director of Long-range Planning" has become, whatever its origins and intent, one of those titular placebos granted to otherwise worthy men whose upward mobility has expired.

But the men coming to the LTV offsite meeting had spent a lot of thought, money, sleepless nights, and sweaty palms preparing the figures and the caveats, writing their speeches, designing and producing the slides they would use as illustration, and rehearsing their delivery. Their audience would be their corporate peers and rivals and, more important, their leader.

The first planeload to arrive at the ranch was special as well as early. With Ling were a group of close associates,

personal and business, in varying degrees: Vanda Davidson, M.D., an obstetrician who delivered the children of
Ling's first marriage, bought a big piece of stock in Ling's
first venture into public ownership in 1955, and, since then,
had been a director of every corporation that permuted
out of that first one; Robert McCulloch, who came to America as an immigrant machinist from Scotland in the 1920s,
built a formidable reputation as an aircraft production man
at North American Aviation during World War II, then
founded his own company in Dallas after the war as Texas
Engineering & Manufacturing Company, later known as
Temco, LTV's middle name; Roscoe Haynie, former president of Wilson & Company, one of the Big Four meat
packers, and, since Ling's astounding and brilliant acquisition
of Wilson, an executive of LTV in Dallas and close counselor to Ling; Sanders Campbell, Dallas real-estate developer,
friend, golf buddy, and lately a director of LTV Aerospace
Corporation, one of the offspring of LTV; and Rich Thomas,
vice president and executive assistant to Ling, an amiable and
thoughtful lawyer who preferred the action of running with
the leader to practicing law. They were down a day early to
explore the terrain, play games, and wait while Ling inspected
the facilities to make sure that all was in place, that the
pecking order was respected and the sensibilities of key
guests would not be offended by the quality and rank of
their accommodations. Shortly, another early batch would
arrive, including Clyde Skeen, LTV president, and his aides
and associates.

The Ling party had left the airport adjoining the company's aircraft plant in Grand Prairie, just west of Dallas,
at midday in a corporation jet aircraft 570L, a Falcon, piloted
by Ling himself. The plane, well stocked, according to
executive-aircraft fashion, with liquor and ice, landed at
Kerrville, Texas, the jetport nearest to Eagle Ranch, where
the Alouette was waiting. Ling did not fly the helicopter,
though he was beginning to learn how. Its pilots were members of the LTV Aerospace staff. Only a few of the guests
arrived at the ranch via helicopter. Other routes included
propeller aircraft direct from Dallas to the airstrip on the

ranch, simpler but slower and less comfortable, or, more likely, company jet to Kerrville and a fifty-mile bus trip to the ranch. Nothing was less than first class, but only the polyglot bird metaphor, Falcon to Alouette to Eagle, was deluxe all the way.

Eagle Ranch, once a boys' summer camp, and at another time a private hunting preserve, covers almost exactly ten sections of land. A section is equal to a square mile, and the total area is equal to enough land for forty Homestead Act farms of 160 acres each, or about 6,400 acres. Even so, the land has little intrinsic value other than its sheer size. Though there is water in the river and underground (landmarks include windmills that pump water out of the ground into tanks for feeding the animals), there is almost no arable land. The vegetation is the typical scrub and cottonwood of that country, good cover for birds and small game but not much else. But as a private hunting park it is splendid. Aside from what the travel folders (there actually was one prepared for Eagle Ranch guests) like to call an abundance of local game, especially white-tailed deer, wild pigs, wild turkey, dove, and quail, the hills and draws are heavy with an odd mixture of imported animals brought in by a former owner. A sportsman can sit in a blind or drive out in a carryall vehicle and sooner or later get a shot at such unlikely game as blackbuck antelope and axis deer from India, two kinds of big-horn sheep—the aoudad from North Africa and the mouflan from Sardinia—fallow deer and red stag from Europe, and sika deer from Japan. There are even a few Texas longhorn cattle and a small herd of buffalo for nostalgia, if not for shooting. And the river is packed with black bass and big fat catfish. It's what they call a hunters' paradise. But it is far more than a rustic retreat, with its dormitories, apartments, meeting, dining, and recreation rooms—including a billiard room—done in a combination of decorator styles ranging from a serviceable contemporary in the dormitories (four-man units) to a kind of baronial conquistador moderne in the top-brass apartments. (Decor is a very apparent aspect of business premises in Dallas and elsewhere among new-style corporate enterprise. It rarely reflects anything of the taste of the owners or of the nature of their businesses but rather the style of a particular interior decorator, and the favorite in Dallas in recent years, though he did not do the ranch, has been John Astin Perkins, who may well give his name to a part of an era of American art history. Perkins adheres to no particular style but rather an excess of several, including French eighteenth century, *haute chinoiserie*, and early-1960s contemporary regency.)

As Ling walked through the dining-and-recreation building that first afternoon, surveying the facilities, he found a guest alone in the billiard room making shots. Since the man had misspent his youth in places other than pool halls, he was an indifferent player who liked to play unobserved. Ling picked up a cue and asked if he could join him for a few minutes. The other man insisted he would be no competition, but Ling assured him that he himself was no expert. The guest figured they would just run a few balls for practice, but before Ling made his first shot he asked where the score would be kept. On those wooden beads on the wire, he was told. Neither player's skill approached the hustler category, and it took maybe ten minutes for the pair to sink all fifteen balls. During the course of the little game, the other man handled the beads, and Ling asked him at least a half-dozen times for the score, sometimes before it had changed. When Ling put up his cue to return to his hosting chores, he asked for the outcome and was obviously pleased that he had outshot his opponent by a ball or two. As Ling was about to leave, the other man told him that he had never before seen a man so eager to score high, whatever he played. Ling shrugged, smiled, and left.

He had lots to see to, small details that could bruise egos if not attended to. And bruised egos could wreck the house he had built and was trying to hold together and expand. One director had to have a suite to himself because he snored loudly and was embarrassed about having disturbed roommates on previous trips. Others, especially the chief executive officers of major subsidiaries, also required special treatment. William J. Stephens, chairman of the board of Jones & Laughlin Steel Corporation, the nation's sixth largest steel maker, was one. LTV owns 81 percent of J&L's stock, which, in ordinary circumstances, would make the relationship between parent company and subsidiary quite clear. But the links between the two companies were twisted and tangled by government intervention in the form of an antitrust suit filed the previous spring, by J&L management and operations problems that could bleed the entire LTV financial structure to death, and by the personal and social tensions that divide upstart Dallas and venerable Pittsburgh.

The room-assignment list showed that Stephens was to share Ling's own quarters. Ling probably figured that with Stephens that close to him physically for three days, he might be able to persuade the steel man to have J&L raise $50 million or more of new capital. Ling could not order him to do that because, even though Ling-Temco-Vought held unquestioned stock control, it was enjoined by the federal government from exercising that control. For Stephens the situation could not have been better. With his retirement only a year or so off, the fact that his principal stockholder's hands were tied meant that he could spend his last active days without having to pursue the aggressive course that LTV's acquisition of his company had originally presaged. All he had to do was hang in there—an enviable position for a man with most of his career behind him. Or at least it seemed that way to one visitor who happened by Ling's apartment one midday while Ling was exhorting Stephens to take steps to get his steel company, and therefore LTV, out of some of its most pressing difficulties. Stephens reassured Ling that he would do something about it when he returned from a lengthy world tour. Ling verged on anger a couple of times, but when he paused to go to the toilet, Stephens seemed to fall instantly asleep, the point of which could hardly have escaped Ling.

Harding L. Lawrence was assigned to share the apartment of W. Paul Thayer. They shared a common business interest: airplanes. Lawrence was chairman of the board and chief executive officer of Braniff Airways, while Thayer held the same position at LTV Aerospace Corporation, an aircraft manufacturer. Both companies were important subsidiaries of LTV, and both men were therefore important subordinates to Ling. But this apparent similarity in their rank and relationship to the parent company was misleading. Braniff was acquired whole by LTV in a complicated deal completed in 1968, and Lawrence came with it. LTV Aerospace had been created in a quite different way, being initially an acquired division of the parent company before it achieved its separate corporate entity, and Thayer had moved up the corporate ranks. But if Lawrence did not seem to fit into the "family" as readily as Thayer, it was for more cogent reasons than their corporate histories.

To look and act like a chief executive can be as important in becoming one as a man's training, experience, and past record as a manager. Take a look through the business press and corporate annual reports. Increasingly, the men pictured there look like top executives. It is extremely unlikely that men in general have, through some genetic quirk, begun to look like their jobs, even allowing for the preponderance of Anglo-Saxon Protestants in high places. It has been suggested that the levels executives reach correlate with their physical height. Hair seems to count too, the amount and even the style and color. (The substantial recent growth of the hair industry seems to support that assumption.) Weight also seems to count, but in an inverse ratio. Corpulence, once a symbol of royal and later of industrial power, is now viewed as a disqualification on some such ground as this: if a man can't control his own appetite, he probably isn't fit to control industrial processes and other men.

That doesn't mean that because a man is cast rather than qualified for his job he is likely to make a mess of it. Chances are he won't. The men who follow the pioneers who build the enterprises (*they* can be short, bald, even fat as long as they are able) create institutions designed to be run by ordinary men. Many of the decisions a chief executive must make are foreordained by circumstances or by the work of subordinates or committees. Others are dictated by competitors who are industry leaders. In normal times when business is good, there are few moments in the life of a chief executive when the decisions he makes entirely on his own are likely to make or break the company. When they do fail to produce desirable results, it often takes years to know that, and then it still may be impossible to assign the blame to one man. There are always external and uncontrollable factors, such as the state of the economy and adverse government policies, that can be cited as the causes of setbacks. And the decisions of previous managements can also be real or putative factors in bad times: they should have diversified, they misjudged the political climate in South America, they didn't spend enough on research and development, etc.

Finally, the very fact that a man has the job makes his actions proper ones. That may sound circular and simplistic, but there is more to it than that. Once he has the scepter and the orb, he is indeed the boss as far as his subordinates are concerned. Who, after all, is going to measure him then? Directors who meet every month or so and devote little time to their corporate responsibilities in between meetings? Shareholders, with nothing more to go on than complex and often disingenuous corporation financial statements and assurances from ignorant but well-meaning securities salesmen? But if a man looks and sounds like an executive, by God, who's to say he's not one?

Harding Lawrence, an aggressive and experienced airline executive, is a man who understands this very well. Hardly a man alive looks more like the ideal head man of an airline than Lawrence. His wavy hair, silvery at the sides, his careful attention to his modified modish dress (especially notable and colorful at the ranch), and the image his airline projects in its advertising and decor (brightly painted planes and a series of Pucci-designed stewardess costumes) all conspire to present Braniff's top manager as a jet-age personality. Even in an earlier day, Lawrence managed to project a special sort of flare by naming a child of a previous marriage State Rights. But that sort of provincial touch was nowhere in evidence at his second marriage, to Mary Wells, the advertising executive who planned the fancy planes and costumes. It took place in the Hôtel de Ville in Paris. In his relations with his principal stockholder, in the form of Ling, he had been much concerned with his compensation and perquisites, especially as they ranked him among other airline heads. Ling himself had been cautious if not exactly awed in his dealings with Lawrence—but not to the point of informing Lawrence that he was engaged in talks aimed at selling LTV's control of Braniff and therefore of Lawrence's future.

Paul Thayer is, in a sense, as appropriately cast in his job as Lawrence, but not as much, it would appear, by design. The main business of his LTV Aerospace Corporation is making and selling military aircraft to the federal government. And Thayer was a World War II Navy flyer and an authentic hero—an ace, as they used to call them. After the war, he went to work as a test pilot for Chance Vought, the principal supplier of warplanes to the Navy. There is probably no job in private industry more heroic than testing new aircraft. And Thayer looks the part even now, years away from the cockpit of an untried aircraft. A steady, straight-into-your-eye man, a "hard-nosed Dutchman," to use a common Dallas description of him. No back-slapper, Thayer is nevertheless, by virtue of his background and manner, a most acceptable man with "the customer," as they call the Pentagon, the buyer of most of what Thayer's company makes. If the fact that he owns and races horses takes him a little out of the mold of tight-lipped determination, the concern he once expressed over the choice of a college for his daughter puts him solidly into it: Thayer dismissed the prospect of schools on both coasts for her out of concern about their permissiveness and radicalism, and thought that somewhere in Minnesota or Michigan she would encounter a more appropriate education. Another aspect of Thayer's experience that would bear on his future was the fact that as a government contractor he was used to working in an environment where political and other external circumstances took a large measure of control out of his hands.

Ling was an admirer of Thayer for his heroic past as well as for his loyal and efficient present. As a low-ranking Navy enlisted man during World War II, and recently an eager amateur pilot, Ling had a special respect for Thayer that their present comparative status did not affect. Many men in industry and the military less powerful and less accomplished than he seemed nonetheless to impress him by their rank. And his associations, particularly outside of business, with top people of all sorts, perfectly natural for a man of his position and interests, seemed to produce in him a special, almost boyish pleasure.

In another of the top-executive apartments at the ranch, Roscoe Haynie and E. Grant Fitts were roommates. Haynie had come into the Ling circle when LTV made its lightning acquisition of Wilson & Company, the giant meat packer and sporting-goods maker. Haynie had been its president. Now a director of LTV and chairman of its executive committee, he was number three in the ranking (after Ling and Clyde Skeen, LTV president) and a close adviser and friend to Ling. A longtime executive of one of Chicago's most important corporations, Haynie was well connected in political and business circles throughout the region. He was a skilled and respected manager widely credited with Wilson's relative success in a day when the huge Chicago meat packers were on the decline. But a curious set of circumstances frustrated his hope of becoming the corporation's chairman, so he was able to make the transfer of allegiance and even the physical move from Chicago to Dallas with less regret than might have been expected. Haynie at this point was probably Ling's closest business associate. And as an avid golfer, as well as an intelligent interpreter of Ling's objectives, he made an excellent roommate for E. Grant Fitts.

That does not mean that he would buddy up to Fitts. Nobody does that. Fitts is a most enigmatic man, a keeper of his own counsel, a loner in a world of goodfellowship, an unknown figure in a day when corporate executives seek their images in press releases and who's whos as eagerly as Narcissus stared into the water. No one in Dallas claims close ties with him, and few men in Birmingham, Alabama, where he built a brilliant career as a lawyer before coming West, recall close links with him. He had been on the fringes of Ling's career for nearly a decade and he would briefly be the most important man in Ling's life, the very instrument of his downfall. But Ling himself knew little about him. The only chink in the tight wall Grant Fitts built around himself is literally on a wall. It is a sign, the first thing in sight when a visitor steps off the elevator on the nineteenth floor of the LTV Tower in Dallas. The top line, all in capital letters, reads simply: E. GRANT FITTS. Almost as an afterthought, beneath it, in much smaller capitals and lower-case italics, the words *Chairman of the Board and President, Gulf Life Holding Co.*, appear, followed by the names of the insurance companies held. The origins of Fitts's Gulf Life Holding Company are intimately intertwined with an LTV deal and with millions' worth of LTV securities. Fitts, a director of LTV but not a man interested in corporate camaraderie or planning meetings, did not come down to the ranch with the first arrivals. His only interest was the directors' meeting slated for the end of the session on Friday afternoon. Fitts is a golf enthusiast, a fine player who came late to the game, recognizing as an adult that it could be an important way to rise in business. A Birmingham law-firm colleague still recalls Fitts's joy upon his admission to an important country club. Another man repeats an incredible legend: that Fitts learned golf secretly, privately, at home, with books, in front of a full-length mirror, and then broke one hundred the first time he played publicly, rather than appear as a bumbling duffer. Fitts himself won't comment on the story, but the fact remains that he is one of the best businessman golfers in Dallas, a city filled with outstanding businessman golfers, including Jim Ling. Fitts is especially renowned for the length of his drives. He likes to kill the ball, a golf companion observes. But the other side of Fitts is a man of irony and barbed wit, especially against intellectual inferiors no matter how closely associated with him, bordering but never crossing into indiscretion. Though a reluctant man in public, Fitts has a formidable reputation as a lawyer that goes back to his early days out of school. The combination of qualities indicates a man who mostly controls his feelings, a man who dislikes "body contact" in business, to use a popular Dallas sports analogy, but a man who is thorough and relentless in pursuit of his goals, which he rarely reveals. His surface manner—smooth, Southern courtly, almost bland—conceals much. For Ling he was a most dangerous man. But that was not apparent those warm, sunny days in Real County.

Clyde Skeen, LTV president, shared his executive apartment with William H. Osborn, another LTV director by virtue of his position as a partner in the firm of Lehman Brothers, investment bankers to LTV. Even a fleeting view of Lehman Brothers—with its mighty reputation, its generations of Montgomery cotton merchants and New York financiers, a New York State governor and United States Senator, a remarkable art collector, the façade at One William Street, the framed documents recording ancient transactions such as the trading of a slave, and all the other ingredients of a century of financial and political power— hardly brings to mind an association with a Texas parvenu, a man building a company with no patience for history, without regard for manicured manners, pushing his way into the fortresses of American industry. Yet their association made perfectly good sense.

Ling's previous Wall Street banking connection was with the firm of White, Weld & Company. Ling and the partner assigned to him had a falling out over Ling's assault, in 1961, on the venerable Chance Vought Corporation. When White, Weld's man withdrew, Lehman's man moved in. During the year 1968 alone, Lehman Brothers received commissions and fees "in connection with public offerings and private placements of securities of the Company and its subsidiaries" of nearly $1 million. That, however, represented only about half of the investment bankers' pie. A hunk the same size went to Goldman, Sachs & Company, another Wall Street firm, of perhaps greater power if not comparable historic weight and image. Its representative on the board of directors of LTV was Gustave L. Levy, absent from the Off-site Planning Meeting, but a man for whom Ling felt great regard. In fact, Ling was almost humble when he spoke of Levy, who, after all, had been chairman of the board of governors of the New York Stock Exchange and was treasurer of New York's most visible cultural institution, Lincoln Center, and chairman of the board of one of the world's foremost medical institutions, New York's Mount Sinai Hospital. And when Gus Levy sat and nursed a drink in Ling's New York hotel suite, LTV staff men would bask in his presence and fondle such terms as "comfortable as an old shoe." That attitude infected Ling, in whose house Levy usually stayed when he was required to be in Dallas. Ling saw this personal association as a friendship. It is unlikely that Levy saw it as anything more than good customer relations.

Neither Levy nor Osborn functioned, despite the popular—and sometimes valid—view of investment bankers, as a counselor and confessor, advising and deterring; rather, they were middlemen between Jim Ling, a man building an enterprise out of acquisitions and a torrent of new securities, and the salesmen who sold them to investors.

Bill Osborn is a cautious man with the style and accent of a Yankee storekeeper, but with family ties to industrial nobility. He is well qualified to say yes or no to the prospect of investor acceptance of yet another securities issue from Ling-Temco-Vought. Osborn, however, seemed bemused and maybe even awed by the financial complexities that are Ling's everyday currency. Whether he shook or nodded his head at Ling's plans to acquire Wilson & Company, Allis-Chalmers, or Jones & Laughlin, it is doubtful whether Ling noticed or cared. But if he said that a particular securities offering was priced too high or that stockholders would want a couple of dollars more before they would accept an exchange of securities, then Ling might listen and amend his plans. Perhaps that merely defines the primary function of many investment bankers: wholesalers who know what the market will take. They also can be useful in providing introductions that lead to loans and acquisitions. At the ranch, Osborn attended meetings dutifully and also pursued a hobby, photography, shooting animals with a reflex camera and a telephoto lens while others stalked game with rifles or clay pigeons with shotguns.

Clyde Skeen, the president of Ling-Temco-Vought, made an amiable roommate for a dignitary from the East. He was a former executive at Boeing who had once been considered for the chief executive's job at the desperately troubled General Dynamics Corporation. He worked closely with Ling, mostly as a second man on finance. Even so, the bulk of the responsibility for operations of LTV and for its mounting operating problems had fallen on his shoulders. He is an intelligent man, outwardly unflappable. But it was apparent even to casual observers that he was becoming overburdened, though hardly overmatched. As the tensions increased, producing chin-rubbing and mumbling among directors who saw trouble but not causes, he would bear the brunt of the initial attacks. He would also be the first of the top men to fall.

The festive side of the offsite meeting began before the arrival of most of the participants. Early arrivals were out in the hills stalking game. Though he had hunted big game throughout the world, Bob McCulloch had never killed a blackbuck antelope from India. Ling and some friends took McCulloch out to find one, but they failed to get close enough for a successful shot. Having sampled the food the first day, Ling counseled the staff toward less ambitious efforts. After dark, the floodlights were turned on at the skeet and trap ranges, and the shooters, aided by a staff of eager young men controlling the launching of clay pigeons and the distribution of ammunition and drinks, spent happy hours demolishing moving targets.

The following day, the planes and buses arrived with their contingents of guests and executives. Altogether there were nearly seventy, not counting ranch hands or the young men who served as ferry pilots, bartenders, and ammunition suppliers. Each man's luggage was deposited at his lodgings with considerably less difficulty than one might expect in ordinary commercial travel. A special staff had devoted many man-hours to the preparations.

The business part of the meeting began after lunch on Wednesday afternoon with Ling himself making some opening exhortatory remarks followed by talks on government and foreign relations by LTV staff executives. The special guest speaker of the afternoon reflected a preoccupation of businessmen in general and Ling in particular. The man was Air Force Colonel Kenneth H. Cooper, M.D., author of the book *Aerobics*, who writes and gives lectures, illustrated with slides, on how to keep fit by running, jogging, cycling, and other exercises designed to defend the cardio-vascular system. Cooper closed the proceedings for the day. "Recreation" was the next item on the agenda, and for the rest of the after-noon, men ran, jogged, puffed, walked, trying to rack up the number of points the speaker had said were required for a stout heart.

Ling would have been with them, for he is a man much concerned with his own physical condition. On the twenty-ninth floor of the LTV Tower, two floors below his own office, he had installed what he called the Spa, a gym filled with treadmills, chrome-plated weight-lifting equipment, and stationary bicycles, which he and some of the other executives used regularly. He even had a stationary bicycle brought to New York for use in the corporation's apartment at the Regency Hotel. Looking younger than his years, even under great strain, Ling is a most compact man, standing six-foot-two and weighing between 190 and 200. His only physical problem seems to be a chronic sinus and allergy condition.

But he did not run that day because he was still trying to get his friend Bob McCulloch a shot at an antelope, which meant riding the ranch in a carry-all bus scouring the hills and washes for herds. On his way past the skeet range, he stopped the car to talk to some men firing their way through the string of shooting stations. A shooter challenged Ling to a contest, and Ling agreed, provided the other man was will-ing to bet money. In a quick round—a carload was waiting—Ling won the bet, missing only a single one of the clay disks. When he gleefully collected the bet, he announced to his victim that he hadn't shot a round of skeet in several months.

McCulloch didn't get a shot at an antelope, so on the drive back for dinner he thought he'd try his luck at some-thing less ambitious—wild pig. Spotting some in the scrubby woods along the riverbank, he left the truck and began mov-ing in. Ling waited by the truck. At the sound of a rifle shot, Ling moved forward to see what had happened. McCulloch appeared and shouted that he had hit one. Ling grabbed a rifle and followed him, looking for the dead or wounded animal. Something had bled on the ground, but there were no other signs of the creature. Then there was a sound, a raspy grunt, from the direction of a bush. Seeming to leap off the ground like a released spring, Ling fired four rounds from his lever-action rifle into the bush with such speed that the weapon might have been a machine gun. But there was no trace of the animal, and, just as suddenly, Ling was the relaxed guide, leading his party back to dinner.

Beginning Thursday morning, each of LTV's subsidiary companies was scheduled to offer its forecast of business prospects for the next five years. Ling himself acted as moderator, ringing a bell when speakers took more than their allotted time, which was considerable. The audience was generally attentive or at least respectful. But it is characteristic of such meetings that the sponsors and speakers take them more seriously than the audience. Captive business audiences are traditionally treated with less concern for their real interests than those who buy tickets. But managements seldom reckon with this. They figure that, after all, the food, liquor, and games are free; why shouldn't the men listen and care? The trouble with this thinking is that it gives no weight to reality. Few men in the audience were so naïve as to believe that anybody there had some magic method of making valid predictions for the long term. They had been involved in their own forecasts enough to know that when they turn out to be true, coincidence is at work as much as anything else. And they all implicitly recognized that the entire session was an exercise in horn-blowing and self-aggrandizement. But even more to the point, if you give a group of men a lot of food and drink and sport, and then put them into a half-dark room and make them listen to a series of nonprofessional speakers bolstered by endless slides of graphs and tables, frequently shown too quickly to be understood and often with type too small to be read, they will be hard put to stay awake, let alone listen and believe.

Nevertheless, the meeting went on, and on, more or less as scheduled. Harding Lawrence spoke glowingly of the future of his airline while its present was falling far short of past forecasts. He did not indicate that he foresaw that, in the quarter which Braniff had entered the previous day, it would lose more than $3 million and thereby deal a severe blow to the stability of LTV itself. Roy Edwards, the president of Wilson & Company, gave a formidable address to the group, full of pictures of animals and juicy cuts of meat. An able, ambitious executive, Edwards spoke in a tone that was exhortatory and inspirational in the manner of a Sunday-school teacher, which he had been, with traces of a political aspirant, which he may be. His dubbing of Ling as the Galileo of American enterprise was easily the morning's climax, and maybe the week's. The sated audience got through an afternoon of more talk and slides with only a few men reacting when a speaker for Wilson Sporting Goods raised the specter of "consumerism" as a possible deterrent to the realization of his forecast.

"Recreation" drew Ling into a heated gambling contest on the hard grass putting green. And dinner, replete with a distinguished château bottling in enormous quantities, was followed by the guest speaker. For Ling, the choice of the main event was a personal matter. The year before, a renowned local impressionist known as Cactus Pryor had posed as a British left-wing economist named Sir Gilbert Peake, and apparently he was so effective in his anti-American, anti-free-enterprise routine, in which Ling himself served as a straight man, that one venerable guest actually believed he had met the man some years before in London. This night, the speaker was an East Texas lawyer named Robert Murphy who doubles as a paid entertainer. Though the Texans present tried to reassure out-of-state guests who might not appreciate the man's regionalisms, Murphy turned out to be a raconteur of remarkable virtuosity. His success, particularly with the non-Texans, was most gratifying to Ling.

The following day, Friday, October 3, was the last one for most of those attending, so the morning was a time of hangovers for those who had not unbent earlier. Actually, the entire event had been relatively free of the sort of roistering that businessmen are supposed to engage in out-of-town. Paul Thayer's presentation of the outlook of his own subsidiary, LTV Aerospace Corporation, was characteristically terse and pointed. He dealt with its principal activities, military aircraft, especially the A-7 Corsair II, a light attack plane used in Vietnam. His company was getting into the domestic marketing of a French-built helicopter, the Alouette that had brought Ling and his party to the ranch. And he described an unlikely diversification, the purchase a month earlier of a tract of land near Steamboat Springs, Colorado, which the company hoped to develop into a ski resort. The proceedings went quickly, permitting the final order of business—the meeting of the board of directors—to be held an hour earlier than scheduled. A typically perfunctory session, it ran less than its allotted sixty minutes.

As the goodbyes were said and the buses and planes carried men and luggage home, there was little evidence that the obstacles confronting the corporation might prove insurmountable. There were cash problems ahead, but they seemed manageable, either through new loans or through some rearrangement of subsidiaries that would give the parent LTV access to their surplus cash. Roy Edwards of Wilson was elected a member of the board, filling a vacancy created by a retirement. And negotiations were under way to sell a subsidiary called Computer Technology, Inc., to the Prudential Insurance Company. Ling's formation of Computer Tech a year earlier as a major entrant in the computer installation and software field had been widely regarded as a triumphant example of his special talent for creating stock-market values with minimum investment and maximum financial invention. And though this new company had almost from the start been encumbered by serious personal abrasions among top executives, the planned sale of its controlling shares promised enormous profits for LTV. The parent company had already offered some of Computer Tech's shares to a public that was bidding up the shares of other computer software companies and had reacted to Ling's as though it were a cross between IBM and a cure for baldness. Grant Fitts must already have felt some concern about the state of corporate affairs, especially the decline in the value of LTV securities he and his insurance companies owned. But he raised no objection when the board asked

Ling to leave the meeting and then voted to lend him nearly $2 million to buy more LTV stock as a reward for the benefits he had produced by creating and now selling Computer Tech. Ling had not received any options for several years, apparently because the board members thought he was wealthy enough without them.

The biggest single problem that confronted Ling-Temco-Vought that day seemed to be finding a solution to the management difficulties created by the federal antitrust suit demanding divestiture of Jones & Laughlin. But Ling already had a fairly good idea of how they could get out of that problem. Money was tight; securities prices of the corporation and all its subsidiaries were down, putting pressure on the corporation and on many of its executives who had used securities as collateral for loans. But LTV was bigger than ever. Its sales in 1969 would make it the fourteenth largest corporation in the nation. Troubles, sure, and a little dissension around the edges, but nothing that couldn't be dealt with. As far as Ling was concerned, the empire was basically sound. And his board of directors seemed willing to go along with his conviction that he could work it all out and that he actually was doing just that.

Over the years, the board had become little more than an extension of Ling's will. Levy and Osborn, the investment bankers on the board, had little reason to dispute any decision he made that would produce more commissions for their firms on the securities sales, exchange offers, and the other deals he would inevitably have to bring off to restore stability to his debt-ridden structure by raising cash and refinancing maturing debt. And if the court went against LTV and the corporation had to divest itself of its holdings of Jones & Laughlin, that would mean even more commissions. The presence of men on the board of directors of a publicly held corporation who are in favored positions to do business with the company is perfectly legal. All they have to do is disclose to stockholders in proxy statements and prospectuses the nature of that business. But their presence creates conflicts of interest that must frequently affect their ability to make objective judgments. Outsiders probably figure that investment bankers on the board assure the corporation of valued financial counsel. But their function often turns out to be limited to providing access to securities markets and profits for their firms.

The directors of LTV were typical of many corporate boards, and their unwillingness or inability to affect major corporate decisions points to what is probably the biggest flaw in the process of managing public corporations. Directors are the representatives of the shareholders. As such, they have fiduciary responsibilities; that is, they are supposed to be looking out first of all for other people's invested money. And they are supposed to know in great detail what is going on, so that when they approve a management decision they are fully responsible for its consequences. But it rarely works that way in practice. There is just too much to know.

Several of Ling's directors were top executives of the corporation and of its subsidiaries. They were certainly close enough to what was happening to see the mounting problems. But they owed their jobs and their fortunes to their ties with Ling. Some of the other board members were old friends and early investors. Others were legacies from earlier mergers. Even Grant Fitts, who would soon begin to articulate his doubts about the way things were going, had done nothing to deter Ling. In fact, it was Fitts who, a couple of years before, had persuaded Ling to acquire Greatamerica Corporation, the holding company created by Dallas insurance man Troy V. Post to hold investments in some insurance companies and other enterprises, including Braniff Airways. That deal had produced a half-billion dollars' worth of debt for LTV, but it had also given Fitts his big chance, because he would later buy those insurance companies from LTV. Fitts was hardly the man to make the first test of Ling's vulnerability.

In these days in October, 1969, Ling was still in command. If there was an undercurrent of doubt among the directors and executives of Ling-Temco-Vought, it was still largely offset by the tremendous personal force that Ling embodied as well as by the vast economic power of the corporation even as its problems became evident.

It is easy to say that the army he led came along for the conventional reasons of greed and the desire for power. His executives were well rewarded. His investment bankers netted millions. The dozens of commercial banks, led by the biggest of all, the Bank of America, made out very well from the endless borrowings that were a fundamental Ling device. For a long time, the scores of insurance companies, mutual funds, and other institutional investors that held the many securities of his corporations reaped capital gains and dividends. And so did tens of thousands of individual shareholders, especially the ones who got in early and got out in time.

As for what was in it for Jim Ling, that too can be answered in conventional ways. His earnings ran as high as $375,000 a year. The value of his stockholdings had once reached about $80 million. And he had all the other trappings: the huge office, the private jets, the château in Dallas, the house in Palm Springs, the expensive apartments and suites in New York, Washington, Chicago, and Pittsburgh, cars and drivers waiting wherever he alighted, club memberships and seats on the boards of civic and charitable organizations as well as a major bank and the Dallas Cowboys, and frequent opportunities to give speeches to business executives, who listened to what he had to say.

He was a very big man in Dallas and in America, and his Ling-Temco-Vought, the thing he had built from practically nothing, was still, even as it began to stumble, a spectacular assemblage of industrial power. In 1969, Wilson & Company sold nearly $1.3 billion worth of beef, lamb, pork, veal, and chickens. In just one plant, that subsidiary could kill and process more than a million hogs a year. Jones & Laughlin poured and shaped more than five million tons of steel worth more than $1 billion. Its Pittsburgh works, ancient and inefficient as they may have been, were an American industrial landmark. When you looked out on the night in the steel city, the fiery sight that you first encountered was a mill owned by Ling's corporation. The planes of Braniff flew all over the country and to Hawaii, Canada, and South America, to the tune of more than $300 million in revenues.

LTV Aerospace sold more than $700 million worth of planes and aerospace hardware, including the A-7 Corsair II attack plane for the Navy and the Air Force, the Scout space-probe rocket system for NASA, and the tail section of the Boeing 747. Wilson Sporting Goods turned out more than $100 million worth of baseball gloves, golf clubs, tennis rackets, and other products, and was the world's biggest manufacturer of sports equipment. Other LTV subsidiaries were making chemicals and drug products, high-fidelity and communications equipment (including the top-secret electronics on ships like the *Pueblo*), $200 million worth of wire, cable, and floor coverings from Okonite, and lots more in factories employing more than 120,000 people scattered all over the country.

Total sales of the whole complex would top $3.75 billion in 1969. While earnings were not going to come anywhere near the $30 million the corporation had netted the year before, Ling didn't know that when he listened to his executives down at the ranch. Even LTV's problems were spectacular, stemming mainly from a total consolidated corporate debt of more than $1.5 billion that required payment of more than $100 million a year in interest by the corporation and its subsidiaries.

The little electrical contracting company that Ling had started the whole thing with wasn't even part of the sprawling enterprise any more, and what he controlled had been established and built by other men. But he had put it all together, and there it was, however briefly, the fourteenth largest industrial corporation in the United States. It didn't work very well, and it didn't stay together. And a lot of the reasons why it didn't were Ling's own doing, even though it is possible—and even valid—to blame it on the stock market for collapsing, on the antitrust people for filing a baseless suit, and on his own supporters for turning against him when maybe they should have let him alone.

None of that really matters now. Nor does the fact that what is left of Ling-Temco-Vought is foundering and isn't very interesting any more. A lot of people lost a lot of money backing Ling's fantastic enterprise (though that has troubled him a great deal). But nobody made them do it. And plenty of money was made by investors along the way.

Ling led his army of executives, financiers, and investors through more than a decade of financial and psychic adventure. In the course of that march, he demonstrated remarkable creativity as he found the parts and discovered the processes for assembling them into a quite beautiful machine, however flawed it eventually became. Without meaning to, Ling used what was at hand to express himself, his drives, his private visions.

Long before the part of Los Angeles called Watts became notorious as the place of a bitter race riot, it was known to some people for what stood on a little piece of land there. An immigrant Italian laborer who could barely speak English or even Italian had appropriated a small part of a city block to build a series of fantastic towers. Made of steel rods, cement, bits of broken bottles (including the easily recognizable blue ones used to pack milk of magnesia), and assorted junk of all kinds, these Watts Towers of Simon Rodia are considered by many to rank among the world's great works of art.

In a sense, the thing that Ling built and the way he built it became a kind of Watts Tower. Business isn't supposed to have any esthetics other than those nice neat numbers like earnings per share and return on investment. The bottom line is all that business is supposed to be for. Ling used it to build something else. The people who followed him mostly didn't understand that. But they knew he was doing something different, and they thought it was something better, even without understanding it. That was why tough, successful, grown-up men replaced their usual skepticism with loyalty, faith, and even love. That is why some of them, including a few enemies, were willing to back him in another adventure after he was routed in the first attempt.

Maybe nobody should be permitted to use a business enterprise in that way. Almost certainly if Ling had not been able to do what he did, he would have found another way to create a tower out of bits and pieces. Jim Ling doesn't need a defender or a critic of his esthetics or his motives.

What he did was worth the try and worth looking at in all its aspects, including the esthetics. Leverage may build shaky towers, but when it works, it has a palpably beautiful quality that demands respect. A lot of people paid through the nose to get a good seat. But they got to be a part of one dandy show. And it could have worked. Maybe the next one will.

2

────

THOUGH Jim Ling himself is unclear about what turned him on to visions of great power and wealth, he surely could not have found himself in a better time or place for his reaching out. What Ling made fulfilled not merely some standard-sized version of the American Dream but the particular one of a young man coming home from the Navy to Dallas. In the years after World War II, Texas provided a climate that many driving and driven men found congenial and useful.

Important finds in East Texas in the early 1930s were to make oil as important to Dallas as cotton, distribution, insurance, and banking. Wartime demand for domestic petroleum products, great as it was, was nothing compared with what the peacetime automobile boom and the burgeoning petrochemical industry brought. Texas had already seen great fortunes made from oil before the war, but they were mostly based in Houston; now Dallas was getting its share of the new wealth. Men nobody had ever heard of before were taking millions out of the ground because they were lucky, smart, or both. Ling would refer to some of them later as geological accidents. But in those early days when he was fresh out of service and trying to build his own little electrician's shop, he could not help being awed by their wealth, however they got it.

The local legends spread across the country. High income

taxes left over from the war years could be mitigated in oil because of the unending depletion allowances and deductions for intangible drilling costs that permit oil men to keep most of their money out of the Treasury. Texas was also the biggest cattle producer, and for a while it was possible, because of tax twists, for some investors to make money off cattle even if they sold them for less than they paid for them. Prospects like these helped feed the fortunes and the yarns. The jokes about Texans who used Volkswagens for bookends became a national pastime, and if they were exaggerated, they certainly weren't groundless. The American public was becoming familiar with Texans like H. L. Hunt, Sid Richardson, and Hugh Roy Cullen, who were said to have daily incomes in the millions. The Murchisons and their fortune backed Robert R. Young, the strange and brilliant Texas railroad man who took over the New York Central. Stanley Marcus, the remarkable Dallas merchant, shrewdly exploited the legends as his Neiman-Marcus became the shopping center for billionaires, with a Christmas gift catalog that offered, perfectly straight-faced, camels and elephants complete with keeper one year, his-and-her airplanes another. All that was something for a young man to work toward.

Making it in Dallas was not so easy, especially for a man with none of the several kinds of credentials and connections of value in that city. Ling is a Roman Catholic, and Dallas, strongly church-minded, is the home of the world's largest Baptist congregation. Money from Baptist philanthropic organizations has controlled a major bank as well as other businesses. Baptist laymen are among the city's foremost figures, and the Baptist view of God and men pervades Texas life. The state's tortuous liquor sales procedures attest to the sect's power in the legislature. Phoney (and legitimate) club memberships and brown paper bags on restaurant tables had long been part of the life of the state. Despite the problems of getting a drink, a cab driver, asked what was his city's principal product, replied, "Empty whiskey bottles."

Ling was an outsider in other ways, too. Because all his schooling took place outside the state, he was not exposed to the required teaching of Texas history. State history comprises some part of the curriculum in a lot of other school systems. But in few other places is there anything quite like being a Texan. Most urban people identify with their city a little sooner than their state. Ask a man from Chicago or Baltimore, and he's not likely to tell you he's from Illinois or Maryland. That may be true with a Dallas man as well, but not as often. Texans are singularly aware of their history and quick to identify with it. Everybody remembers the Alamo, and the Lone Star flag is almost as commonplace a sight on Dallas flagstaffs as the Stars and Stripes. Texas, after all, was a republic for ten years before it joined the Union, and along with the almost fierce national patriotism of Texans, they take their state seriously. It is almost as though there is an ethnic Texan. But Ling, however much he has become the symbol of the aggressive Texan, is somehow not quite an ethnic.

Not that a man has to be a Baptist, bear the name of some Texas hero such as Sam Houston or Mirabeau Lamar, or come off a dirt farm. Stanley Marcus is a Jew, and so was Fred Florence, who built Dallas' Republic National Bank into the state's biggest. And Erik Jonsson, one of the founders of Texas Instruments Corporation and longtime mayor of Dallas, is from Brooklyn. In fact, of course, the city, like so many others that have grown up since World War II, has more than its share of newcomers who have worked their way into the foundations of the community. That does not say the community is some kind of melting pot that wipes away the distinctions. Religion, birthplace, ethnic origin, and the age of a man's money still affect the degree of his acceptance. Even at the height of Ling's ascent in Dallas, when he had been taken onto the Citizens Council—the quasi-official body of businessmen who rule the city—sat on the boards of the First National Bank and the Dallas Cowboys, and was a member of the most prestigious country clubs in town, there were still men who had made their money twenty or thirty years earlier and considered him an upstart.

The economic climate of Dallas when Ling came onto the scene was made of more than oil, cattle, and cotton, although, whatever a man's other businesses, he would usually put a little money into one of the many oil deals always available. Real-estate speculation and development made other fortunes and bolstered many of the big ones. Families named DeLoache, Wynne, and Caruth gave their names to streets and suburban developments and still are often heavily involved in big new projects downtown and around the rim of the city, where office buildings have been springing up alongside the houses, apartments, and shopping centers for years. As with oil, most of the real-estate activity was backed by a kind of round robin of investors, with participation sometimes open to relatively small money. Half the tables at most of the private clubs of the city might be occupied by men putting together deals along with their drinks. That kind of buying and selling, certainly not exclusively a Dallas activity, has almost a social aspect to it, like a high-stakes gin game. A local deal-man once explained how a not very bright but very wealthy Dallas man made his fortune: "He's a nice fellow and never gives you any trouble in a deal, so everybody is glad to give him a piece of the action."

When the war ended, Texas suffered the loss of many military installations and aircraft factories. It probably trained more soldiers and pilots than any other state and ranked high as a builder of planes. But the hardships that came with peace were soon minimized as the Iron Curtain, the Truman Doctrine, the Marshall Plan, the Korean War, and NATO created a kind of permanent garrison economy that President Eisenhower, in his curious and unexpected parting shot, labeled the military-industrial complex. Influential Texans in Washington—including Senator Tom Connally, House Speaker Sam Rayburn, and rising young Lyndon Johnson among others—made sure their state got at least its share of the money spent in defense of the free world. But the going was slow in the first days after the war. Dallas got a small shot in the arm in 1946 when Bob McCulloch got some federal backing for his attempt to build Flying Boxcars in the plant he had run for North American Aviation during the war. Ordinarily anybody who would try to build military aircraft in those days would have been written off as quixotic. But McCulloch had built a reputation as a production wizard, there was a huge plant out there making nothing at all, and the area had a lot of unemployed aircraft workers. So Mc-Culloch managed to persuade a few investors that it was worth a try, and he set up Texas Engineering & Manufacturing Company. The company would sweat out years making everything from planes to aircraft parts and sub-assemblies, washing machines, and finally missiles and electronic systems. However shaky its beginnings, it was in a far bigger league than the little home-wiring business that Jim Ling started in the same place at about the same time.

As government military business became increasingly important to the area—Bell Aircraft, Convair, and Texas Instruments among others were there—men who were otherwise apolitical adopted strong views on freedom and aggressive foreign policy. It does not require a cynical turn of mind to associate the economic interests of Dallas, of Texas, or of any other place or industry with national and international politics, nor need one impugn anybody's sincerity or patriotism to make that connection. What was good for Dallas was good for America: that was an idea that a bright young man trying to make his way in a powerful business community could readily assimilate in his increasing contacts with his economic betters, and without the slightest bending of his strong sense of personal morality and integrity.

After all, what had brought America out of the depression and given it back its power and its sense of rightness was the remarkable growth of its industry and the victory that produced. To be big and powerful was clearly good. And, of course, Texas was still the biggest state of all. Everybody knew that Texans would think nothing of driving a hundred miles for a malted. Stories like that were told seriously around the country. A Texas man at a convention listened to several other grown men exchanging such bits of folklore and finally said: "Sometimes we drive two hundred miles for no reason at all." But the country believed the myth, and Texans enjoyed the feeling of prominence it gave them. Big was good everywhere. The nation measured itself in every conceivable way that made it feel bigger and more powerful than it had been in the past and than its allies and its enemies were. It was impossible to argue with the Gross National Product and with our military supremacy, or at least few were willing to try. Men who might have been expected to be more watchful and critical of national excesses and imbalances managed not to be, because there was more than enough of the gross national pie for everybody. And men whose sense of the past was shaped by dim, lifelong memories of wanting to fill some void of their own reached out for what was there.

When Edna Ferber's *Giant* was published in 1952, Texans hated and, as much as they could, boycotted the novel. But many of them also read it and recognized the big-rich oil people on whom it was loosely based. The book was probably unfair in its focus on the vulgarity of big new Texas money, because the style it excoriated is not singularly Texan, except maybe in degree. Big new money buys big new things wherever it turns up. The palazzos of Newport and the châteaux of Fifth Avenue were not really less vulgar in their day than the stately homes of Texas. And men of great wealth have always sought to attain the trappings of power commensurate with their money. It is probably true, however, that when the money comes as fast and big as it came to some Texans, especially when it comes from lucky holes in the ground, it tends to bring with it an oracular quality. A man who was stone-broke yesterday and is hugely rich today wants to believe that there is something in *him* that got him his wealth. Texas is full of rich oil men who have tried to demonstrate their inherent qualities by investing their oil money in other business ventures, often fruitlessly, or by trying to make themselves into authoritative public figures in one way or another. The wave of right-wing extremism in Dallas politics that produced coarse public demonstrations against Adlai Stevenson and the Lyndon Johnsons in 1964 has been characterized by a local Republican politician as the doing of the sons of rich oil men trying to find useful employment. Many others, of course, have been content to take the position that better nouveau than never and weave their way into the social and cultural fabric of the city.

Dallas likes to think of itself as the most cultivated and sophisticated city in the state, and maybe it is. In Houston, which is south and east of Dallas, they still wear a lot of those big white hats that Yankees think of as cowboy attire. But these are rare in Dallas, where the local business community favors clothes such as are worn in Detroit or Chicago, perhaps with a little more color and a slightly higher frequency of sports jackets in top-executive offices. On the other side, dinner clothes and even formal white-tie attire are probably a little more common in Dallas than in Denver or Cleveland or even New York. Fort Worth, about thirty miles west of Dallas and actually a part of the metropolitan area, likes to think of itself as where the West begins. A bigtime Fort Worth attorney flying up to New York for a Wall Street meeting is likely to wear modified-cowboy with square-cut jacket, pleated pockets, and maybe even hand-tooled boots. But not a Dallas man.

Dallas people are big on culture and pride themselves on their colleges and universities, their civic opera company, their local theater center, and the fact that they are a stop on the Metropolitan Opera road trip. Some will even insist that their cultural institutions are part of a tradition that has its roots in the middle of the nineteenth century, when a group of French utopian followers of Charles Fourier set up a colony in what is now West Dallas, the city's principal enclave of slums. But whatever influence these Fourierists may have had, it was probably less pronounced than that of local businessmen who have encouraged culture from the conviction that it is good for business and for the city, not necessarily in that order.

In Dallas, money is out in the open. It is *the* subject matter. The power structure is much more clearly a matter of money than it is in other, older places. Dallas is a hard-edged community, a kind of new frontier town even though it is more than a century old. Old buildings offend people there. A local man complains about the old courthouse overlooking the place where John F. Kennedy was assassinated. He calls it an eyesore. He resents the town's decision to let it stand, a handsome, archaic building. It ought to be torn down and replaced by something tall, angular, and modern, like the LTV Tower with its lights that spell out words and symbols on the night skyline.

An outsider can make it in Dallas society by having money,

dressing neatly, giving away money, and putting in time on community projects or assigning subordinates to the work. It takes a little time. New money is defensive about newer money. But seasoning doesn't take long, not even as long as it took Cornelius Vanderbilt to change from a boat man and a con man to the founder of a socially acceptable family or for John D. Rockefeller to change from predator to philanthropist.

The ruling group in Dallas is open to anyone who meets its qualifications. It is a democracy of money, an open society of businessmen. As such, it runs a tidy city of clean streets, well-publicized civic projects, and a minimum of visible urban trouble. People obey the traffic signals in Dallas. A stranger used to taking a slight lead-off before the light turns green and the "wait" sign turns to "walk" will earn an angry frown from pedestrians who wait dutifully up on the curb. And the downtown streets seem so clean that a man may carry a cold cigar butt for blocks until he feels sure nobody is watching him ditch it in an immaculate gutter. The city was one of the first in the country to move on school integration, once it became clear that was the law of the land. However deeply Dallas may feel its prejudices, its leaders determined early that they didn't want any messy publicity over the school segregation issue.

The assassination of President Kennedy brought to light statistics that established Dallas as a place of violence where such a monstrous crime might almost have been expected. Ridiculous as such a conclusion happens to be (who holds the murder of President McKinley against the brawling mill town of Buffalo?), it had an understandably painful effect on the consciousness of the city. Without referring to the act, people in Dallas often felt constrained to mention the relatively lower level of other kinds of crime in their city and generally to boost their town as a good place to live. Homicide and manslaughter, they seemed to imply, were after all not as much measures of the quality of law enforcement and of civic worth as were crimes against property. Besides, Dallas scores well on clean and safe streets and pleasant neighborhoods. A man can live his whole life in the city, drive to work every day, visit his business associates and friends, play golf, see football games, catch planes, and never encounter the city's black and Mexican slums.

The effect of federal antitrust law and policy after World War II was to create an environment in which an enterprise could be reasonably sure that it was out of reach of the trust-busters only if it acquired businesses patently unlike or independent of its own. The war had brought a tacit moratorium on the prosecution of antitrust cases that had been so aggressively pursued by New Deal trustbuster Thurman Arnold in the 1930s. But in 1949, the Justice Department filed suit against du Pont, demanding that it give up its controlling stockholding in General Motors. By then, Arnold had become a founding partner, with former New Deal associates Abe Fortas and Paul Porter, of the Washington law firm of Arnold, Fortas & Porter. Years later, that firm would represent Braniff Airways and then defend Ling-Temco-Vought itself when the Justice Department filed its suit against Ling's acquisition of Jones & Laughlin. But when the Justice Department went after du Pont and General Motors, the issue of vertical integration—in this case, the control of a major customer by a supplier—or any antitrust problem held no interest for a young electrical contractor. How could it? All it meant was that it was no longer possible to create a General Motors by putting together a collection of automobile manufacturers and suppliers as William C. Durant had done, or to create a United States Steel Corporation by combining raw-materials producers with steel makers and fabricators as J. P. Morgan had done after the turn of the century. A textile company that wanted to expand would be better off buying a hardware maker or a chicken farm than a dress manufacturer or another textile mill. An electronics maker would be relatively safe if it picked up a shipyard or a restaurant chain. In other words, the strictures of antitrust provided the context for the growth of what would come to be called conglomerates.

The yearning for virtue, for strength through rectitude, infected Wall Street after the war as much as or more than it did other institutions. In the days before the war, the financial community had suffered grievously at the hands of the New Deal as well as by its own acts. The virulent decay of the economy that followed 1929—the collapse of the great utility empires of Howard Hopson and Samuel Insull and of the investment trusts of the great houses of Wall Street, and the bank closings that wiped out the small wealth of the thrifty—was followed by waves of investigation and sanitizing legislation. And then came the revelation of the crime of Richard Whitney, brother of a J. P. Morgan partner, president of the New York Stock Exchange, and wearer of a noble name. Whitney had dipped so heavily into money he held in trust for the innocent that he went to jail. When the war ended, the archons of the Exchange were determined to carry forth their efforts to create a new image, and they did. They chose as their president not one of their own but an amiable, bespectacled college president named Keith Funston. If the new man seemed something of a bumpkin alongside his employers, that at least made him what their recent history denied them: he was trustworthy. And when he stood up and proclaimed the people's capitalism and exhorted Americans to buy a share in America, the public came back to investing in securities. Whether they were responding to the belief that Funston was just like themselves or simply to the desire to get a bigger pay-out from the new miracle of America is impossible to say. But the point is that they came back in, cautiously at first, and then less cautiously. They traded their waning skepticism for the zeal of the gambler on a hot streak.

It felt safe to come in. The market had sputtered for a few years after the war, but then it took off in the first of a succession of bull markets. There were downs as well as ups, but not nearly so many or so steep. After all, the market was simply recognizing and giving proper value to the American corporate industrial machine. Early fears of another depression, an idea that captured Sewell Avery and nearly ruined his Montgomery Ward, were soon dispelled. It wouldn't, maybe couldn't, happen again, because everybody was more careful, better financed, knew what he was about this time. In the year 1954, the market made its biggest gain, more than 40 percent over the year before, according to one indicator. And the next year, it continued to climb, carrying up with it a wave of new issues, mostly new little companies that sounded good and performed phenomenally for a while. That was the year that Jim Ling edged his way into high finance, selling shares in his own electrical contracting business. The success of that first move was, in a sense, to set the pattern for all that followed.

If the Stock Exchange could learn the ways of public relations, anyone in business could. "Corporate image" used to be an expression to be put between quotation marks as the tongue went into the cheek. In the early postwar days, a young business-magazine reporter was lectured by veterans on the almost sinister intent of the p.r. men to mislead and conceal. When one of them called at the magazine's editorial office, the young reporter was dispatched to find out what the man wanted, because he ranked lowest on the staff. Press releases were invariably deprecated as "handouts," and the phone call to the corporate public-relations office was usually to check a published figure on the number of employees or to arrange an appointment with a higher-up.

Soon, however, the press began shedding its wariness, the tongue came out of the cheek, and public-relations men became the usual and often the most useful sources of business news. Reporters felt no concern when they were seen drinking or lunching with a p.r. man. Industry generally followed the early lead of General Motors and made the p.r. man a top corporate executive. The clubbiness this produced often blinded business, as it certainly did General Motors, to the fact that their press did not necessarily reflect public sentiment, however well it might respond to blandishments from the public-relations department. Generally, though, the public was content to believe what it read in annual reports and in the business pages, no matter how sterile and patently unbelievable the material would have sounded if it were describing men and institutions in government, for example.

Somebody once observed that public relations does for

businessmen what Walt Disney does for animals: it makes
them almost human. To a degree, that was its purpose. By
dehumanizing the people who made and ran the corporations, the p.r. men were creating the impression that the companies they represented were totally rational, virtually omnis-
cient, self-regulating machines free of human error. That
might not make them very interesting, and it would rarely
get them off the back pages, but it was a lot safer than letting investors, suppliers, customers, and regulators see corporations as the vehicles of real people with the same human
drives and faults that they themselves had. It also made their
occasional errors seem incomprehensible and more disen-
chanting than they deserved to be. Even the most astute
outside observers sometimes failed to recognize that often
the errors had been made because the men inside believed
the images that their enterprises had projected.

One of the earliest of the companies that came to be
called conglomerates was General Dynamics Corporation.
(Even its nebulous name—changed from Electric Boat Company—was a precocious invention.) The ordinary shareholder
out in Peoria who looked at the annual reports and institutional advertisements saw his company as the ultimate fric-
tionless industrial machine. He saw expensive graphic design,
abstract photographs of complex electronic circuits, cold-
eyed technicians, and a coordinated system of symbols of
its many divisions. He knew it was moving into many mili-
tary-related fields and he saw its stock price climb for years.
He never got close enough to learn that behind the cool image it was a one-man company still being run by its brilliant,
quirky, hard-drinking, mortally ill founder. He had no sense
of the management shambles that the founder had created
and that his successor all but drowned in. For the rank outsider, the confidence-breeding image of far-out technology
persisted almost to the day General Dynamics abruptly shed
its shimmering image and announced a loss of $425 million
on an incredibly mismanaged venture into commercial jet aircraft. The corporation had misread completely the market
for airplanes, had got lost in a progressive breakdown of its
internal management process, and had bet heavily on one

airline customer, TWA, a company then controlled by another erratic, demanding, oddball genius, Howard Hughes.

The postwar metamorphosis of the Ford Motor Company involved a monumental instance of corporate self-deception. The Ford family was determined to undo the founder's crank image and his near wrecking of the company in his declining years. They cleaned out old Henry's cronies and surrounded his young grandson with an assemblage of talented executives from outside the company, including a group of ex-Air Force officers known as the Whiz Kids, who were said to have practically invented operations research, systems analysis, and all the other trappings of modern scientific management. In stamping out the old man's cult of warped personality, they replaced it with their own new gospel. For several years things went well as the company undid a lot of the damage done by the old management, at the same time creating a marvelous new corporate image. Much of the work was pretty basic stuff, such as putting in cost accounting and spreading responsibility around. The postwar years were not times when it was difficult to sell a car if it had four wheels and an engine. Then, as competition returned to the industry, Ford began making long-range marketing plans. One thing they discovered was that when people got a little more money and wanted to move up, many of them traded their low-priced Fords for other manufacturers' middle-priced cars, especially those of General Motors.

A lot of people were buying small European cars, which gained a foothold in the U.S. market during the shortage years after the war. But that didn't seem to concern or even interest anybody in Detroit in those years. What Ford needed, their exhaustive research apparently demonstrated, was another full-sized, middle-priced car besides the Mercury, to run against GM's Pontiac, Buick, and Oldsmobile. Then followed one of the most publicized corporate moves in history, the birth of the Edsel. Everything about the process was researched and publicized, including the market studies by resident social scientists and a search among poets for the appropriate name. ("Edsel," of course, the winner, was the first name of the founder's only son, and, by any law of perception or esthetics, it was as good a name as Chevrolet or even Ford.) The abject failure of the car, with a loss of at least $200 million, not counting the damage to the company's new glass-and-stainless-steel image, has been well documented elsewhere. But whatever else can be said, the Whiz Kids—or whoever finally was nailed for the error—made one false assumption that never was undone: that because the *company* needed a new big car to balance its product mix, the public also did. That happened not to be true. Probably no other company ever laid its image and its belief in the efficacy of impersonal science so totally on the line and lost so much in the process.

When it was all over, Ford's managers had the good sense to shrug, take the write-off, and not bother to explain how so brilliantly conceived an enterprise could have followed so disastrous a course for so long. That is the way of corporate public relations. If you get a flat, change the tire; the machine's still good. Whiz Kid Robert McNamara was promoted to president shortly afterward, and then, after Henry Ford II's important support for the Democratic candidate John F. Kennedy, in 1960, McNamara went off to Washington as Secretary of Defense. Rumor vendors around Detroit have tried to connect these events, implying that McNamara was kicked upstairs to the Pentagon. Their version makes no sense from a political, historical, or business standpoint. But that doesn't mean that it didn't happen that way.

If a man was infected by the national growth syndrome or by whatever else drives men to build big things, and if his vision did not encompass some marvelous technical development such as computers or xerography or a camera that developed its own pictures, and if he was not a patient climber up the corporate ladder, he was going to become a conglomerator, whether he knew it or not at the outset. And he was going to do it with other people's money and with all the tools of finance, management, and public relations he could assemble. Jim Ling came of business age in that context. It was his time, and Dallas, Texas, U.S.A., was his place.

3

In at least two published interviews, the towering Professor John Kenneth Galbraith has singled out Jim Ling as an object of scorn. In one, he jeered at *Fortune* magazine for taking seriously certain of Ling's ideas, and in another, he exhorted Ling, among others, to "reflect on how good it was while it lasted and how little they deserved it." There is a curious parallel in the lives of these two men, Galbraith and Ling: both were born poor, in marginal and inhospitable country. Though they both used their wits as currency to buy themselves bigger and better places in their worlds, they played the game quite differently and for different stakes.

Galbraith bet shrewdly and cautiously, so that an occasional loss was endurable. But when Ling recently observed, "I won eight times and only lost once," he omitted the crucial fact that he parlayed his winnings brilliantly though dangerously, suffering his one loss at the end—the Jones & Laughlin acquisition, a disaster that cost him almost everything but his nerve. It was indeed good while it lasted, and anybody who saw at close range the way Ling lived and worked, the businesslike joy with which he flew his 570L Falcon jet across the country, had a sense of how good it had been. That the professor, a renowned observer of our national life, should see fit to focus on Ling, even to deride him, puts Ling near the center of contemporary business history, where he surely ought to be, whatever else he may or may not deserve.

Unlike Professor Galbraith, Ling is self-taught in just about every aspect of his life and, as such, does not see the gaps in the fabric of his life as Galbraith can. Ling does not see himself in history. In fact, he once actually stated that he thought 1922 was as far back as he ever needed to go to investigate the precedents for a course of business action he was being questioned about. The last day of that year happens to be the date of Ling's birth, and to the limited extent that he has ever concerned himself with history, that is when it all began.

Ling is quite capable of recalling and occasionally reflecting on some aspects, even the more painful ones, of his early life. But he does not generalize from them. What happened happened. To understand, he must almost literally taste or touch an experience. As a man who seems always to have lived in a world of telephones and jet planes, his early days in the little towns on the Texas-Oklahoma border—he was born in Hugo, Oklahoma, and raised in nearby Ardmore—are not merely remote, they are prehistoric, however formative they may have been. The forces that shaped him in those days do not seem to connect or relate to the present man. He seems to read his own past the way others do, as disjointed pieces that have been made into a press legend. When he tells of his early life, the effect, for the most part, is inspirational, the story of a boy who came up the hard way and turned out well. His memories are often of adversaries and victories, occasionally of forbearance and eventual escape. Though he never resorts to the third person when he recalls the past, it is as though he were talking about someone else, someone who had to fight like hell against the many "them" who attempted to thwart him. Even those he feels were directly responsible for his defeats are viewed with irony rather than rage. The fault lay in his trusting them, a fault he hopes to correct in the future as a result of what he calls "twenty-twenty hindsight," one of his favorite expressions.

But, except in one area, the crucial one of financial technology, Ling rarely abstracts from experience. He makes almost no use of this hindsight. His turn of mind is a much more literal, almost physical one, like biting a coin to test its authenticity or, more accurately, like thinking, at the moment when the coin is turned back to you as spurious, that you should have bitten it when you got it.

Ling's last official biography from the LTV public-relations department states simply that he was born in Hugo, Oklahoma, the son of Henry William and Mary Jones Ling, and grew up in Oklahoma and Louisiana. Good, solid, middle America only a little after the best of the good old days. But the press releases and the bulk of the clippings refine and rehash until they merely reinforce the legend and further obscure the man. It is all true, or close enough, but with truth and accuracy that lack reality. Ling comes out of it all largely uncharted. Psycho-history and psycho-biography, even at the hands of perceptive scholars, are difficult, and psycho-journalism is presumptuous at best and more likely meaningless. But Jim Ling wasn't born and raised in a couple of paragraphs of familiar facts, after which he ascended, emerged, or appeared. He was there somewhere all the time, growing up, playing, fighting, winning, losing, hurting.

Ling's mother's family, the Joneses, had produced three or four generations of lawmen around Sulphur Springs in northeast Texas, near the Oklahoma border. His father, Henry William Ling, the son of a Bavarian immigrant, was a Roman Catholic convert who settled in Oklahoma across the Red River from Texas. It must have been a special hell to be Henry William Ling in that time and place. America was going through one of its periods of overt expression of fear and hatred. Anti-foreign and anti-Papist feeling ran high. Those were days when the anti-German sentiment of World War I was still a fresh memory. During the war, the German language had been dropped from the curriculums of schools all over America. Hasty name-changing had extended even to the switch in 1917 of the British royal family's name from Wettin (Prince Albert's family name) to Windsor. The bad guys in the kids' games were the Germans long before America had heard of the Nazis and Hitler. In 1924, Congress cut off most immigration of the more "foreign" foreigners. At the Democratic convention that year, the Ku Klux Klan was a powerful and respectable force. The Klan was electing public officials throughout much of the country, including the Mayor of Detroit. At one time, even the late Justice Hugo Black held a card in the Klan. In slightly less (and sometimes more) virulent forms, super-patriotism, purity of heart, and simplicity of mind offered refuges not merely for scoundrels and ambitious politicians but for all kinds of decent, frightened men.

The Ling children were raised as Catholics, and so were at least partial outsiders in the place of their birth, this heartland of anti-Catholic Fundamentalist Protestantism. For their father, that conflict of traditions proved devastating. He worked as a fireman in a train crew whose other members were devoted and strongly anti-Catholic Masons who apparently regarded him as an affront to their high principles. They harassed him to the point finally where he killed another train man. The elder Ling pleaded self-defense and was acquitted, but the fact that his victim was a Negro may well have influenced the decision. Jim Ling says that his father never got over the guilt of killing another man, and after working a few years in the oilfields, he withdrew into a Carmelite monastery in San Antonio. But Ling himself didn't get over it either for years. Just as Roman Catholicism has always been an impenetrably sinister force to men like the Oklahoma train crew, Freemasonry remained a source of fearsome mystery to Ling. After all, here he was, indisputably American, small-town, and all the rest, yet threatened by this thing that seemed to have destroyed his father.

Even when he grew up, it gnawed at him. But Ling is not a man to display his fears. He could not see Freemasonry as just another source of camaraderie for men who themselves felt threatened and needed the protection of its ritual and secrecy and of its charitable purposes. He read what he could about this organization that he believed had caused his father so much pain. And he knew that it was proscribed for adherents to his faith and that it had great power in the country where he was born and raised. He could see that. He encysted his fear of it somewhere in the back of his head and waited.

Years later, when he was an adult, Ling did manage to come

to grips with it and neutralize it in a characteristic way: he joined it. He actually became a Mason and studied for the first three degrees, at first looking for the key, the potent mystery, but soon knowing there was none in the dreary rites performed by unimpressive men in the back of the firehouse. Then the awe dissolved, and he simply dropped out, satisfied that there was nothing here to fear any more.

The picture of Ling as a boy, created by business journalists quite naturally more interested in other things, shows a scale model of the man, with the same tight-lipped determination. But a boy whose father is racked by terrible guilts and whose mother dies when he is only eleven—and from something as trivial and meaningless and tragic as blood poisoning from an infection caused by irritation from the earpiece of her eyeglasses—may be hard outside, but he is still a wounded boy. One of six children and the oldest of the three sons, Jim Ling was too old when his mother died to go off with his brothers, Michael and Charles, to Father Flanagan's Boys Town and then to college. Instead, he began his own patchy education. He got shunted off to an aunt, who had turned her home into a boardinghouse, in Shreveport, Louisiana, and he attended a Catholic boys' prep school called St. John's College. Somewhere in his boyhood he had thought of going to Notre Dame and becoming a priest, an ambition he says dissolved when he discovered girls.

In school, he was an aggressive competitor, moving ahead of his class as fast as the teachers would let him. That gave him some sense of his remarkable intelligence but it also put him into classes with much bigger kids and made him feel even more out of place than most adolescent boys feel, wherever they are. He learned to play chess at school and still remembers his suppressed rage at a nun who beat him with a Fool's Mate: "I said that I let her beat me because she was senile. She was about thirty-five, and I didn't even know what the word meant." Though he had nearly completed the entire high-school curriculum by the time he was fourteen, he was not allowed to graduate early. He recalls the horrible embarrassment of not having enough money to buy a pair of football shoes. Se he quit school and took off for a long stretch during which "I was a bum," he once said, drifting around the country, working at odd jobs including keeping books in "cafés," which is what they called greasy little restaurants out West. By then, he says, he had a clear idea of how bright he was, and between his wits and his strength—he was already big and tough—he managed to find work wherever he went. But it is not a time he talks about easily.

Ling is not the sort of self-made man who boasts about how he came up the hard way. His lack of formal education didn't thwart him much—Dallas was not Boston or London. And it may even have helped him to the extent that he was free from intellectual distractions and perhaps some caution. But he has never seemed particularly comfortable with his incomplete schooling. He still sometimes bridles at being called a "drop-out," insisting that he almost completed school "but I never did get a high-school diploma. I had enough credit, but it was in the wrong subjects." His mother sometimes taught school, though she had no formal teacher training, a situation not uncommon in many parts of the country even fairly recently. And Ling remembers her often correcting his grammar and his tendency to drawl. Probably as a result, his occasional lapses are no more frequent than those of many of his business contemporaries with college degrees. Even so, if Jim Ling had presented himself for a job at the employment offices of any of the components of Ling-Temco-Vought during the past twenty years, he probably would have been turned down out of hand for anything but the most menial jobs. As it happened, however, from the time he came out of the Navy at twenty-three, Ling never has worked for any company other than those he created and controlled.

There's an old joke—Somerset Maugham even made a short story out of it—about a man who loses his job as sexton of the church when it is discovered he can't read and write. He goes into business and becomes enormously wealthy. When an interviewer discovers the fact of the man's illiteracy and, in wonderment, asks where he would have been if he had had the advantages of a proper education, the rich man replies, "I'd be sexton of the church." The answer makes a better story than his replying that he probably would have become a bishop or a Pope or a big manufacturer of vestments and altar cloths. But the question itself is irrelevant in Ling's case, even though one is tempted to ask what he would have been had he managed to get an M.B.A. or a Ph.D. from Harvard and to speculate about the role that his lack of higher education played in aiming him and driving him to where he went.

In the simplest sense, Ling was an opportunist. He finally drifted to Dallas and, after another round of what are now called dead-end jobs, became an apprentice electrician with a local contractor. It was a lot more substantial than anything he had done before, and besides, by this time he had reason to stay put: still in his teens, he had got married. The first Mrs. Ling was a secretary at the telephone company. She was also a devout Seventh-Day Adventist, a sect as alien to Ling as the Masons. Her church's strictures on education of the children, who began arriving in 1943, would eventually undermine their marriage. After determined efforts to keep it going —and long separations—it finally ended in divorce.

But in the war years, as Ling's family grew, he devoted practically all his waking moments to moving up. He compressed his apprenticeship into a few months and soon became a journeyman electrician. At the same time, he managed to hold another full-time job working nights in an aircraft plant. That also kept him out of the draft. By the time he went into the Navy in 1944, Ling had managed to save the down payment for a small house in Dallas and enough more to help the family through his time in the service. The Navy sent Ling to electrical school in Gulfport, Mississippi, where he graduated second in his class. He spent time in the Philippines stringing power lines and studying a correspondence course in electrical engineering he traded his beer ration for. In those days, Ling didn't drink, probably a carry-over from his boyhood in the Bible Belt, and, in fact, he didn't have his first hard drink until he was a grown man.

Ling didn't rise very high in the Navy and was only a Fireman First Class when he got out, still a long way from golfing with admirals. Despite his training and experience in electricity, he developed a curious theory that the more current your body could take, the healthier it was. But he also describes high-voltage work as "like kissing a cobra." And in explanation for his desire years later to acquire the Okonite Company, a maker of wire and cable, he recalls that, in the Philippines, he considered the company's products "the Cadillac of the industry." His voyage home was spent mostly in the hold of an aircraft carrier in excruciatingly close contact with a man who chewed gum incessantly. That event reemerges in his conversations when he attempts to explain his inordinate dislike of the sounds of crunching and chewing. They tend to reinforce a feeling, stemming from a slight hearing loss on one side, that he has failed to hear something important.

When he got his discharge in 1946, Ling decided not to go to work for somebody else but to start his own business. A kind of legend, which Ling himself has become a party to, begins with the initial investment in the business, the seed for all that followed. He sold his house, paid off some debts, and had a little money left. The amount has varied somewhat in several printed versions of his rise, but a company document, begun in July, 1962, shortly after the present corporate name was adopted, entitled "Chronological History of Ling-Temco-Vought, Inc.," establishes what has to be considered the official figure. It reads: "Having invested $2,000 in war surplus electrical equipment and a used truck, Mr. James J. Ling on January 1, 1947 organized LING ELECTRIC COMPANY as a contracting and engineering firm in Dallas, Texas." The anonymous historian who began the assembly of this looseleaf account managed to embellish the story very slightly: "engineering" was hardly the right word at the start.

Ling moved his family to rooms behind the shop from which he began lining up work, at first mostly installing doorbells and lighting fixtures and doing a little wiring of new houses. The first year, the little company grossed $70,000, barely enough to pay his handful of helpers and cover operating expenses. He had invested everything he owned in the business, but, according to one story, when a chance to buy some war surplus materials priced at about $500 and worth a lot more came along, he bought them with a check that reportedly required a lot of hasty emptying of pockets and piggy banks to make good before it got to his bank. Even now, however, Ling insists the check was good when he wrote it. His total volume came to $200,000 in 1948, more than double his first year in business, and the little company managed to turn a profit as well. Ling quickly recognized that residential wiring was not the way he wanted to go, so he began selling himself and his firm to construction contractors who did industrial and government work. In 1949, Ling Electric doubled its volume again, to $400,000. Aggressive and persuasive, he was the kind of bright young man that other businessmen liked to work with. His earnest manner said that Ling Electric could do the job, and he spent many nights with a friend who was a CPA studying accounting and cost control. He was now bidding on and getting work for outfits that built hospitals, Air Force base buildings, and other large-scale installations. The firm opened a field office in New Orleans for one hospital job, and it was doing work as far away from Dallas as San Diego.

As the company grew, Ling began to recognize that he was living on the edge of a big-money world. Pretty soon he discovered a new power source that would turn his burgeoning contracting business into a stake—in much the same way that his legendary $2,000 had a few years earlier—in a game that, in the Pentagon technological jargon that has increasingly become the language of business, would create "a different order of magnitude." This discovery would give him what he came to call a growth rate of "exponential" proportions. Ling discovered public investors.

4

J I M L I N G attributes his discovery of the dynamics of corporate finance to a loss he took on a flyer in the stock of a local insurance company, a kind of business extremely common in Texas. Ling has often told the story of how he invested $40,000 in the company and watched it dwindle to $22,000 before he got out. But it was all worth it, he adds, because for the first time "I had become acquainted with a prospectus." He called the stock salesman and said, "Thanks, you have just made me a million dollars." That turned out to be an understatement of a different order of magnitude.

The prospectus is a most forbidding form of literature. It is the document you and your lawyers and investment bankers must prepare to describe securities you are about to sell to or exchange with the public. The rules and policies of the Securities and Exchange Commission and of the state securities commissions governing prospectuses intend that they should provide the prospective investor with all the information necessary for him to make a prudent decision about his money. But it rarely works that way. The effect of this regulation is usually to produce a document so abstruse as to make interpretation impossible to an ordinary man, whatever the intent of the seller. If the name of James J. Ling is ever associated with literature in any form, it will be as the creator of some of the longest and perhaps most awesome prospectuses in American financial history, delineating, in their curious and twisted ways, some of the most imaginative deals ever put together.

The $18,000 education Ling speaks of was little more than learning the alphabet compared with what was to come. For the differences between a single proprietorship, however substantial, and a corporation owned at least in part by public shareholders are vast. The man who controls a corporation has far more than mere access to the great increases in capital that the public can provide, though that is difference enough. But the resulting diffusion of ownership, if not of control, changes the business as well as the attitude of the man in charge. For one thing, formerly his only outside observer was the Internal Revenue Service, to which his responsibility, however substantial, did not extend to actual operation of the business. As long as he paid his taxes, he could do pretty much what he pleased with his own business. But with public stockholders, no matter how large his own shareholding, all his decisions and actions are in a sense monitored by other stockholders, government regulatory agencies, lawyers looking to promote derivative suits, the financial community, and the public at large. He is now clearly in a vastly different and more delicate position. What he does now involves other people's money, and his ego trips and perquisites now are paid out of the pockets of others as well as his own and the Treasury's. Performance is exactly that: the entrepreneur is now on camera, he is before an audience. For a man with a yearning for great power and influence, there are few launching devices that offer more upward thrust than going public. Granted whatever you do is unlikely to make the front pages (though Ling managed to make page one of *The New York Times* on at least two occasions, neither of them happy), nevertheless your corporation's name, even restricted to the financial pages of a local paper, passes under the eyes of the most powerful people. The head of a publicly held corporation must explain his actions in terms of the interests of the shareholders, however much they may be mere means for him to win rewards other than dividends on his shares. Though Ling didn't build his company for that reason, one of the greatest satisfactions he derived from his position as chief executive of

LTV was flying a Falcon jet. When, in 1969, the corporation's earnings problems began to surface and austerity required that LTV forgo the operation of a Boeing 737 commercial-sized jet it had ordered, Ling expressed sadness that he would never get to fly it. And after he had been forced out, when he flew to New York on a commercial airline, he remarked that the thing he missed most was flying his own plane. What he most certainly missed more was being chief executive. Flying a jet aircraft is just one of the trappings of power, however pleasurable; having the power is what counts.

By 1954, Ling had reached a point in his business and personal life when he was ready for something new and different. His first marriage was in the final stages of dissolution, and his contracting business—now grossing better than $1 million a year—was no longer enough of a challenge. He had begun spending a large share of his working hours playing golf at Preston Hollow Country Club, of which he later became president. He was in virtual retirement at age thirty-two. He recalls 1954 as the year he brought his handicap down as low as five from around eighteen. It was also a year of soaring prices in the stock market and the beginning of one of those periods when investors become infatuated with stock issues of new companies. It has been said that, in 1955, an Iowa pig farmer could have incorporated his farm as Hogotronics, Inc., and found a ready market for his securities. Even so, Texas had just had a period of disastrous speculation in new insurance-company issues, which led to reforms of its lax insurance-company laws. Besides, a regional electrical contracting firm was not the sort of business the public would embrace. It is a service business whose assets, aside from a few tools, supplies, and office furniture, are mostly people's skills and the relationships that provide applications for those skills. Not that a service business is without intrinsic value, but it is difficult to price. Too much depends on particular people and their ability to get and deliver the work. When the work dwindles, the value often drops precipitously, because there's nothing there that you can melt down and sell in a liquidation. That may be an unrealistic basis for evaluating a going business of any kind, but it certainly reflects the traditional view of assets.

None of that deterred Ling once he decided to go public. He tried to interest several local investment bankers in his plan, but none would handle his offering. One recalls with a smile a tour of the company's facilities guided by Ling and his brother Charles, who was associated with him in those days. The premises were anything but pretentious, but it sounded to this banker as though he were being conducted through a vast enterprise. Undaunted, Ling got together a group of his friends and their friends, mostly medium and smallish investors, businessmen, and professional men with a variety of connections around the community, including an ex-Texas Secretary of State. They were his board of directors. Then, to give his new corporation a little extra boost, he got together another group, including Doak Walker, the former All-American football star from Southern Methodist University, as "advisory directors." In the prospectus for the new company, their presence, almost unheard of in a corporation of any kind, was explained this way:

> In preparation for the planned national expansion program for our firm, we have created an advisory board of directors who are leading businessmen, or specialists in their field. We are very happy to have these gentlemen associated with us in our expansion program. They will lend their vast knowledge and support to our program.

It was a cheeky grandstand play, but Ling needed all the cachet he could get, so he settled for this version of a "letterhead" organization. Of course there was a lot more to the company than his friends and their friends. For the first five months of 1955, the company that was now known as Ling Electric, Inc., had grossed $833,000 and showed a net after-tax profit of $90,600.

Ling's way of converting his contracting firm into a corporation with a "planned national expansion program" and an advisory board of directors was a more or less traditional public offering, except for the nature of the business itself. A new corporation was set up with nothing but an authorization to issue a million shares of stock with a par value of $1. That corporation, which became Ling Electric, Inc., paid to Ling 474,000 shares of its stock for his contracting business. At this point, it might be said that Ling had received the equivalent of $474,000 for his business, which was probably more than it would have been worth in liquidation. But that is not quite accurate, because there was not yet a market for the stock, so you can't be sure how much it was worth. Ling had this paper and still controlled the company, being the only stockholder until the time of the offering. Now for the public sale. It was a little bumpy at first, but he was determined, even to the extent of appearing in a booth at the Texas State Fair to push the stock. Later he was quick to point out that he had been merely distributing copies of the prospectus, not selling anything. The public was offered most of the rest of the shares, 450,000, at $2.25 per share. It took three months to sell that stock. When the offering was completed, Ling still held his own stock plus control of the corporation, which now had all his former assets plus the proceeds of the public sale, or about $800,000 after sales commissions. But now Ling also had something else: outside shareholders for the first time.

The net effect of this series of transactions, in addition to the wealth it created for Ling, was to give him a new source of power and a rather special introduction to the meaning of assets. Since the bulk of what he had sold successfully to the shareholders was intangible, he began his life as a financier with a somewhat different, rather more flexible view of the nature of assets than he would have had if his initial business venture had been a store or a lumberyard with most of its value in inventory and real estate (the initial assets of Ling Electric did in fact include a real-estate subsidiary that Ling had sold to the company sometime earlier) or a tool-and-die shop with a lot of high-priced machines and gauges. But by going public the first time with a service company, Ling could not help but view assets as anything that produced earnings, however intangible it might be. To a degree, everybody in finance now holds similar views. And, after all, a going business, however firmly rooted in bricks, mortar, and machines, always derived a part of its value from its relationships, shown on the books as "goodwill," though that term has lately been stretched far out of its original business meaning.

As soon as he had completed the offering, Ling was impatient to begin moving. He had the vehicle now, a publicly held corporation with a thriving business, a boxful of cash, and the power to issue stock. His first move was a small one, not very far from where he was. Ling Electric paid stock and cash for another electrical contracting firm, in Glendale, California. Hardly daring in itself, that deal put Ling in the right spot to take his next step. His company was doing fine, but it was still doing pretty much what it had always done, on a larger scale and over a broader area.

The bigtime was not in electrical contracting. It was in manufacturing something, and the most interesting "something" to investors and to the general public was electronics. Ling, who was looking for a way out of the service business, was certainly aware of that, especially when he began visiting California to look after his newly acquired contracting firm in Glendale. The West Coast was seething with electronics. But, aside from Texas Instruments, which was becoming a major producer of transistors, there was as yet little important electronics activity around Dallas. As Ling once said, "It dawned on me that this was the thing to do."

Pretty soon he got his chance. One of his stockholders, who happened to be an executive at Texas Engineering & Manufacturing Company (the Temco he would one day own), told him about an outfit in California that was developing a piece of electronic equipment of great value to aircraft and missile manufacturers. Building planes and missiles required some way of testing their parts and sub-assemblies for resistance to the stresses of vibration. Most of this testing had previously been done with cumbersome mechanical shaking devices. But, lately, some companies had been working on equipment that could do the job more reliably by applying sophisticated electronic controls. One of these companies, Ling's informant noted, was L.M. Electronics, which was burdened by the financial problems typical of a lot of undercapitalized new entrants into the electronics field. It had, Ling was told, a chance to do well if it could hold out financially.

Ling liked the sound of the situation, and he flew out to

the Coast to have a look. He says it took him only a day to size up L.M. and make the deal. But when he got back to Dallas, he recalls, other members of his board of directors objected to his plan to acquire L.M. They had already made substantial paper profits from the increase in the value of their Ling Electric shares, and they thought that Ling was moving precipitously. But when he threatened to buy L.M. for himself and actually approached a Dallas bank for the money, they backed down and approved the acquisition. Ling Electric wound up buying control of the company and its patents and retaining its operating executives for $27,500 in cash, another $50,000 for working capital, $60,000 in installments to settle with a creditor who was owed $90,000, plus some stock.

In the minutes of a board meeting of Ling Electric held on April 11, 1956, a report from Ling urging approval of the acquisition of L.M. Electronics said it "would open the field for Ling Electric, Inc., and broaden its base and at the same time provide a product which would be used nationally in the government missile program and promote the name Ling Electric, Inc.," among major aerospace and research organizations. It was clear enough where Ling wanted to go, and now he had started to move.

5

As soon as Ling completed the deal for L.M. Electronics, which bore the initials of founder Leon Mooradian, he changed its name to Ling Electronics. It was a smart buy for Ling, not just because it was available and cheap and had the right word in its name, but because it was in a part of the electronics industry that was becoming important, however small the scale. The newly named Ling Electronics could make needed products that would, as the minutes had put it, "be used nationally in the government missile program." That was a step toward the bigtime.

The new company, of course, was merely a subsidiary of Ling's electrical contracting business, and, however significant the move would become, it did not even make the Dallas papers when it happened. Ling was already known among construction people in the region, but what may have been the first mention of his name in the local press had occurred only a few months earlier when a local Dallas insurance investment company had sent out his picture with a release announcing that he had been made one of its directors. The picture was a standard studio head-and-shoulders. The young man on the page appears younger than his years—he was already thirty-two. But the face seems less that of a man on the way up in a highly competitive business than of a shy country boy with a country haircut. Long after his haircut style became more sophisticated, he still retained something of the look of those days, and, even under great strain, he never quite looks his age.

But the young man from Oklahoma was building a tidy little pyramid that already consisted of four corporations. At the top was Ling Electric, the parent, and suspended underneath it were Grady-Ling, the California electrical contractor; Lingco, the real-estate company he had sold to Ling Electric just before the public offering; and, of course, Ling Electronics. There was nothing complicated about this structure and nothing intended to obfuscate, despite the willingness of some detractors always to see in the complexity of Ling's later moves a desire to screen his activities from close scrutiny. Folding the four companies into a single enterprise would have entailed a lot of financial and legal reshuffling, since the units had separate credit and customer relationships and conducted their business in different places. It was actually simpler to maintain the structure as it stood, for a while at least. And, to the degree that men like Ling, however earnest, enjoy the game, it must have been more fun to count four companies bearing his name than just one.

One day he would become the best known of conglomerators, even the symbol of all of them, but in those days the only place he managed to get his name in lights was over the Pittman Street office of his contracting company in Dallas. He was already becoming adept in the sphere of corporate technology—a term he would use years later to describe his approach to empire building—but he had yet to learn very much about the uses of image making beyond putting his name on his enterprises.

Ling's first lesson in the value of publicity as a business tool came not through his own business but from his attempt to stage the city's first major golf tournament in years. The Dallas Centennial tournament was scheduled for May 24, 1956, only a few weeks after he had buttoned up the L.M. deal. He and his associates in the golf venture, an organization called Golf International, guaranteed to put up prize money of $100,000. That was a lot of money for golf, especially in those days before television had turned it into a major spectator sport. Ling and the other backers figured that the scale of the prizes and the golf stars the money would draw would provide enough push to sell plenty of tickets. So they did little promotion to support their commitment. Heavy rain compounded that mistake, and hardly anybody showed up to watch their tournament. As a result, Golf International dropped something more than $100,000, and when some of the other backers walked away from their obligations, Ling paid off their debt unassisted. Only a couple of the others ever came through with their shares of the loss, a fact Ling still recalls with irony if no longer with any bitterness. A local sportswriter called him "golf's leading money loser," and Ling concurs, citing the fact that the $100,000 loss cost him the chance to buy additional Ling Electronics shares later worth as much as $17 million.

Despite the fiasco, Ling didn't pull out of the promotion the next year. He got Dallas *Times Herald* golf writer Jim Lawson to help him with the tournament's promotion, and in its third year the Dallas Open was producing enough profit to finance a few college scholarships. At the beginning of 1958, Lawson became Ling's administrative assistant in charge of publicity, advertising, and just about everything that came under the heading of corporate relations. Mostly it was a one-man job, but on occasion, such as before the little corporation's shareholders' meetings were held, he would hire a temporary girl to help him tally the proxies. (After eleven years of working closely with Ling, Lawson finally left to try his hand at running a corporation and started one called Resalab, Inc.)

But even before Lawson got there, the electronics side of Ling's enterprises was growing. When a local promoter named S. Mort Zimmerman came to Ling with a low-cost closed-circuit television system and persuaded him that it could sell as a teaching device, Ling Electric formed another subsidiary called Electron Corporation to try to develop and market the system. (Nothing much ever came of that effort, but it may at least have headed off any desire to participate in the "knowledge industry" bubble that seduced many major corporations into making large and imprudent investments in publishing, teaching machines, and programmed learning to cash in on developments that never quite found their way over the horizon.) Now there was a parent plus four, with Electron Corporation.

Within months, Ling took in another company, a small one that designed assemblies of wire and put them together for electronics manufacturers, called Electronic Wire & Cable Corporation. It was in financial trouble and was bought for all of $200 plus a loan of $50,000 for working capital. But what was interesting about the acquisition was the fact that the company was bought not by Ling Electric but by Ling Electronics, itself a subsidiary, and thus Ling had added a brand-new third tier to his business. Without hindsight, there would be no significance to this aspect of the move. At the time, the little wiring company was simply available and cheap and brought into Ling Electronics a service it was buying outside. But it is impossible to dismiss altogether the thought that by bringing in Electronic Wire & Cable in this particular way, Ling was beginning to move in a style that had a special appeal for him—and for his stockholders when they eventually got caught up in the excitement of his virtuosity. The ways corporate imperialists have chosen to build their empires, in view of the structural alternatives generally available to them, can be seen as expressions of their drives and their personalities, going beyond purely legal and financial considerations.

At this same time, in early 1957, Ling made a public offering of securities of Ling Electronics. The sale was handled by a local securities dealer and most of the securities went to holders of Ling Electric shares. The offering consisted of $1.3 million worth of common stock and convertible debentures. (Ling himself bought some of the shares and then agreed to put them and all his other Ling Electronics securities in escrow as an act of good faith until the company's earnings climbed substantially.)

There is nothing unusual about this method of raising new capital, as any sophisticated investor knows. Yet there is something worth considering about convertible debentures: their designedly amorphous nature. A convertible debenture stands—or falls—somewhere between a stock and a bond.

Precisely where is a matter debated by financial people, accountants, and tax collectors, and it is determined in a particular instance by the success of the enterprise during the period when the security is outstanding.

A debenture is something less than a bond and more like a promissory note to begin with, in that it is issued for a fixed period—in this case, ten years—and draws a fixed rate of interest—6 percent for those of Ling Electronics. Corporations regarded highly have no difficulty borrowing long-term money through bonds, which are usually secured by assets, or through straight debentures, which are not. But a fledgling like this subsidiary of Ling Electric ordinarily cannot borrow long-term money easily and cheaply by selling straight debt securities. It usually must offer a special added attraction to lenders, what financial people call an equity "kicker." Making the debenture convertible is one way to do that. A convertible debenture provides the lender with the opportunity to become an investor in the corporation by converting his debt security into common stock at a price set at the time of issue, one that is higher than the market price then. That way the holder of the debenture has the company's promise to pay interest and ultimately principal, plus a chance to profit, along with common shareholders, from any increase in the value of the common shares. The selling price of the Ling Electronics shares was $3 and the conversion price was $3.75. Once the market price of the stock rose to about $3.75, the debenture holders could convert their securities at the rate of one share for every $3.75 worth they held and ride the stock, or just hold the debentures, whose market price would reflect the increasing value of the stock and also give them some interest income. And if the stock price fell below the conversion price, they would still have their interest and, presumably, their principal. But convertible debentures tend to carry a lower stated interest rate than straight debt, because of the value of the kicker. Thus if a stock-market price lower than the conversion price reduces the effective value of the conversion feature to nothing, debentures tend to sell for relatively less in the market than straight debt.

From the standpoint of the issuing company, there are obvious advantages too. For one thing, it gets needed money without immediately diluting the voting power and per-share earnings of its common stock, as it would if it raised all its new money by selling stock. For another, if the price of its shares goes up and debenture holders tend to convert, its debt and interest charges are reduced, and the pain of dilution is not so great as at the time of issue. Though the holder sees a convertible as access to equity, the issuer deducts the interest as an expense, which he can't do with the dividend he would pay on stock. What is more, the issuer usually can call the debentures in for redemption when he is in a better cash position and figures that his common shares will soon be salable in the market for far more than the conversion price he would get if debenture holders converted. That is what Ling Electronics did less than two years after the convertibles came out. But the stock was already selling at more than the conversion price, so none of the debentures came in; they were all converted at $3.75.

As soon as Ling Electronics had completed its stock-and-debentures offering, Ling put his enterprises through the first of the many restructurings that would become characteristic of his particular style of operating. Slightly oversimplified, the reshuffling went this way: First the name Ling Electric was changed to Ling Industries, Inc. Then another company named Ling Electric was formed, and Ling Industries transferred its electrical contracting business to this new company in exchange for its stock. So now the parent company was called Ling Industries, which was both more accurate and more impressive than its old name.

Later that year, Ling Electronics, still a subsidiary, picked up American Microwave Corporation, a maker of relays for communications systems, for stock plus about $50,000 to cover debts plus working capital. By the end of that fiscal year, July 31, 1957, total sales of all of Ling's enterprises amounted to less than $4 million. The biggest part of that was still coming from the contracting business, where Ling was landing electrical contracts for such projects as the new Air Force Academy in Colorado and a naval hospital in San Diego.

One of the first jobs Lawson faced when he joined Ling at the beginning of 1958 was yet another reshuffling. That one worked like this: Ling Industries went out of existence, and its holdings were acquired by Ling Electronics, which now became the parent company. Then Electronic Wire & Cable was merged into American Microwave, and the name of this merged company was changed to Ling Systems, Inc. But calm did not return to the Ling executive suite, because, a couple of months later, Ling Electronics paid $750,000 in borrowed cash plus some stock to the seven owners of United Electronics Company, a Newark, New Jersey, manufacturer of vacuum tubes and capacitors. Though still a very small entrant, Ling was broadening the scope of his activities in electronics. By July 31, 1958, Ling Electronics, the new parent, had total sales of nearly $7 million, a jump of about 75 percent above the year before. And electronics at last was a bigger part of total sales than electrical contracting, though perhaps not of total profits.

Now came what was for those days another major acquisition. On the heels of United Electronics, Ling Electronics laid out $320,000 in borrowed cash and six-month promissory notes for the Calidyne Company, of Winchester, Massachusetts. Calidyne was also in the business of assembling equipment to test aircraft and missile parts electronically, but it made only one component of the complete units, the principal one that Ling Electronics did not make and had to buy from others. By bringing in Calidyne, Ling Electronics became an integrated manufacturer of complete units for testing resistance to vibration, one of the two biggest in this field, ranking it alongside a subsidiary of a major industrial corporation, Textron, and giving it increased prominence among suppliers to the aerospace industry. Ling now controlled an enterprise that spread from California to New England.

All this gobbling up of companies had built up Ling Electronics' bank debt to about $1.5 million. Back in 1956, when he had acquired L.M. Electronics, he had also established for it a line of credit with the Bank of America of $100,000. That small line with the world's largest bank grew frequently as Ling acquired more and more capital-short companies. But now he wanted to turn his bank debt into long-term money through a securities offering. His last one had been handled by a small Dallas investment house. But Ling now looked first toward San Francisco and then toward Wall Street, and, at the right moment, he made contact with the venerable house of White, Weld & Company.

As it happened, one of the people who came into Ling's operation as head of L.M. Electronics, Cameron Pierce, had been a college classmate of Paul Hallingby, Jr., who had recently joined White, Weld, and on a trip to New York the three met for dinner. Though the purpose of the dinner was strictly recreation, at least as far as the investment man was concerned, it marked the beginning of a business relationship. Though Ling can be relaxed, warm, and casual in a social situation, he usually remains, even over drinks and dinner, consumed by his own business activities. And when he expresses this interest, however inadvertently, it can be most infectious. That dinner meeting led directly to White, Weld's handling a significant securities offering for Ling Electronics. White, Weld arranged a private placement—an offering to a small number of investors that does not require a registration of the securities with the SEC—of $2.2 million worth of convertible debentures payable in ten years. The interest rate was 5.5 percent—low for a corporation as relatively obscure as Ling Electronics—and the debentures were convertible at $10 a share, well above what Ling shares were selling for in the over-the-counter market. What is more, under the terms of the private placement agreement, the buyers of the debentures could not convert their holdings into common shares and sell them publicly, because the Ling shares had not been registered with the SEC, although Ling indicated that he would soon register them. In other words, the investors were not only putting money into Ling's company but they would be locked in for some time to come.

What was important about the deal for Ling was who put the $2.2 million into securities of this barely known company in Texas. White, Weld found twenty prestigious institutional investors, including the endowment funds of Swarthmore and Wellesley colleges and Princeton University. Private placements of this sort are by no means unusual for raising capital for obscure but promising companies. Hallingby knew Pierce well, and he knew that L.M. Electronics' products could be the basis for a profitable new entry into the electronics industry. Ling had commissioned a study of L.M.'s field by Stanford Research Institute. Its apparently bullish report and Ling's almost fanatical determination to become a major force in that industry were not lost on Hallingby. And since the firm of White, Weld numbered among its customers many major institutional investors, the working out of the deal was relatively simple. Money managers do it all the time, often without even having to get more than routine approval from their customers' portfolio managers and trustees. In fact, investing a little money in the securities of small outfits with good growth prospects is not only prudent for institutions but necessary if their assets are to increase with their growing needs for capital. Investment bankers such as White, Weld are always looking for likely growth candidates such as Jim Ling was in those days.

The $2.2 million was not a lot of money for this group to risk, even on an unknown, especially divided twenty ways. But for Ling the offering was a stroke of great fortune. Securities of Ling Electronics now sat in the portfolios of some of the most distinguished institutions in America, placed there by an eminently respectable Wall Street banking house. Whether Jim Ling jumped for joy or celebrated in any special way, he was nevertheless enormously pleased with this first breaking through the bastions of what outlanders often viewed with mixed feelings of disdain and awe as the Eastern Establishment. But beyond the ego satisfaction that this acceptance must surely have afforded, there was a practical gain of even greater value to his future plans. "Whether we like to admit it or not," one investment banker observed about Ling's offering, "there is such a thing here as investment by crony, and Ling managed to get into a lot of cronies' portfolios." To that degree, Ling had arrived, and that was important to him and to what he had in mind. (That offering turned out extremely well for the investors. Before the end of 1958, within weeks of the sale, Ling's stock, which traded over the counter, passed the $10 mark. When the company called in the debentures for redemption three years later, none came in; they all had been converted to common stock, which traded as high as $44 a share and never at less than the conversion price.)

When Ling came East for his new money, he told his new investors of his big plans for expansion in electronics. Within months, he was ready to close another deal, bigger than anything yet. Ling had already had his sights set on the Altec Companies, Inc., a major manufacturer of commercial and consumer sound systems. Altec, once a part of Western Electric, the manufacturing arm of American Telephone & Telegraph, was based in Anaheim, California. It also happened to be about twice the size of everything that Ling had managed to put together. The idea of approaching what was, compared with Ling Electronics, a giant may have seemed like a nervy move for Ling. But that was what he wanted next. And, as Ling had discovered, if he didn't get Altec, somebody else probably would, because Ward Carrington, its principal shareholder, was mortally ill, knew it, and had considered selling Altec to several bigger companies. "He was dying of cancer," Ling once said, "and, frankly, he had estate problems." Ling developed a plan that would permit Carrington to solve at least his financial problems while it brought Ling his company. Negotiations went on for several months.

Once Ling had convinced the dying man that Altec would be in good hands if it became part of Ling Electronics, he put his plan into operation. California corporation regulations are, in normal times, rather stringent compared with those of other states, not only covering the issuing of securities but also requiring approval of mergers and acquisitions. And, during those days, the incumbent commissioner tended toward an interpretation of the laws ranking him in sternness with John Calvin or Girolamo Savonarola. Ling Electronics happened then to be a California corporation, stemming from its origins as L.M. Electronics though its headquarters remained in Dallas, and the prospect of this constituent acquiring a far larger neighbor apparently did not sit well with the commissioner. Instead of confronting this potential adversary, Ling elected to move his corporation's "place of domicile" to Delaware, the choice of most of the nation's major corporations and many of its minor ones. Though other states have recently modernized their corporation and securities laws to render themselves more congenial to corporate business, Delaware was by far the most hospitable for many years.

(The place of domicile of a corporation has very little to do with the location of its headquarters and the places where it actually does its business. Incorporating in Delaware does not free a corporation from any significant legal obligation to stockholders, creditors, employees, customers, or suppliers. It does allow it considerably more freedom from routine administrative problems than is permitted by the incorporation laws of other states. To comply, a company need only maintain an address in the state, usually in care of a local representative who handles the minimal filings of papers, certificates, seals, and so on. In the case of Ling Electronics, the transfer was effected in what is a standard way: a Delaware corporation called Spring Valley Corporation was set up under the state's laws. At that point, it owned nothing but shares of its stock. These were then traded to Ling Electronics for its holdings, and the original Ling Electronics was dissolved. The name of Spring Valley was then changed to Ling Electronics, and the shareholders received their new certificates, the principal difference being that their corporation was now domiciled in Delaware, though it continued to be based in Dallas. Often such corporations as Spring Valley are set up by corporation lawyers and held in a file cabinet as impotent dummies until they are required for such transfers.)

As soon as Ling Electronics became a Delaware corporation, it filed a registration statement with the SEC. When that became effective—implying, as the SEC invariably points out, neither approval nor disapproval of the securities involved —Ling Electronics offered to exchange those newly registered shares for stock in Altec. By the spring of 1959, virtually all the shareholders of Altec had exchanged their stock for Ling shares, and Ling now owned the company.

This particular exchange offer—though it followed a common pattern—had a quite remarkable, almost magical effect. The former shareholders of Altec received registered and therefore salable Ling shares worth about $5 million, which can be said to be the purchase price of their company. But from the standpoint of Ling Electronics, the cost of acquiring Altec was zero, at least as far as any actual outlay was concerned. Of course there was now in existence a lot more Ling stock. But since the substance of Ling Electronics had now been augmented by the value of Altec's business, the market value of each share of Ling stock not only was not diminished but actually increased somewhat. What was reduced, of course, was the voting power of each share of the corporation's stock. But Ling's own position as controlling stockholder was not seriously affected, because the bulk of the shares received by Altec holders went to Carrington. Had he held them, he would have remained a significant power in the new company's management. His interest in those last days of his life, however, was not corporate control, and, as part of Ling's acquisition plan, White, Weld arranged a public sale of his new shares at a far higher price than they had sold for before the Ling deal was made. That gave Carrington the cash he needed to provide for his family and help them pay his estate taxes, and it assured Ling of continuing control of his enterprise by dispersing Carrington's large block of stock among many new shareholders.

The shape and the scale of his enterprise had altered markedly. Ling was still in electronics manufacturing, but of a considerably different type from what he had got into with L.M. In a few weeks, he moved deeper into the acoustical industry when his corporation bought the stock of University Loudspeakers, Inc., and some associated companies from its two stockholders for $2.3 million in cash, most of it borrowed, and short-term notes.

Now Ling changed his corporation's name again. This time he didn't just replace somebody else's name with his own. In Altec, he had bought a name prominent in its industry, one well known also among consumers in the growing home high-fidelity field, and one certainly better known at that point than Ling's. He recognized that and capitalized on it by adding it to his own name, and his corporation became Ling-Altec Electronics, Inc.

By mid-1959, it had become clear that the limits on Ling's ambition had finally dissolved. In the past, anyone watching him might have felt safe in forecasting his ultimate goal. When he became an electrician, it seemed reasonable to assume that he might settle for building a substantial contracting firm. When he happened into electronics through the discovery and acquisition of L.M. Electronics, his drive clearly was taking him out of contracting, but there was plenty of room to grow as a supplier of military electronics equipment. Altec and University did not quite fit that pattern. But the term "electronics" was broad enough—at least for laymen and even for a lot of investment people, whose understanding of it was imprecise and mixed with awe—to give these acquisitions consistency with what went before. For Ling, however, electronics was becoming what electrical contracting had been and what everything else would be, a vehicle for the expression of what was driving him. He said it in an interview in the Dallas *Times Herald*, July 1, 1959, part of a series titled "Tomorrow's Leaders." A drawing of Ling, almost photographic in detail, stares earnestly at the reader. He holds the model of a missile in his hands, over the headline "He Rockets Ahead." The piece recounts his career "to the chairmanship of a mushrooming electronics empire . . . meeting major needs of the nation's defense . . . the acknowledged leader in the field of electrical vibration and acoustical testing equipment for missile systems." And then it tells where he is going: "By 1961, Jim Ling hopes to see his company listed as one of the nation's top 500 businesses, and he aspires to see its name become 'immortal' in the business world for the quality of its inventions."

That forecast turned out to be wrong only in a detail: Ling made the *Fortune* 500 list a year earlier than he said he would. That would indicate that he was not making a mere boast so much as describing the outcome of a feasible plan he already had in mind. Ling's references to the celebrated list of industrial giants occurred with increasing frequency. He seemed at times to regard it as the only objective measure of business success. The list includes only corporations at least half of whose business is in manufacturing or raw-materials extraction, and the sole criterion for ranking among them is sales volume. Though regarded by many other businessmen besides Ling as the yardstick of accomplishment, and with good reason, the list admittedly is flawed: Major enterprises that cannot qualify as "industrial" are omitted altogether, and some that are large in no other way than that they rack up high sales do find their way into its ranks. What is more, corporation rank by sales in no way reflects other aspects of economic power or management quality. Thus a preoccupation with rank on the list, if it is permitted to affect basic management decisions, is apt to sacrifice concern for earning power and long-term stability to sheer volume. Observers of Ling's career, both in and outside his enterprises, have faulted him for this preoccupation.

At the time Ling joined Tomorrow's Leaders, he projected total sales for Ling-Altec for the year 1959 (he had by then adopted the conventional calendar year) of about $28 million, far less than what his augmented company actually grossed, because Ling was not finished with acquisitions for 1959. A couple of months later, Ling-Altec paid $3.25 million in borrowed cash plus notes and stock worth another $300,000 to James O. Weldon, his wife, and another shareholder for the stock of Continental Electronics Manufacturing Company, and Weldon came along to run it. The company Weldon had founded was a pioneer in the design and installation of extremely powerful radio transmitters for such customers as the Voice of America. By the end of the year, Ling-Altec's sales hit $48 million, nearly doubling Ling's midyear forecast. The least of the 500 companies had sales of less than $72 million, and shortly before the year ended, it looked as though Ling might close the gap even further. Continental beat out RCA to win a prime Navy contract, worth about $50 million, to develop and build a very low-frequency radio station for communicating with submerged Polaris submarines. Though the development work and the bid preparation had taken place at Continental before Ling-Altec bought the company, Ling nevertheless took great personal pride in what he saw as a victory over corporate giants. "It whetted our appetite," he said, "to become what is called a prime systems contractor."

The University Loudspeaker and Continental acquisitions put Ling-Altec in heavy debt to the banks again, and White, Weld took the company out by arranging another private placement, this time a fifteen-year, 6-percent loan from a group of financial institutions headed by Mutual Life Insurance Company of New York. These investors also received stock warrants, securities that gave them the right to buy 50,000 shares of Ling-Altec stock from the company for $33 a share any time during the next ten years. Among the other terms of the $5-million loan were Ling's continued adherence to his expressed plans to build a major electronics enterprise. Electronics still seemed to be the best way to grow, so Ling had no qualms about agreeing to what did not then appear to be an important tying of his hands.

That loan no sooner had been made and the banks paid off than Ling was confronted with a chance to feed his appetite to become a prime contractor and at the same time vault, not squeeze, his company onto the 500 list. Colonel D. Harold Byrd, a Dallas oil man, was also a large investor in Temco, having been one of the original backers of Robert McCulloch when he founded it as Texas Engineering & Manufacturing Company after World War II. Byrd's first money came, as he is fond of telling, from an oil well he brought in after drilling fifty-three dry holes. His distinctions, according to a film he had produced for a syndicated television show called "The Sweet Smell of Success," include a range of Antarctic mountains named for him by his distant cousin, the polar explorer Admiral Richard E. Byrd, and the largest drum in the world, a gift he made to the University of Texas marching band. One of Byrd's trademarks is a tie-holder with a picture of an Antarctic penguin. Byrd had been hearing a lot about Ling's aggressive style, and he thought it might help Temco, but he had never met Ling. So he asked his broker's customers' man to arrange a meeting. When Ling-Altec and Temco finally worked out a merger, the stock salesman got a finder's fee of $25,000 for the introduction.

McCulloch and Ling had gone into business for themselves at almost the same time. McCulloch's venture—trying to make money out of a military-aircraft plant without a war —probably was a lot riskier than Ling's venture into home electrical work. But McCulloch was able to get a lot more backing, because local finance people saw McCulloch's project as a hope of keeping at least some of the community's wartime facilities operating. McCulloch struggled for years to get the company on a paying basis, and by the time Byrd approached Ling, Temco sales had passed the $100 million mark and the company was looking toward real prosperity from a Corvus missile contract it was about to get that could be worth $400 million in sales.

Ling found the Temco prospect irresistible and he almost ran over to McCulloch's office to make an offer. Ling had little trouble persuading McCulloch and his number two, Clyde Skeen, that they ought to swap stock and merge. The problem came from Hallingby and some of the financial institutions that had put up the $5-million long-term loan. They couldn't see how Temco, a company whose biggest success had come from rebuilding old C-54s, the military version of the DC-4, and fabricating all sorts of metal products from popcorn machines to aircraft sub-assemblies for other companies, would in any way move Ling-Altec closer to its goal of becoming an electronics giant. Ling came to New York and talked to his lenders. He pointed out that Temco had little debt, a large complement of engineers, that it had been doing electronics work on aircraft it was overhauling for the military, and that it would do more on the Corvus missile. He said that the combination of an airframe builder and an electronics manufacturer was logical, since many new developments in electronics would involve aircraft and aerospace. And to overcome any lingering doubts about the soundness of the combination, Ling agreed to sweeten the loan deal by giving the lenders, in his words, "their pound of flesh," another 15,000 warrants to buy the company's stock (they already had received 50,000) in exchange for amending the loan agreement to permit the merger. He did not make a point of what was for him a most compelling reason for the deal: that Temco was on the 500 list and that the merged company would start out nearly halfway to the top. But to make certain that there would be no doubt about his intention of hewing to his plan from here on out, he brought the Temco business into the combination via a new subsidiary comfortingly named Temco Electronics & Missiles Company.

6

T H E merged company promptly got a new name, Ling-Temco Electronics, Inc., and Ling called it a financial springboard for even bigger things in a front-page article in the *Wall Street Journal*, "one of a series of stories about new millionaires and how they made their fortunes." The story was illustrated by a drawing of Ling smiling triumphantly. It did not say very much about how Ling ran his enterprise. It might have noted that Ling was beginning to devote the bulk of his time and interest to the financial aspects of his business, leaving operations increasingly to subordinates and division managers, and that as time passed he would become almost totally immersed in finance and acquisitions, though Ling certainly did not think that was happening. And when he did, he would insist that he managed "by exception"—to use a piece of business jargon then coming into currency which meant that the top man only had to take action when something didn't look right in the reports he received from down the line. Like other corporate constructors, Ling was an architect and a leader rather than a manager or administrator. To ask how he managed his companies was almost to miss the point of what he really was doing.

In quoting Ling about the financial springboard, the *Wall Street Journal* article that made him a front-page news story nationally for the first time did not, of course, suggest where the springboard would hurl him, probably because his next opportunity, though literally right next door, had not yet come into mind. It would happen a lot sooner than anyone expected in those spring days of 1960. And when it did occur, it would change Ling's public image for all time. At the moment he took over Temco, Jim Ling was a small but increasingly visible speck on the national business scene. His presence was still a happy one: a buoyant and interesting upstart who was working minor miracles with credit and stock swaps. Within a year, another image would attach to him: a dangerous intruder on the ramparts of established industrial power, an uncouth predator making raids on the innocent. That is where the divergence between the reality and the myth becomes worth noting.

The evolving figure of Ling as a self-made financial wizard has always been distorted, leaving out significant pieces of the man and never even attempting to explain him satisfactorily to anyone who did not know him well. Ling himself has done little to correct the distortions and fill in the omissions that would bring the myth closer to the reality, partly because he has been flattered by the acclaim. Not all the modesty he has expressed at the continuing interest of the press in his career has been false. With no more skill at introspection than most men of large action, he has never been able to answer one question about himself: why? The many accounts of his career spell out over and over the details of his rise and the methods he used, remarking at the daring and occasionally even recognizing the brilliance. But they seldom even hint at the deep-rooted forces that prohibited him from remaining a drifter or an electrician or a contractor or an electronics manufacturer or anything else for very long. And when the comments became harsh, as they soon did, Ling's response would be defensive, because the criticisms impugned his motives when they attacked his actions.

The distinction between private motives and public actions is just about impossible to make in dealing with a man whose character is as heavily cloaked in official statements, reports, and formal speeches as that of a businessman. What meets the eye is all that can be taken into account anyway. It would hardly seem to matter that assaults on Ling's motives wound him deeply, however thick-skinned the public man has learned to be. It matters more that no one who has known him well seems ever to have questioned his integrity, even when they doubted the soundness of his objectives or his judgments, even when they chose not to do business with him.

Two minor episodes in Ling's career reflect this aspect of the man. Some time before the Temco merger, a large block of shares in a Denver electronics corporation, Hathaway Instruments, became available. Ling and a group of Dallas investors heard about the block and decided it was an attractive investment, so they bought it as individuals. But, since Ling was the chief executive of an electronics company, it could be argued that he had deprived his enterprise of what is known in law as a "corporate opportunity." That is, he should have acted first for his corporation by offering it the chance to buy into Hathaway. And he did in fact get sued in an action brought by Abraham Pomerantz, a lawyer renowned for his efforts on behalf of shareholders against corporation executives. Often in such actions, a defendant will seek an out-of-court settlement, especially if the amount involved is not significant. But Ling, who felt his integrity was being questioned, insisted on fighting the case. It took a couple of years and cost him, he says, "hundreds of thousands of dollars." In the end, in a courtroom in Wilmington, Delaware, he did settle by giving his company 4,000 shares of Hathaway stock.

From Wilmington, Ling took a train to New York, the same train Pomerantz took. Pomerantz, according to Ling, came into his compartment and proposed that the two have a drink. Ling recalls that he regarded Pomerantz at the time as an enemy but reluctantly agreed. Pomerantz spoke about conflicts of interest in corporation law and of his suits against some of the biggest names in American business. But what is of consequence to Ling, even now, is that he felt he was able to convince Pomerantz that, despite the outcome of their case, Ling was, in his own words, "innocent in principle." Pomerantz, he notes with considerable satisfaction, never sued him again.

During this period, Ling and some friends created a small business investment company, a type of financing enterprise established by federal statute to invest in fledgling businesses. Theirs was called Electro-Science Investors, Inc., and its special domain was electronics companies. Companies such as Electro-Science are supposed to invest their money only in the companies they are financing, usually by buying new issues of their securities. They are not empowered to buy already outstanding shares on the open market, since that would not serve the statutory purpose of investing in small businesses. In 1961, Ling personally bought outstanding shares in a company in which Electro-Science had an investment. Three years later, the SEC sued Ling, charging that he had made $485,000 from the stock, money that should have been made by the investment company. Ling's defense was that he had been advised by his lawyer, who had been with the SEC for several years, that Electro-Science was prevented from investing in the stock and that he therefore was free to buy it. Ling still recalls with bitterness the newspaper coverage at the time the suit was filed. But he was not about to go through another protracted court case, so he settled out of court by paying Electro-Science $225,000, while denying any wrongdoing whatsoever.

In fact, an inordinately thick sheaf of papers in the file of the case in the Dallas federal courthouse is devoted to a hairsplitting disputation on the precise wording of the settlement document itself, concerned with nothing more than the problem of making pellucidly clear that Ling was not conceding any conceivable imputation of misbehavior. Settling civil cases of this sort is, of course, a commonplace in commercial law, because, however wrong a businessman may believe an accusation against him to be, it is often simpler and frequently cheaper to settle at some nice compromise figure. People generally don't get very hung up on large issues of justice in such cases.

There are certainly sound legal reasons for paying careful attention to the precise wording of a settlement, reasons affecting further liability by Ling. But at least one man close to the case felt that Ling's concern for the way the document read exceeded any legal consideration and stemmed from a determination to eliminate any lingering doubt about his innocence. Years later, Ling was still reluctant to talk about the episode and even then gave the impression he would have preferred fighting for unqualified exoneration. But he insisted, as his legal answer had at the time, that he was acting entirely on the basis of what he believed to be sound legal advice. And then he added, "They didn't tell me the right rules. Just tell me the rules, that's all I ask." Ling has always abhorred a missed opportunity, but it would no longer matter that the rules prohibited him from taking some, because he was developing an astonishing skill for making others where they did not seem to exist.

The springboard of the Temco deal, completed in the summer of 1960, almost immediately began sagging badly. Within weeks after the closing, the government decided to cancel the Corvus missile program, the $400-million contract that was going to thrust Ling-Temco skyward. Ling, for whom politics had never held more than a casual and largely pragmatic interest, had become an active backer of Lyndon Johnson's candidacy. But the prospect of a Texan as President soon dissolved at the convention in Los Angeles. Meanwhile, Ling bided his time, buying a big Texas manufacturer of air-conditioners and refrigerators for $6 million and picking up some small stuff too. (He had also made a move of minor historic interest when he sold off his original enterprise, the electrical contracting operation, to the people who were managing it.) His corporation's stock had passed $40 in late 1959 after Continental Electronics landed the Polaris transmission deal and then ambled downward, finally diving by summer to $20 on the over-the-counter market, probably from the effect of the canceled Corvus program as much as from the increase in outstanding shares that resulted from the exchange for Temco shares.

At that point, a new proposition came to Ling. John Coughenour, a broker then with a small Denver investment firm, called Ling with an idea. Coughenour was one of the first investment people outside of Dallas to develop an interest in Ling's activities, going back to the early days of

Ling Electronics, and he and Ling had become friends and occasional business associates in the ensuing years. Among the widely touted stocks in those days, a favorite of financial publications, was Chance Vought Corporation. After taking a close look at the company, Coughenour decided that it didn't rate the confidence investors were giving it. It was loaded with assets, but they were not being used effectively. By the time he contacted Ling, Coughenour had already been in touch with some large holders of Chance Vought who had indicated they would be willing to sell. "So one day I called Jim and said I thought we could put together enough stock to take over the company," he recalls. "I went to Dallas to meet with Ling, and he said let's just start buying it."

The company had been founded in 1917 by Chance Vought, a pioneer aircraft engineer who learned to fly with the Wright brothers. Full of the romance of helmets, goggles, and flowing white scarves, the company became a part of the movement that began in Wall Street to combine airplane makers, component producers, and airlines into holding companies that in some ways were forerunners of the conglomerates of later years. In the late 1920s, Chance Vought joined with Boeing, Northrup, Pratt & Whitney, Sikorsky, and other plane and equipment makers as well as the predecessors of United Airlines to form United Aircraft. In the early days of the New Deal, United and other plane makers had to get rid of their airlines, but United Aircraft held onto Chance Vought, which became one of the major suppliers of planes, notably the beautiful and deadly Corsair, to the Navy during World War II. Immediately following the war, when the Pentagon became nervous about the heavy concentration of the aircraft industry in New England and Long Island, United Aircraft was asked to move its Chance Vought division out of Connecticut and into a portion of the huge government-owned aircraft plant outside Dallas, part of which would also be occupied by Temco. By the 1950s, United found itself in an increasingly untenable competitive situation. Its biggest division, Pratt & Whitney, which sold engines to other airframe makers, was encountering resistance from its outside customers because they feared that Chance

Vought might be gaining access to their design and development secrets when they dealt with Pratt & Whitney. Rather than risk further strains on the customer relations of its most profitable division, United Aircraft decided to get rid of Chance Vought. In 1958, it was made into a separate corporation and then spun off through the distribution of its stock to United's shareholders as a dividend.

Chance Vought had developed and sold the Pentagon the Crusader Navy fighter and the Regulus guided missile. But when the missile contract was canceled, and the end for Crusader orders was in sight, management began spending cash and going into debt to diversify into other industries that sounded good, such as data processing and mobile homes. But it is difficult to imagine that they were particularly concerned about threats of the sort that Ling would soon represent. After all, Chance Vought was a grand old name, and from the day they arrived in Dallas from the East, its managers had worked hard to dig themselves into the life of the community and were eminently acceptable. As one former Chance Vought man recalls, "The top brass had a very Ivy League attitude. They had come down from Connecticut, they were class, and they didn't let anybody forget it." To a community like Dallas, still preoccupied in those days with style, Chance Vought was important for its image as well as for the jobs it provided the townspeople, the deposits it carried with the banks, and the time its executives contributed to the community's charities. However interesting the rulers of Dallas may have found Ling, they could not be expected to take kindly to his or anybody's efforts to shake the status quo.

From the moment Coughenour first proposed the idea to Ling, even though he had his hands full with Temco, he wanted Chance Vought, first of all because it was big: sales in 1959, $254.6 million. By the end of 1960, total Ling-Temco sales would reach $148.4 million, more than triple Ling's 1959 sales and enough to put the company at No. 285 on the 500. But that was nothing compared to what the combine with Chance Vought could be. The Continental Electronics Navy contract had made Ling-Temco a prime military contractor. But building airplanes was far more than making and installing radio transmitters. Chance Vought was a piece of American industrial history: Gull-wing Corsairs taking off from carrier decks during World War II, John Glenn making the first supersonic transcontinental flight in a Chance Vought Crusader. Once Ling glimpsed that prospect, it became irresistible.

Presumptuous as the deal may have initially appeared, it was plausible for one reason: Chance Vought's executives owned almost none of the company's stock, so they couldn't offer any resistance by virtue of the power of shareholdings, and Coughenour had tentative commitments from holders of at least 15 percent and maybe 25 percent of the total shares. That seemed like a big head start.

Before Ling could move toward his new goal, he had to try to persuade his institutional lenders to let him change plans again. They had yielded grudgingly on Temco, after getting more warrants. But another aircraft company was not what they had been led to expect as Ling's next move. He was still supposed to be building a major electronics concern. Besides, they didn't like being involved, even at one remove, in a messy fight for shares against a good old company like Chance Vought. But Ling was determined to pursue that company, and he spoke openly to his lenders of climbing another big step up the 500 list. Neither White, Weld nor Mutual Life of New York found his arguments compelling, and they withdrew. Mutual, which had put up more than half the original loan, was taken out of its share by the Bank of America, and the interest rate was increased .25 percent to 6.25 percent for all the lenders, including the five from the original group who remained.

Paul Hallingby, the dissenting White, Weld partner who withdrew his firm from its investment-banking relationship with Ling-Temco (Ling says he was "encouraged"), has always insisted that there had never been any other basis for his decision than a developing difference in philosophy and objectives. "I certainly never questioned Ling's honesty. He told us right away what he wanted to do and why," Hallingby said. "I have always liked the guy and wished him well." The

difference in philosophy, however impersonal, was a fundamental one that had grown out of differences in origin, history, psychology, and whatever else contributes to the relationships between what men are and what they do. It
determines which side of battle lines they choose to take and
the ways they fight. Though there are significant exceptions,
it is no accident that the aggressors in the corporate wars
have frequently been poor or Jews or immigrants, men who
felt themselves to be outsiders and who certainly were not
welcomed by the good gray types in charge.

There was no animosity on Hallingby's side, and on Ling's
side there was only his growing impatience with those who
could not comprehend what he was trying to do. Dr. Van
Davidson, Ling's friend, early supporter, and director, tried
to keep White, Weld behind Ling by arguing that Ling's
great talent was for creating and executing incomparable
deals and that that ought to be supported. Davidson's argument, though it somewhat oversimplified Ling's qualities,
nevertheless did offer an explanation of his most apparent
source of fulfillment. Anybody who has watched Ling up
close for any length of time has seen him range from abject
boredom when there was nothing to occupy him but operations to total concentration and unbridled excitement when
there was something to be won.

By the time Ling decided to go after Chance Vought, he
had become a popular figure in Dallas. If he had strong feelings about the Dallas Establishment or any other, he did not
voice them. He was working his way into the community
steadily, and his successes had none of the flavor of winning
and losing. Before he went after Chance Vought, Ling—as
far as the community was concerned—seemed to know his
place. The merger with Temco was essentially friendly, and
few felt Ling had overreached himself then. But Chance
Vought was another matter altogether. Ling's battle would
split the town and create acrimony that would not subside
for years. And even when Ling had regained grudging acceptance in Dallas, he would still be known elsewhere as a
dangerous man, to be fought, not to be trusted.

Coughenour's proposition did not come to Ling at the best

of times. With the Corvus program down the drain and working capital dwindling, Ling-Temco was not in strong financial condition to get involved in a big stock-buying war. But Ling knew that Coughenour would take his idea to Litton or Textron or somebody else. So he decided to try it anyway. He went to New York to find out if the stock Coughenour thought he could buy was actually available. It certainly seemed to be. At first some Wall Street people scoffed at the idea because it came from a Denver man in a tiny firm unknown in the East. But, win or lose, the buying would generate a lot of commissions, so they agreed to go along with the effort. One of them, William H. Osborn, had just become a partner in Lehman Brothers. Later, he became Ling-Temco's investment banker and a member of its board.

Ling and Coughenour ran into trouble almost at the outset. First of all, a lot of people who had originally offered them Chance Vought stock turned reluctant. They recognized that Ling was making a daring play that would surely be opposed by Chance Vought. That meant that he would desperately need every share he could get. So they began holding out and raising the price on him. In October, he called a special meeting of the Ling-Temco board to get official approval for the venture and to get the company to commit about $10 million, most of its working capital, to buying Chance Vought stock. At first, the directors were uneasy about the size of their commitment. They finally gave in, when Ling painted the big picture of what the company would be. Word of Ling's intentions started leaking through the financial community, and a ferocious opposition began to form.

Among the ways in which Chance Vought's executives had endeared themselves to the city was by serving and contributing heavily to local charities. Frederick O. Detweiler, Chance Vought's chief executive, himself headed the building-fund drives for two Dallas hospitals and the YMCA, among other good works. That was particularly gratifying to Fred F. Florence, the city's leading commercial banker and civic leader.

Florence's role in Ling's assault on Chance Vought was

complicated. His bank, Republic National, had lent Ling money to invest in Electro-Science Investors, and their relations were generally cordial, according to Ling. Ling-Temco did business with the Republic, but so did Chance Vought. When Ling approached Florence to tell him of Ling-Temco's plans for buying into Chance Vought, he says, he pointed out to the banker the conflict of interest created by that fact and also by the presence of a Republic executive on the Ling-Temco board. Florence said he thought Ling-Temco ought to have a Dallas bank as its principal lender. Ling told Florence that he intended to maintain his relationship with the Bank of America as his corporation's principal lender, but he suggested that the Republic bank might also participate "parallel with" the Bank of America or separately in some way.

Ling says that Fred Florence agreed in that meeting to act as an intermediary to Chance Vought's management. Sometime later, however, Florence apparently decided that there would indeed be a conflict of interest if the Republic became involved in the acquisition effort, and he sent James W. Aston, his number two man, to tell Ling that while Florence supported Ling's objectives, the bank would have to remain neutral in the controversy.

Some people viewed this change in Florence's position as opposition to Ling. But Ling points to the fact that Florence sent him a Christmas present as evidence that the banker was still on friendly terms with him. When Ling called to thank him for the gift, he learned that Florence was in the hospital. A few days later, on Christmas, 1960, Fred Florence, the one man who might have mitigated the intensity of the battle, died.

But Ling persisted, putting up everything he owned to borrow money, including $6 million from Troy V. Post, the rising insurance magnate, and guaranteeing loans for people on his side who were also buying stock. A couple of weeks later, Ling announced—as he legally was required to do— that he and Ling-Temco owned more than 10 percent of Chance Vought. He asked its management for a meeting. Two encounters took place in mid-January. Detweiler refused to consider the possibility of merger, and instead launched a publicity campaign with a letter to Chance Vought shareholders vilifying Ling. Ling countered with an offer to Chance Vought shareholders to buy 150,000 of their shares at $43.50. He already controlled more than 200,000, bought at prices ranging from $33 to $43.125.

Chance Vought struck back with a civil antitrust suit against Ling-Temco. It would later be reinforced by the announcement of a proposed antitrust action by the Department of Justice. Some people have suggested that the government's action was brought simply as the result of Chance Vought entreaties to Washington. Ling blamed it on Attorney General Robert F. Kennedy and from then on considered him his enemy. The announcement seemed like nothing but an effort to defeat Ling. When the suit itself was finally filed, it appeared to be an attempt to punish Ling. It made the hypothetical charge that this merger might "foster other mergers and acquisitions involving electronics and aerospace firms, thereby causing a lessening of competition and a tendency toward monopoly."

Ling's continued buying finally got him nearly 40 percent of Chance Vought's stock, and in March the aircraft company's management agreed to a merger. Ling had said that Detweiler could keep his job, but when the boards of the two companies approved the arrangement, Detweiler quit. Ling was exhausted. He and his second wife, Dorothy, took off with the Troy Posts for a tour of the Far East.

When he returned, the Justice Department was trying to hold up combination of the two companies. But Ling beat a federal injunction against the merger by about two hours, and the suit was ultimately decided in favor of Ling.

The atmosphere of ill will in Dallas persisted. Robert McCulloch and other executives concluded that maybe the birth of Ling-Temco-Vought would be a happier event if Ling himself were not the chief executive. The board concurred, and McCulloch became chairman and chief executive and Gifford K. Johnson, Detweiler's successor at Chance Vought, became president. Ling drew the titles of "vice chairman of the board" and "chairman of the executive committee," and he has called this demotion "my purgatory." Losing the power implicit in the title "chief executive officer" cut him deeply. There is nothing in corporate management quite as useless as a "vice chairman of the board." But, purgatory or not, Ling was not about to go into limbo.

7

WINNING had changed irrevocably Ling's place in the consciousness of the city. The lines drawn would never be erased completely. Men who supported him, whether openly or not, for the hope of financial gain alone or to be on the side of a battler against the top people, became fans and allies from whom he would get support again, sometimes to his surprise. And those on the other side, who once had seen him only as a relatively obscure comer, now knew he had arrived. Whatever else happened, he would be noticed—and watched. Watching men like Ling is a pastime in places like Dallas among people who see themselves as somehow removed from the field.

The move to drop Ling from the top spot, though it muddied up the lines of authority, had little effect on who actually ran the corporation. If anybody had had a thought of pushing Ling very far into the background, it quickly evaporated. The new Ling-Temco-Vought was born in trouble. Some it had bought, the rest it already owned. Chance Vought had several losing operations, including at least one that was approaching bankruptcy, none of which Ling had any idea of until he got inside the company. Moreover, the Ling and Temco parts had some shaky units too. Something had to be done quickly to shore up the company, and with or without the chief executive's title, Ling was the man who was going to do the job. "Coaching from the sidelines" was how he described his role at LTV in those days. Whatever the formal procedure and the efforts by others to participate, nothing big was decided or carried out without his OK, whoever else's may also have been involved.

Refloating the company was an urgent and demanding job, but it was by no means all that Ling would have to contend with. To raise more money to buy control of Chance Vought after Ling-Temco's money ran out, Ling had borrowed on his own and had pledged most of his personal assets, including his Ling-Temco stock. Once the battle was over, the new LTV's shares dropped sharply, especially when it became known that the new company would have huge write-offs. That put Ling under personal financial pressure. But, on top of everything else, Ling was then heavily committed to the reconstruction and furnishing of a house, a venture that, whatever its intent, was going to give the watchers a large eyeful.

Big houses have always been part of the folklore of big new money, whether it was made in banking, movies, mining, railroads, oil, or corporate imperialism. That is inevitable, because if a man builds big enough, no matter what he puts into the place, the statistics are what get talked about: how many millions the place cost, how many thousands of Italian artisans worked how long carving the balustrades, how long the weavers worked on the tapestries, how many kings had sat in the chairs, what queens had bathed in the tubs, and all the rest. Dallas has been perhaps more than typical of that tendency in recent years.

The Lings compounded the problem because they were new at the taste game and left the bulk of the job to the renowned Dallas architect and interior decorator John Astin Perkins. By the time he was done, the price tag—including eleven choice North Dallas acres and the original house, a smaller mansion built in the 1930s by a cotton and oil man named C. Dick Andrade—came to $3.2 million. Ling ran into trouble paying for it because he was buying Chance Vought at the same time. He had to borrow $750,000 from one of Troy Post's insurance companies to keep the contractor working. Before it was done, Ling had begun to sense that the taste he had bought from Perkins was more than he had bargained for. Living in it was not going to be an easy matter at first. But what do you do when you have laid out more than $3 million for land, buildings, fountains, statuary and paintings, marble floors, twenty-four gold Louis XV chairs around the dining table among other antiques, monumental bathtubs, a Japanese teahouse, and a water bill that would run to $700 a month in the dry season? It is not something you can change your mind about and unload on a waiting buyer. Nor can you eliminate the gossip by hiding behind the iron gates and keeping people out. That would be even more extravagant and hardly courageous. So the Lings lived in it, and despite the fact that its excesses were not easy to forget, they eventually came to ignore them and made it a happy and comfortable home.

The Ling place was viewed from the start as a crass attempt to crash into Dallas society. It has always invited relentless comparisons with every other palace in the city, including the even more ornate and ormolu one built for Troy Post, the automated structure of Clint Murchison, Jr., and lately the one that Braniff's Harding Lawrence and his advertising-executive wife, Mary Wells Lawrence, bought and redid. Whether their house in any way affected their ability to move deeper into the community, both Jim and Dorothy Ling increasingly became involved in the social politics of the city—the committees, fund drives, and opera associations that seem to occupy a more prominent place in the news in Dallas than they do in other large cities. Ling has always insisted that none of those activities, however worthwhile, was nearly so important to the welfare of the city as the jobs its industry created. While he was still defending himself against the charges that he did not contribute as much as Frederick Detweiler or Fred Florence to Dallas charity, he often argued that by acquiring Chance Vought he kept it from being bought by someone who would move it away. Unlikely as that may have been, it was a prospect Ling used in describing how he had saved a major employer for the city.

Even before the lawsuits against the merger were withdrawn, Ling was beginning to realize that his enterprise was in a rather untidy state. In September, 1961, soon after he returned from his Far Eastern vacation, he was told that Chance Vought would have to charge off losses of close to $2 million from unprofitable contracts and research and development expenses that had produced no profitable business. A couple of months later, he was told that there were also going to be losses at Ling Electronics as well as in some Temco divisions. He told his people to keep looking until they knew how bad things were. A few days later, he got word that the losses would exceed $3 million and might run as high as $5 million. Next time around, the range had reached $7.5 million to $9 million. A short time later, the board of directors was told the losses would reach $11 million. By this time, Ling decided that they had better prepare for even more trouble, so a reserve of $2 million was set up to take care of additional trouble spots, which soon appeared.

Ling-Temco seemed to have bought a turkey, and it can be argued that Ling should have known better. But whether he could have is another matter. Despite some well-publicized defense-contract cancellations, Chance Vought seemed to be producing a modest profit. All that meant was that some profitable divisions were carrying a lot of losers. Ling denies having any sources of inside information from Chance Vought during his stock-buying campaign. Chance Vought's top people apparently were not facing the reality that some of their units were near collapse. Businesses used to subsisting on the once certain nourishment of government contracts frequently have not made out in their efforts to operate in the outside world of competition. Free enterprise is often little more than a myth, and its strongest champions are just as quick as anybody else to run to Washington for help from foreign competition, high costs and taxes, climbing interest rates, or any other painful effect of their free-enterprise system. The chief executive of a corporation that manufactures bowling-alley equipment actually attempted to use his Washington contacts to get bowling included among a list of approved sports in a physical-fitness campaign sponsored by the White House. The problem as he saw it was not that his company had made and financed the purchase and installation of too many bowling alleys. What the nation desperately needed was more bowlers.

Though cronyism and favors from friends and governments take some of the sting out of competition in the marketplace, even this modified form of enterprise had been less protected and more difficult than the secure life of a government contractor as long as the flow from Washington held up. (Years later, Ling himself dismissed the idea that his own military-aircraft people could make a profit by building small private planes, because he doubted that they could compete in the "real" world.) But whether Chance Vought was worth what Ling paid for it is beside the point. He wanted it, and that was what it had cost him.

When he got his first close look at the insides of the company, he was furious. Business lenders usually protect their money by setting limits on working capital, net worth, and ratios of debt to assets. LTV, as a result of what had been uncovered at Chance Vought and within divisions of Ling's existing enterprise, was in violation of its commitments to its bankers. Though such violations can often be viewed as technical matters that will right themselves soon enough, lenders have to be told about them. If they are minor, the lenders may permit temporary exceptions. But, in this case, it was clear that Ling's corporate financial troubles were not going to go away of their own accord. As a matter of fact, the hope that they finally would go away was probably what permitted them to get as serious as they had become. Corporate managers are just as prone as anybody else to refuse to distinguish between a headache and a brain tumor until the distinction becomes unavoidable. Some of the great corporate disasters have come about as corporate executives have blinded themselves with hope or otherwise have lived out their fantasies instead of taking action. But the scale of the troubles Ling confronted dashed the hopes and wiped out the margin for dreams.

Drastic moves would have to be made quickly just to keep things from getting worse. But no matter what was done, Ling knew that the company was sure to come out looking very bad to the city, the bankers, the investors, and the pub-

lic. There was an outside chance to avoid an unpleasant public exposure, and that was to amortize the dogs over several
years—that is, write them off gradually against earnings.
Other LTV executives preferred that course. That would
produce several lean years, but the effect would be to spread
the disaster and make it appear as something less than it was.
If earnings failed to cover these annual write-offs, of course,
the result might be to make Ling and LTV look even worse.
So Ling decided to clean up the whole mess in a single year.
It would be a bloodbath, and it would drop the price of LTV
shares, including Ling's, a prospect he foresaw but accepted,
which gained him the admiration of the Bank of America.
But that move would offer certain advantages aside from
commendations, assuming that Ling's investigators really had
found all the troubled areas of the combined enterprise. One
very bad year followed by a string of relatively good ones
might erase more quickly the public memory of Ling's folly,
as the acquisition would inevitably be viewed. The alternative was a series of mediocre years at best. Besides, taking all
the losses at one time would produce a big tax-loss carry-
forward, and that would increase net earnings in future years
by keeping federal income taxes down.

So Ling went to work to clean up the mess, selling what he
could, which often amounted virtually to giving away some
units. The biggest single loss came with the sale of Vought
Industries, Inc., Chance Vought's entry into the mobile-
homes field. An investment on Chance Vought's books of
more than $20 million was sold for less than $12 million,
yielding a loss of more than $8.7 million, before a more re-
alistic value was put on the shaky unit. Another major loss
came about through the disposal of a former Chance Vought
holding called Information Systems, Inc., which went for
$6.34 million less than its value on the old books.

The shake-out continued for months, with Ling and his
staff people chasing deals all over the country. And when it
was all over and they were ready to close the books on 1961,
the net loss for the year came to more than $13 million. What
that represented was a write-off of nearly $34 million reduced
by the $5 million or so that was earned by the healthy limbs
of the corporation and by write-ups of some $15 million of

sound assets. That is a gross oversimplification of the process by which the gory financial situation at Ling-Temco-Vought, Inc., was untangled in those frantic early days.

In the best of circumstances, the writing of annual reports to corporate shareholders is a craft not accorded a very high place in the realm of literary culture, and rightly so. Yet the conditions under which such reports are produced, even in the healthiest of companies, are murderous. Though little but their figures is ever read and most of them go from the mailbox to the wastebasket with hardly a riffle, corporate managers generally view their creation with a measure of anxiety that could have been equaled only at their first adolescent sexual encounter.

The conditions under which the anonymous author of that first annual report of Ling-Temco-Vought, Inc., for the year 1961, labored have gone unrecorded. But even if they were only typical, he worked under an excruciating deadline. You can't do the job until you know a little about how the figures will look, and at LTV, 1961 didn't end until well into 1962. Printers always outrank writers, so the production schedule determined the writing timetable. And with the ranks and titles of the upper echelon—if not the actual power—a mass of confusion, the normal second and third guessing by top executives must surely have been far more than usual and severely taxing on even the most durable of men.

However wearing it may have been, the end product, the medium for a message—that your company, dear stockholder, dropped more than $13 million, and you lost $4.99 for every share you own—was a masterpiece of calm, trending up toward the dawn of a new day. Unlike most, including its successors, this report carried no "financial highlights" up front, because there were none. It spoke calmly of "adjustment and consolidation" and "proven capabilities." The revaluing upward and downward of assets was the result of "an intensive review of each operating unit's policies and practices" followed by "certain financial adjustments necessary to place each operating unit on a common basis." This opening section twice mentioned the unlucky $13-million loss, but managed to convey the impression that improvement was not only likely but inevitable. That of course was certainly true, because, whatever else the company was or wasn't at that point in time, it was still an important manufacturer of military aircraft and electronics with an order backlog of more than $300 million. And even with only four months of Chance Vought sales on the books of the consolidated company, sales for the year approached $193 million, enough to move LTV past the midpoint of the 500 list to No. 244.

A year later, in a private report to LTV's directors, Ling used less measured tones to characterize the debacle:

> The public image of LTV, from stockholders and public relations viewpoint, was severely impaired, if not completely shattered, by the reporting of such a substantial loss so quickly after the merger of these two large companies, with no prior warning. The investment banking fraternity immediately washed their hands of LTV and even to this date has made only a cautious reappraisal of the Company. . . . Ling-Temco formerly enjoyed the reputation of a hard-driving, aggressive "go-getter" concern in the eyes of the investment public, but LTV has since become one of the "untouchables" in the securities market. For the record, I would like to state to the Board of Directors, as I have stated to the principal bankers of this firm, that I had absolutely no knowledge of the losses that were inherent in the LTE picture at the time of the merger with CVC. . . . My defense, our only defense, was the fact that we entered an aggressive campaign in the latter part of 1960 which carried us to the late part of 1961, which totally and effectively utilized the top talents and time of the operating officers of LTE in fighting the various antitrust actions and corporate action relating to the merger of LTE and CVC. Immediately prior to this period, these same LTE operating personnel had been engaged in the Ling-Temco merger activity; therefore, the better part of

two operating years of extraordinary merger and legal activity had severely diluted the efforts of our operating managers. I believe equally well that the officers of CVC did not really understand that their investments had depreciated so badly below the amounts carried on their books at the time of the merger.

If, as critics have asserted, the assault on Chance Vought was a "raid" to get at a rich potful of assets, the result was an unqualified failure. Obviously, when Ling made his move, he expected better than he got. What was confirmed without doubt, however, was John Coughenour's original promise, that Chance Vought was nowhere near as good as the smart money back East said it was. In later years, Ling became fond of playing what he calls "the game of ifsy." But did he play it as he watched the stock of his company lose more than half its value in the market as the facts about the first year of the merger sank in and his "go-getter" company become an "untouchable"? It is difficult not to wonder if he would have undone the move had he been able to, like running the film of a football play backward with the blitzed quarterback strangely getting to his feet, the defensive linemen floating back to the instant before the ball was snapped.

Such speculation is useless in almost any case, but not where Jim Ling is involved. For the fact is that he got something that he wanted enough to risk all he had, and it is hard to believe that he would not have pursued it even if he had had better information about the state of his quarry. He might not have told his allies what they would have to go through before he could produce Ling-Temco-Vought. And he may not have told himself the whole truth during every moment of the battle. But it is difficult to imagine that he would have backed away. He remembers how he had to deal with bullies in the days of his early adolescence in the little towns on the other side of the Texas-Oklahoma border: "You had to fight them once and beat them. Then they'd have a different look on their faces the next time they saw you."

8

————◆————

F OR the better part of three years, the investors' image of LTV was a line on a stock chart that plummeted to around $15 a share in 1962 when a major break in the stock market followed the announcement of the LTV disasters of 1961. Then the line remained almost horizontal. Ling, the former "go-getter," had been quite accurate when he said that his sprawling enterprise had become an untouchable. But a man who had hawked his first stock from a booth at a state fair when nobody else showed any interest in selling it for him could be expected eventually to figure out some way to overcome the indifference of the market to his corporation. Ling had a good sense of the way Wall Streeters respond to winners and losers. He knew that it would take more than just a better year next time before he could expect them to reconsider LTV.

What happens when Wall Street loses interest in a burst bubble is fairly predictable: You lie there at the bottom of the chart while people who used to recommend your company pretend they never heard of it as they turn to some new hot phenomenon. Meanwhile, you scrape yourself off the mat and clean up your statement. After a while, some smart young security analyst for whom your lousy financial report is at best only a dim memory asks, "Hey, whatever became of that Chinaman down in Texas?" Then maybe you are redis- covered as a "sleeper." But if all you have done in the interim is make a modest recovery, the renewed interest is only slight and you become just another company. Ling had come to understand that very well, and he would soon set his mind to work to develop something that would wipe out the wretched past and recapture the old awe. But not yet.

The chopping and pruning and selling went on for many months, and the result was a gradual stanching of the losses, a rebuilding of the financial structure, and a return to a semblance of corporate health. Once the unprofitable divisions had been sold, earnings bounced back in 1962 to more than $8 million compared with the $13-million loss in 1961, and they were tax-free because of the 1961 loss.

Ling was only beginning to encounter a problem that would grow with the corporation, a problem that confronts every expanding diverse enterprise: management. When he was an electrician running a small contracting firm, he could see and run it all. As the firm began winning contracts for bigger jobs—missile sites and Atomic Energy Commission installations, among others—Ling still managed to keep up with the increasingly complex technology required. It was, after all, still electrical contracting, though of a considerably higher order than home wiring. An inordinately quick study, Ling had little difficulty mastering each additional technology his company acquired, even when he moved over into electronics. That enabled him to keep in close touch with the managers of his acquired companies, most of whom stayed on after being taken over. Inevitably, in the transition from Ling Electric to Ling Electronics to Ling-Altec to Ling-Temco, he became increasingly removed from operating management and immersed more deeply in finance.

But he still kept his hand in to some degree. When the Continental Electronics division was installing its enormous Navy communications transmitter at Cutler, Maine, Ling himself came out to look at the project and even climbed the towers in a high wind, an event he still recalls with some pride in his ability to overcome his fear. But that sort of thing was already becoming as much a matter of ceremony as of direct involvement with operations.

When it came to Chance Vought operations, Ling sensed

that he was in over his head. You don't have to know how to design a plane or a missile control circuit to make top level decisions. Frederick Detweiler had been an accountant who worked his way up the management ranks at United Aircraft. The problem of operating Chance Vought grew out of the fact that there was just too much of it. Even the go or no-go decisions, for the most part, had to be made considerably closer to the action. Major policy matters, such as tactical versus strategic aircraft, space versus military, or commercial versus military, would still be decided at corporate headquarters. But Chance Vought had full ranks of qualified technical and production men who could run the operations.

Ling's value, as he saw it, was to provide that elusive quality called leadership. And in the confusion and shattered morale that followed the merger, he recognized that he would have to provide it quickly. The fact that Gifford Johnson, who had been number two man under Detweiler, became president of the merged corporation and Paul Thayer, another top Chance Vought executive, became head of the division certainly helped relieve the anxieties and smooth the transition. Furthermore, aside from the departure of Detweiler, relatively few heads rolled. Ling has always insisted that he buys management in his acquisitions, and that was, for the most part, true in this instance. Even John W. Johnson, the Chance Vought public-relations man who worked with Detweiler in his battle against Ling, not only kept his job but soon moved over to LTV corporate headquarters. In the years to come, he was to play a key role in the difficult job of removing the "untouchable" label and communicating a dazzling yet believable new Ling image.

In the course of trying to weld the units into as happy a family as was possible in the circumstances, Ling called a series of meetings of LTV's recently acquired management groups. They were to be informal, friendly get-togethers. That was the intent, at least, though the invitations to the 300 or so executives must surely have seemed more like command confrontations, with each man's job at stake. Ling, however, was determined that the gatherings be a means of relaxing tensions. He got the personnel department to send him photo-

graphs and information about every man on the guest lists
for the half dozen or so meetings. Then he sat up the better
part of the nights before the events matching names, faces,
and functions. Ordinarily rather a shy man in large social
gatherings, Ling circulated easily among the guests, always
using their names, correctly in almost every instance. The
effect, apparently, was what he had hoped for: he emerged
as an impressive and conciliatory leader.

Whatever the reasons, Chance Vought racked up some
major successes in its competition for important new government contracts. Though some never went beyond the development stage and one, the V/STOL (vertical and short
take-off and landing) XC-142 aircraft had a tragic ending,
the successes of this acquired unit helped LTV significantly
during the next few years. The activity of Chance Vought in
a broad range of high-technology fields—lunar vehicles, space
probes, manned-space-flight simulators—began to create new
interest in the corporation. And one key contract provided
more than a billion dollars' worth of volume and substantial
profits for several years to come. That grew out of the successful competition for a light attack aircraft that became known
as the A-7A (through A-7D in its several versions) Corsair
II. The division's principal aircraft had been the Navy's all-
weather F-8 Crusader fighter, and it was close to the end of
its production run when the designers went to work on the
new project. A top executive of a major competitor called
Chance Vought's successful entry in the competition "in-
genious," because the division managed to develop a completely new airplane that was nevertheless an adaptation of
the outgoing F-8. The remnants of any morale problems
seem hardly to have affected the functioning of Chance
Vought.

By the end of 1962—a year in which Chance Vought businesses accounted for LTV's entire earnings—Bob McCulloch
realized that he was not the man to hold the chief executive's
title. "I knew that what Jimmy was trying to do was what
ought to be done," he once remarked, "but I never really
understood that kind of financial activity. I'm strictly an aircraft production man." McCulloch held the title of chairman

for a while, but Ling became chief executive officer again in January, 1963. The announcement was made at one of those pseudo-events created for local coverage: the ground-breaking ceremony for the new LTV Tower. McCulloch and Ling appeared together wearing construction workers' hard hats and took turns wielding shovels.

Now that Ling had repaired the profit-and-loss statement by cleaning out the bulk of the losing operations, he began his new regime by presenting the board with a plan for remaking the balance sheet by reducing the long-term debt. The bulk of it stemmed from the $44.5 million worth of convertible debentures that were issued by Ling-Temco in exchange for those shares of Chance Vought that Ling and the company had not bought outright in the assault. Total long-term debt came to more than $64 million, and the interest the corporation had to pay on it amounted to more than $5 million. The plan he outlined called for selling of some additional operating divisions and other assets to raise cash, calling in and paying off some debt, exchanging other debt issues for new ones that carried lower interest rates, and offering preferred stock. That would get LTV out of the troubles with its bankers created by excessive debt in relation to net worth. It would cut down on its heavy interest costs. Ling also recommended that LTV declare a small cash dividend in 1963.

What is especially notable about this plan that Ling laid before the board was the attention to detail aimed at gaining the greatest advantages from the available opportunities. With consummate skill, he combed through an enormous number of possibilities, weighing complex relationships among various kinds of securities, their potential values after issue, the dynamics of the securities markets, and the effect of various moves on the corporation's public image. Though Ling consulted his own financial people and his investment bankers, the total plan was his own. And whether it was apparent to anyone else or not, it made clear that Ling's interest, his energy, and his quest for fulfillment would be found more than anywhere else in the financial management of assets. To the extent that success in that pursuit depended on being in one line of business rather than another, he would be there. And to the degree that investor acceptance of his enterprise stemmed from certain public aspects, he would attend to them. But manufacturing electronic equipment and building airplanes would no longer offer ends in themselves. Making the finance processes work to discover and establish new values and thus increase the corporation's power would now absorb him almost totally. The proof of that power would remain LTV's position on the 500 list.

Like all plans that involve uncontrollable elements such as market behavior and public opinion, Ling's did not work precisely as he had outlined it. But the result was good enough. Within the next year or so, he managed to reduce the corporation's debt and its interest costs by almost half.

The document itself is a mass of financial detail, speculation, and justification. But just a few pieces of it will serve to demonstrate Ling's particular talent. One of his major concerns was to reduce the possibility of dilution of the common stock through conversion of the 5.5-percent convertible debentures put out in exchange for Chance Vought stock. The conversion price was $34.80 a share (that is, for every $34.80 of debentures you held, you could get an LTV common share instead), and since LTV shares were selling at about $15, nobody was going to make the swap soon. But Ling figured that the company's improved performance would raise its stock price quickly, so he wanted to eliminate some potential dilution.

His solution was an exchange offer to the holders of these securities. It worked this way: Each holder of 5.5-percent convertible debentures was invited to turn them in and receive for each $100 worth a new $60 5.5-percent *nonconvertible* debenture and a $40 4.75-percent convertible debenture. At first glance, that wouldn't appear to be a very good deal for these security holders. They were losing the convertible feature of part of their holdings and getting a lower interest rate on the rest. But it was in fact a pretty fair exchange, because the new $40 4.75-percent securities were convertible at $18 a share, which was a lot closer to reality than the old $34.80 price. That gave those who made the exchange a ride on roughly the same number of common shares they had before, but sooner and cheaper.

As it turned out, when the exchange offer was made in the summer of 1963, most debenture holders swapped their securities. But before the year was over, and just about the time that LTV common shares seemed to be climbing out of their long torpor, the corporation called those new convertibles in and redeemed them for cash, which was always its expressed prerogative. The money had come largely from a sale-lease-back deal—that is, certain plants and equipment were sold for cash to investors and then leased back on a long-term basis. Ling had contemplated sale-leaseback arrangements in his original plan, though he had hoped that improved operations of LTV would generate enough cash to redeem the convertibles. Before conversion could create a major dilution problem, the bulk of the convertibles had been removed from the market.

Another aspect of the plan covered the future of the nonconvertible debentures. Here is the way Ling viewed them:

> Historically nonconvertible debentures with similar interest characteristics of the new issue will sell between 70% and 80% of par range. It appears most likely therefore that LTV, during the next 3-year period, could buy in approximately $15 million (par value) of its long term debt at a cost of between $11 million to $12 million. This saving of $3 million to $4 million would be taken into the ordinary income account as earnings.

The point here is simple enough: Nonconvertible debentures tend to sell at less than their face value if they carry interest rates that are relatively low. Somewhat oversimplified, that means that if you can borrow a dollar at a low rate of interest, your loan paper won't be worth the full dollar at the beginning, even though it will to whoever holds it at its maturity date. In the meantime, however, if you get some cash, you can go into the market and buy the note back for maybe only 75 cents. If you do that, you have consumed assets of 75 cents, but you have reduced liabilities by the full dollar of debt. That saving of 25 cents can be considered as money earned. In later years, when LTV's debt rose sharply and sold at similar and even greater discounts, Ling found the dynamics of this kind of transaction especially fascinating. In a curious way, the fact that your debt is selling in the market at less than you have promised to pay back in the future can be considered almost a benefit. The problem of converting it into a tangible asset depends, of course, on your ability to find the cash to buy it back cheap. But one of the reasons why there is a discount from the face value is that investors have become less sanguine about your chances of repaying it. Another is that interest rates in general may have risen in the meantime.

The whole idea may seem at first to be tainted with double dealing. After all, Ling is saying that the corporation will offer securities with a face value he knows the market will not support. How, in good conscience, can he justify such conduct? First of all, the old convertible debentures were selling at a discount, and if Ling could know that nonconvertibles of the sort that he was contemplating would also sell below par, so could any other investor. Second of all, the new convertibles with a lower conversion price seemed likely to sell at par or maybe even at a premium. "Therefore," as Ling reported, "the individual security holder's position has not materially changed even though substantial savings have been effected by the company." In fact, the new offering brought investors a premium of about 15% above their old debentures, so, as Ling saw it, everybody won.

Ling did not lose sight of the need for a neat and even contrite public appearance in the midst of his efforts to refloat his enterprise. The corporation sold not only its bad losers but some good divisions as well in its efforts to raise cash. Referring to this housecleaning, his report noted:

> The divestment of a number of noncomplementary divisions not only made sense from an operating and financial point of view but clearly shows a policy of retrenchment by LTV to the familiar surroundings of the electronic and aerospace industry. This

makes a great deal of sense to our bankers and the investment public as well.

Words like "noncomplementary" and "familiar" are a long way from the random diversity associated with what would come to be known as conglomerates. At about that time, a banker who felt he understood Ling said, "I think he's outgrown his acquisition phase. He wants recognition as a businessman and he realizes he'll get it only if he makes LTV work." Ling's own progress report barely mentioned acquisition, but the idea was, even then, not beyond the realm of the many possibilities he dealt with:

> Should the company come to a future position where its primary need were to acquire broader technical prowess to enter advanced growth areas of technology, a solution to both the technical and the long-term debt problems might well be a substantial merger with a carefully chosen company with solid assets. The company involved may not necessarily be engaged directly in the market and technical areas covered by LTV.

There, buried deep in Ling and his plan, was a conglomerate.

While Ling was putting his corporate house in order, he was also struggling with the personal financial problems that arose from his own investment in Chance Vought stock. At one point during the 1961 acquisition battle, he himself owned nearly 10 percent of that company's stock. But in 1962 he had sold his holdings in LTV to cover his loans and wound up with less than a dozen shares of LTV when he took over again as chief executive.

Ling gained a new grip on the company the following year with the help of Colonel Harold Byrd. The two men set up a private holding corporation called Alpha-Omega, into which Byrd put some LTV stock and other securities and Ling put just about everything he had in the way of assets. Alpha-Omega then liquidated its other holdings and during the next several months bought enough LTV common, preferred, and convertibles to become the largest single shareholder, with around 10 percent of the votes. Though each man held half of Alpha-Omega's shares, Ling was permitted to use its LTV votes to reassert his control of the corporation he had built, which was one purpose of setting up the holding company. Another was to regain for Ling a substantial financial interest in the enterprise he had built.

To that point, Ling had demonstrated that he was aggressive and imaginative in the realm of corporate finance, already able to achieve major objectives with relatively few corporate and personal assets. He had shown himself to be extremely skilled in making opportunities largely by finding imbalances and disparities among the market and book values of various securities. However well he had done all of this, he was still mostly doing what had been done before. Even so, the increasing complexity of his moves had already caused consternation among some of his staff people, especially some of those who had been with him since earlier days.

McCulloch was not the only one who could not quite understand what Jim Ling was up to. And Ling, whatever else he may be, is not especially adept as a communicator of his ideas. He can talk at great length about a plan and still fail completely to get it across to anyone not totally plugged in to Ling's way of leaping from thought to thought ("touching only the peaks," as someone once described it). His remarkable mental agility is only part of the problem, however. Compounding it are other factors. One is his assumption that the listener has a grasp of corporate technology equal to his. Another is his impatience with those who try to slow him down. "Let me finish this point; we'll go back over that later" is almost a Ling trademark, but mostly the conversation doesn't get back to those unexplained points. And sometimes the confusion stems from Ling's highly individual if not imprecise use of language (he once described a period of concentrated, uninterrupted effort as "celibacy") and his lack of concern for exact dates and figures when he is scaling the peaks. Then there is a corollary: some who do not follow him hesitate to admit it, figuring they will work it all out later by themselves, which they may or may not do.

Often people found themselves nodding to Ling, which

meant to him that they understood. But what they were really expressing was not comprehension but conviction. They didn't quite know what he was constructing, but they believed in it anyway. The turnover of members of his financial staff in those days was as much as anything a product of men of adequate intelligence not being able to keep up with him sufficiently well to implement his ideas. There always have been some who could keep up well enough to carry out the programs. Clyde Skeen, who came with Temco, eventually worked his way to the role of number two, though the line between his finance and operating management functions was never defined clearly enough and eventually caused him and the corporation considerable difficulty. George Griffin was hired away from McDonnell Aircraft in St. Louis in 1961 to serve as a special financial operative for Ling. A brilliant lawyer and accountant and an ex-Air Force bomber-navigator, Griffin was one of the few men around Ling who could follow the leaps and turns well enough to interpret Ling to others. Not that men who couldn't keep up were in any sense retarded, although some very bright ones occasionally came away from Ling thinking they might not be so smart as they had thought.

Also some people exposed briefly to Ling were overly sensitive to his lack of formal education and conventional social credentials and concluded that Ling simply was not very bright. Their reactions are not unlike those of literary intellectuals who express disdain for painters and composers who don't articulate well what they are doing and instead assume that the painting or the composition speaks for itself. But what Ling had done and would continue to do was a kind of creative improvising based on something he could see and feel somewhere in himself and couldn't get across to anybody who wasn't plugged in, at least at the time he was creating it. Afterward, all kinds of minds have been able to sort through the notes, the tapes, the reports, and the prospectuses and know very well what he had been up to. But only a few— including Skeen, Griffin, Bernard Brown, the treasurer, some of his legal advisers, and a handful of men who came to LTV via later acquisitions—could keep the gap between him and themselves manageably narrow.

The problem of defining Ling is futher complicated by the fact that, in those days at least, he elected—wittingly or not—to be judged in conventional terms by conventional people. That accounts for the house, the furnishings, and the change in his attitude toward community involvement that saw the Lings serve such civic activities as the opera. It also accounts for an art collection that mixed personal taste with sure things. It is a lot easier to see Ling surrounded by his favorite classical, monumental, and not very fashionable paintings by the eighteenth-century Hubert Robert, along with portraits of his wife, children, and grandchildren, and photographs of Eagle Ranch and its game, than by his "high-class" paintings such as a Camille Pissarro. Ling probably sensed that too when, in describing the Chance Vought deal, he told an interviewer, "I stood to lose six million myself. I could have quit and still been wealthy, but maybe I couldn't buy the Impressionist paintings that I wanted; on the other hand, I didn't feel badly about not having Impressionist paintings before."

The bookshelves of the forty-foot den included a couple of yards of Walter Scott's Waverley novels that came with the house. Ling never claimed to have looked at them, even referring once to the author as "Waverley" as he ran his hand along the shelf. But anyone who didn't know him well might view the presence of the works of the British writer as pretension rather than mere decor and maybe an investment. Ling's own reading taste—aside from his voracious consumption of business matter—is diverse and runs from stuff like the novels of Irving Wallace, Leon Uris, and Robert Ruark to chess and popular history. After several false starts, he found himself hooked by Barbara Tuchman's *The Guns of August*.

Generally Ling tends to be excessively respectful of the printed word and reluctant to criticize anything he reads, not untypical of a man with his education. But where he starts on even terms, as he does with chess, the quality of his mind is evident. One day, while playing through a historic game in which the *ante bellum* chess prodigy Paul Morphy defended Black and won, Ling discovered that Morphy's adversary missed a key move that would have produced checkmate for White. The chess column that described the game made no mention of White's oversight. Ling was concerned that, good as he was, he might have been overreaching in his assumption that he had outsmarted *The New York Times* chess columnist, or at least the losing player in a game that made the history books. So he phoned a friend and asked him over to play through the game a couple of times with him to make sure. Ling, it turned out, was right. White had missed an opportunity to beat Morphy, and Ling had not. Then he decided that if *he* could figure it out, the *Times* ought to have mentioned it, and he even briefly considered writing his first letter to an editor.

Ling's public personality—a shrewd, tough, abrupt man surrounded by obvious and impersonal trappings of wealth and power—is unquestionably of his own making, however inadvertent. His impatience with slower heads, however, is often tempered, at least privately, by recognition of his own flaws. One of his aides froze and became tongue-tied while making a presentation to a group of New York bankers, and, after an embarrassing moment, Ling took over and completed the job. Afterward, when the man abjectly apologized for what had been a most unfortunate occurrence, Ling took him off the hook by observing that he himself had done the same thing more than once. What persisted after the event for Ling was the pain the man had suffered and his own memories of awe and fear in such encounters.

His personal sense of values seems in no way affected by the size of the numbers in his public life, another aspect of the man that escapes the notice of outsiders. A man who visited him at home noticed that he had been poring over a stack of paperbacks for something to read that evening. He offered Ling one he had been carrying. Several weeks later, in a letter devoted to business, Ling began with "I enjoyed reading" the book. The giver was astonished that Ling had even remembered where he had got it, let alone bothered to thank him for so trivial and casual a gift.

At times, Ling's generosity can be remarkable. At one point when he thought that LTV's stock was due for a sharp increase, Ling used his own money to set up a kind of investment trust to buy LTV's stock for a group of corporate staff executives who held none of the corporation's stock options. When the stock did rise, as he had predicted, the holding was liquidated and the substantial gains were turned over to this group. A recent prospectus revealed a long list of names of people who either had received shares of stock as gifts from Ling or had been lent money by Ling to buy shares from him at very low prices before a public offering at substantially higher prices. Some of the people on the list were Ling's children and his brother, but others were not identified. It turned out, however, that they included a former secretary, old friends and former associates, an LTV executive jet pilot, and several servants. The least that any of them made from the transaction was $12,500, with no investment at all.

Ling's performance as a golfer seems also to shed some light on his private nature. Golf is as much a part of modern business life as big houses and art collections. And Ling is a dedicated and excellent golfer. A natural athlete, almost unobtrusive in his physical power, Ling might have been a top pro if he had jumped into golf as fervently as he has pursued finance. And when he misses a putt, he is as concerned as the next man, and perhaps a little more embarrassed and defensive. But he is not a consistent winner, though he attributes that to the fact that he cannot devote as much time to the game as some of the country-club crowd "who have nothing else to do but watch the family money." The image of a totally self-contained, stainless-steel personality disappears when he goes out on the course. However little he may enjoy losing, he seems able to make a distinction between golf and the larger aspects of his pursuit, which is not a common quality among the driving, self-disciplined types who "play to win" at everything they touch. If that is a weakness, it is surely not without a certain appeal.

Where winning did matter to Ling—on the big playing fields of the *Fortune* 500 and the stock market—it was not merely everything or the only thing; it was an objective that always seemed attainable—one way or another. In 1964, with the big merger digestion problems out of the way and the refinancing going more or less according to plan, Ling was confronted with the unpleasant fact that the market was still not responding to the company. Earnings in 1962 topped $3 a share, but that was all tax-free. Had normal corporate taxes been paid, the figure would have been sliced to $1.64. The following year, after more write-offs of losses and with a lot of the tax credits used up, earnings per share dropped from $3.03 to $2.12 and would have been only $1.54 if fully taxed. The year 1964 did not look as though it was going to be a big winner. Ling had already forecast to his board the year before that sales, particularly at Chance Vought, would be tapering off sharply as some government contracts expired and before other development projects became important new contracts. That forecast was coming true. What is more, pre-tax earnings were not rising noticeably either, and since they would be fully taxed for the first time, net income was bound to decline. That in turn meant that the ultimate measure for many investors, earnings per share, would be down.

Ling acted to prevent that indicator from turning against him again. Since his common stock had not recovered to his satisfaction, he took the position that it was underpriced and, therefore, as he said at the time, a good buy for the company itself. In mid-1964, LTV made an exchange offer to its common shareholders. For every three shares of common they turned in, they would receive $15 in cash plus a new issue of preferred stock (convertible into 1.25 shares of common) paying $3 a year in dividends, twice what they were getting on their three shares of common, and callable at $75, more than three times the value of three common shares. It was an attractive offer to anybody who wasn't enthusiastic about the corporation and yet didn't want to sell out, either because he had higher long-term hopes or had paid more for his stock than it was currently selling for. The swap gave the exchanging shareholder some cash in his hand and a security with double the income he was getting before and with more stability. And if big growth did take place, the convertible feature of the preferred stock would give him a chance to ride with it.

For the corporation, one effect was that the exchange offer

took 797,490 common shares off the market, and that auto-
matically increased per-share earnings on the rest. The original offer had asked for up to 1.5 million shares, though such
goals often are set above realistic expectations. A week after
the offer expired, LTV began buying more of its common
shares in the open market. This buying was spread over the
rest of the year, and by the close of 1964 the corporation had
taken another 200,000 of its shares off the market, at an average price of $18 a share. As a result, even though sales for the
year were somewhat below 1963 and earnings rose a little and
were taxed a lot higher, LTV's after-tax earnings per share in
1964 climbed to $2.31 compared with $2.12 the year before.
What accounted for this earnings "growth" was the fact that
the number of common shares outstanding had been cut
from 2,824,772 to 1,849,982. Without that, earnings per share
would have been only $1.74, once again proving an ancient
axiom: the next best thing to a bigger numerator is a smaller
denominator.

LTV had cracked the 200 level of the *Fortune* list back in
1962, its first full year of combination with Chance Vought,
reaching No. 158. But general business growth was big in
those years, and even with a slight increase in sales in 1963,
the company dropped to 168 and then fell to 186 the following year with its slight decline in sales. But long before the
books were closed on 1964, Ling's mind was focusing on a
new plan with a whole new set of opportunities. In keeping
with the military-industrial atmosphere in which the corporation was now operating, the plan got a Pentagonian name:
Project Redeployment. Though it would at first receive a less
than enthusiastic reception from investors and the public,
eventually it would prove to be a quite remarkable demon-
stration of Ling's skill at discovering, almost creating, assets
and the beginning of a revival of interest in Ling-Temco-
Vought and its founder.

Long after it was launched, a young security analyst, sitting
in a restaurant in New York, carefully drew the outlines of
the plan on a tablecloth. When he was finished, he put down
his pencil and, without a trace of irony, said, "That proves
you *can* get something for nothing."

9

ONE Saturday morning in early October of 1964, Ling sat in his headquarters office in the new LTV Tower in downtown Dallas and talked about the future. It was the weekend of the Big Game, the annual meeting between the University of Texas and Oklahoma University in the Cotton Bowl. Later, Ling would go downstairs to the National Bank of Commerce, of which he was a director and stockholder, to attend one of the city's traditional pre-game receptions. Mayor Earle Cabell, who was running for Congress, would stop by. So would former Governor Allan Shivers and many other prominent local business and political people. Before the weekend was over, the nearby intersection of Akard and Commerce streets, between the Baker and Adolphus hotels, would be covered with a fine layer of broken glass from whiskey bottles, and the hangovers would be numberless. But in the clear air of that morning, amid the elegant John Astin Perkins orientalia of his new office, Ling spoke to a couple of reporters from New York about the way it was going to be at LTV, largely unmindful of their questions, which were not about Ling or LTV at all. He explained that LTV was buying in its own stock because there was no better bargain around at the time. He didn't mention Project Redeployment either by name or by shape, but he talked in the special relentless and quite winning way he reserves for his favorite subject. Not yet forty-two, he looked and sounded much younger in a sports jacket, slacks, and loafers. He is a powerful man physically, yet he is so compactly built and moves so easily that he at times seems smaller.

As he spoke, Ling gave few clues to the pressures he was operating under. The corporation's sales for the year would be down to their lowest level since 1961. And while total pre-tax earnings were up a little, the per-share figure would depend on the corporation's stock-buying program. There were internal management problems, and before the month was over, Gifford Johnson, LTV's president since the Chance Vought acquisition, would resign, which might create a bad taste in the community and the stock market. The Electro-Science Investors case had just just been settled out of court, and it still troubled him. He was also in the process of buying out Colonel D. Harold Byrd's interest in Alpha-Omega, their holding company, and that was putting Ling heavily into debt. Besides all that, the development work on the A-7A was still under way, and it would be a year before the plane, on which the future of the corporation then seemed to hang, would pass its flight tests.

None of that showed that morning. He was the picture of a confident entrepreneur on the move, one of the prominent members of a group who had recently signed a newspaper ad as Businessmen for Johnson. At one point, he casually remarked to his listeners that LTV stock was selling at 3.5 times earnings. At that moment, the stock was selling at maybe $18, and the company showed no signs of earning anything like the $5 a share that would have validated his figure. The audience did a double-take, and one reporter interrupted to gasp. "That's three and a half times 1966 earnings," Ling quickly explained without further comment on the fact that he was forecasting more than two years in advance, a practice rarely undertaken for the press.

As it turned out, Ling was wrong. LTV actually was selling at less than three times the $6.51 the corporation earned in 1966. But that required some major changes in the scale and the nature of LTV, changes that were already moving out of Ling's head and into the legal and financial actions that would give substance to his prediction. The slashing and reshuffling after the acquisition of Chance Vought were all in the past. The machine was on the track again, and Ling was expressing his conviction that nothing could stop him now, concealing whatever lingering doubts he must have felt.

Before 1964 was over, Project Redeployment was under way. It would not go quite as Ling had planned it, but it would work beautifully. The first step was to set up three new corporations in addition to Ling-Temco-Vought. Next, LTV "sold" each of them assets in exchange for their stock. The new LTV Aerospace Corporation got most of what was left of Chance Vought; LTV Electrosystems, Inc., got the military electronics-systems business that had largely been Temco; and LTV Ling Altec, Inc., took over the sound-equipment and Ling Electronics testing-systems businesses.

The next step, scheduled for the spring of 1965, was an exchange offer through which LTV, the parent corporation, would ask its shareholders to turn in shares of their LTV stock and, in return, receive cash and some of the stock in these three new subsidiaries. If they accepted this offer, what had formerly been divisions of the parent company would become publicly owned corporations. But since LTV, the parent, would retain for itself most of the shares of these subsidiaries, they would still be controlled and largely owned by their parent.

Early in 1965, Ling and his public-relations director, Johnny Johnson, began a campaign of press contact, including a trip to New York, to explain the series of events that was taking place at LTV. The aftermath of Chance Vought followed by the complex refinancing and exchange offers of the previous couple of years had changed LTV's image from pariah to enigma, which probably was an improvement. But as Ling unfolded Project Redeployment, the eyebrows, if not the interest, of his listeners rose. The typical reaction to Ling's matter-of-fact spinning out of the plan, even among financial writers who considered themselves sophisticated, was: What's he talking about? It was Johnson's sincerity and obvious faith in his leader that, as much as anything, made Ling credible if not wholly comprehensible at that time.

It took an eighty-page prospectus in April ot that year to lay out what Ling was talking about, and even with that, Project Redeployment raised more questions than it seemed to answer. What the prospectus covered was the complex exchange offer creating the three new publicly held corporations, and nowhere in its pages did the term "Project Redeployment" appear. The Securities and Exchange Commission doesn't go for anything that can be construed as promotional or, it often seems, literate or even explanatory. Mary Wells Lawrence and William Shakespeare both would have failed abjectly as prospectus writers.

What the exchange offer specifically proposed was that holders of common stock of Ling-Temco-Vought turn in their shares and receive for each of them one half-share of each of the three new subsidiary corporations—Aerospace, Electrosystems, and Ling Altec—plus $9 in cash. The prospectus asked for at least 400,000 shares of LTV by May 7. On that date, only about 175,000 shares had come in, and the offer was extended three weeks. But even by then, fewer than 250,000 shares of the parent were offered for the package of subsidiary shares and cash. One reason might have been that if the financial community was having trouble figuring out what it was all about, stockholders were apparently even more confused.

Even so, Project Redeployment was off the ground, and what it had accomplished at that point, in the simplest terms, was to make LTV into four publicly held corporations. With fewer than 125,000 shares of each of the three *new* companies in the hands of public stockholders and with more than a million each of their "outstanding" shares in the vaults of LTV, their parent, they were still essentially parts of their parent. But as corporations with outside stockholders, they would get their market value from investors' opinions about *their* earnings prospects rather than from accountants' rules about the value of assets on the books of a corporation.

In other words, Ling's Project Redeployment had started with LTV's corporate assets, created three new corporations, traded LTV's assets to those new corporations for their stock, and then put a little of that new stock on the market. The effect was to convert those assets into marketable securities. Now, if investors thought that an aerospace, a military-electronics, and a communications-equipment company were worth more than a company that had owned all three, LTV would have increased the value of its assets. That is because the market value of its shareholdings of its subsidiaries would, presumably, rise with the market price. There are some rational explanations for this phenomenon, having to do with the increase in the number and kinds of shares producing more market interest and opportunity. But none of these really explains an essentially irrational behavior pattern. None of these new companies was going to earn any more now that it was no longer a part of LTV than it would have as a division of its parent. None of them was going to be run any differently or by different people, at least not at the outset. Nevertheless, investors were now going to be willing to pay more, a lot more at some times, for these parts of LTV than they had been before. And since LTV owned most of these shares, and the shares were acceptable to banks as loan collateral at higher values than the assets they now represented would have been, LTV would literally create new borrowing power out of the air as the prices of subsidiary shares rose on the stock market. The effect of the plan was to increase the value of LTV's assets and thus increase its ability to grow by acquisition.

Still another view of the process may come from this simple analogy: Assume that LTV has an asset on its books worth $100. It might mortgage it, sell it and lease it back, or just sell it. But if the $100 figure accurately reflects the value of that asset, from an accounting standpoint, the very most the company can expect to get for it is $100. Now assume that a corporation called LTV-XYZ is set up with $100 worth of common stock. Then LTV, the parent, trades the $100 asset for the $100 of common stock in LTV-XYZ. Next, it offers shareholders of LTV a swap: turn in $10 of LTV stock and get $10 worth of LTV-XYZ. Suppose also that LTV is selling at ten times its earnings, not a very large multiple. But here is this new LTV-XYZ, a company in an industry most of whose companies are selling at twenty

times their earnings. Now, as the $10 worth of LTV-XYZ
begins trading, its price rises to reflect the multiple of other
companies in the industry it has entered by being separated
from its more diverse and less valued parent. Suppose it
rises to $20. The parent, which retained 90 percent or $90
worth of the subsidiary's stock, now has marketable securities worth $180. It may not be able to show them on its
books at that figure, but as collateral they are now worth
$180. And what that increase in value actually cost was
very little. The parent had to give out $10 worth of *its* LTV-
XYZ stock to achieve that value in the market, but it also
got back $10 worth of its own stock, which increased slightly
the value of the remaining parent shares outstanding and
also raised the parent's earnings per share. The parent's ownership was also large enough so that it could consider the
subsidiary's earnings as its own, for reporting purposes, less
the portion that would be attributed to the holdings of the
outside minority stockholders of LTV-XYZ.

That example describes Project Redeployment and its
effects hardly better than the simple statement of Newton's
Third Law of Motion describes the operations of the Apollo
moon-landing project. It attempts only to express the underlying dynamics of the process.

Beyond that, the subsidiaries themselves, as separate corporations, could engage in their own financing activities, always, of course, with the guidance, advice, and consent of
their overwhelming majority stockholder, LTV. Project Redeployment also had the effect of making public, in the form
of the now requisite financial statements to outside shareholders, the results of their operations. Corporations are
generally reluctant to divulge the profits and losses of their
divisions. If they have losers, they prefer to bury the losses
among the profits of healthier divisions. Ling made this
necessary "visibility" of his corporation's activities a virtue
in that the public now could see how well or how badly each
of the former LTV divisions was doing. He also hoped
that with the major divisions separated in this way, losses
in one would not affect the profits and therefore the market
prices of the shares of the others, although they would cer-

tainly affect the consolidated earnings of the total complex as though it were still a single corporation. Another anticipated benefit was the management incentive it offered. Executives of the new subsidiaries would receive their options in the shares of their own subsidiaries. So if one subsidiary did well, its executives would presumably benefit more now that they were redeployed than if they had remained together, because the losses of other subsidiaries would not affect the value of the options of their own company. That seemed to solve a problem of many large corporations: managers of profitable units have to carry the losers, often cutting down their own bonuses, profit-sharing, and stock-option values.

Project Redeployment created some problems, too. For one thing, though the public did in fact bid up the prices of the subsidiary shares almost from the start, it was never clear what effect LTV's own holdings of them might have on the market then and later. The preponderance of the total outstanding shares—around 90 percent at the beginning— might seem poised like a thunderhead over the market. The parent never intended to unload much more of that stock on the market, because that would undo the entire purpose of the plan. But the possibility must have been some sort of factor in the subsequent dynamics of those shares in the market.

This relationship between parent and children also raised some questions about decisions affecting matters where the interests of the parent and the subsidiaries might not be the same. The management of a corporation with wholly owned divisions can dip into their cash and other assets as it requires them for any legitimate corporate purpose. They are all, in effect, in one big pot. But under LTV's new structure, the parent's management, though it represented the unquestioned largest shareholder, was more circumscribed in how it could operate its public subsidiaries. Though earnings, less the minority's interest in them, could be reported as earnings of the parent, they could not be taken at will but only as dividends on the stock held by LTV. But when Ling decided that the subsidiaries ought to pay their public shareholders dividends to increase their market acceptance, the parent company's shares in them were converted into non-dividend-paying shares specifically to conserve subsidiary cash. That meant that just about the only source of actual cash to LTV for payment of its own dividends, interest, and operating expenses was the fees it charged the subsidiaries for computer and bookkeeping services and for the operation of the corporate research laboratory.

Later on, when the LTV complex began running into cash problems, Ling would devise means of getting money from the subsidiaries by converting LTV shares in them into dividend-paying stock, by getting one of them to buy from LTV some of its own shares held by the parent, and of course by selling more shares to the public and all of some subsidiaries to other corporations. However careful he had to be of conflicts of interest, he managed to find enough ways of keeping the enterprise afloat so that even his successors could continue the jettisoning process, using his plans, long after he had left.

But in those days of 1965, there was no cause for concern about sinking. Project Redeployment was a masterful effort, and its financial devices were working well. Its success was helped by a generally rising stock market, by the successful flight test of the A-7A in the fall, and by a major acquisition, the Okonite Company. Despite the contribution of these factors, in those days and for some years to come, Project Redeployment had a brilliant life of its own. By the middle of 1966, with the book value of the assets of Aerospace worth about $18.4 million, the market value of LTV's shares in the subsidiary—a figure Ling called a "working asset"—stood at $117.7 million; Electrosystems' asset book value stood at $8.6 million and LTV's "working asset" value of its shares was $47.1 million; the figures for Ling Altec were $4 million and $17.3 million; and for Okonite $17.7 million and $24 million. And the market value of none of those subsidiaries had yet hit its peak.

Ling first began negotiating for Okonite in the midst of the first exchange offer for Project Redeployment in April, 1965. When he testified before a congressional committee studying conglomerates some years later, he said:

I was in electrical work during the war [with the Navy in the Philippines], and I was highly impressed with the cables they were using, which were very critical at the time. Later, in the formative years of my company [in the electrical contracting days], we used a lot of Okonite cable which was a superior or Cadillac product. Thus I watched with a great deal of interest for years this hassle between the Justice Department and the Kennecott Copper Corporation.

He was referring to the antitrust action against Kennecott aimed at forcing the copper company to undo its acquisition of Okonite, a maker of wire and cable, and a competitor of another Kennecott subsidiary. But what put Ling on the trail of Okonite was not only his wartime memories or his continuing interest in Kennecott's antitrust proceedings but a man from Philadelphia named Robert Mayer. He sent Ling a draft of a brochure being prepared by the investment banking firm of Hayden, Stone, Inc., offering Okonite for sale, and later introduced him to the president of Kennecott, for which he received a finder's fee of $150,000. At least seventy prospects took a look at Okonite, and none pursued it. Ling at first thought he could buy it for about $18 million and finally worked a deal for $31.7 million in cash, much of which he initially borrowed from banks using LTV subsidiary shares as collateral. Part of the deal also included Kennecott's agreement to sell copper to Okonite at low prices for some time.

Though Ling's original interest in Okonite may well have grown out of respectful nostalgia, LTV could not have picked a better time to buy it. Okonite had not looked especially attractive to the other prospects because a fabricator of copper wire and cable without its own copper production is in a chancy business. It is at the mercy of a volatile world commodity market for its raw material, and it must compete with integrated copper producers, who often make enough from mining and refining the copper to be able to sell their wire and cable cheap when that market shrinks. But what interested Ling, aside from Okonite's image, was the prospect of redeploying into the securities market a company with $53 million in assets. It also happened that while LTV was negotiating, Okonite began recovering from a cyclical slump and started showing a profit after a period of losses.

Sales for LTV in 1965 hit a new high, $336.2 million, largely because Okonite's volume for the last quarter was consolidated into the total. Even so, LTV lost more ground on the 500 list, dropping out of the magic 200 down to No. 204 for 1965. If that hurt Ling at all, he must have gained considerable relief from the performance of LTV's stock toward the end of the year. At one point nearly $60, it closed the year at $50, compared with a low, back in January, of $16.75. That meant Ling's own holdings, worth about $3.5 million at the start, ended 1965 with a market value of nearly $11 million. The figures were better than ever before. But for Ling what must have been especially gratifying was the way that all the pieces had fallen into place, wiping out the bitterness of Chance Vought and demonstrating to the doubters that here was a man to bet on because, whether you knew where he was going or not, *he* most certainly seemed to.

IO

A SIDE from all the financial advantages it offered, Project Redeployment, in theory at least, seemed to provide a solution to the growing problem of managing the farther- and farther-flung empire that Ling was building. Each of the subsidiaries had its own corporate officers and a board of directors. But, at the beginning, nobody at the subsidiary level was called "chief executive officer." Ling held that title, and he was on all the boards, whose members were either insiders or men only once removed, such as Bill Osborn of Lehman Brothers. The implication of the structure at that time was clear enough: LTV headquarters was where the power resided.

Management theorists like to make distinctions between authority and responsibility, between line and staff executives, between direct and delegated functions, and between a lot of other real and not so real aspects of running big organizations. There are all kinds of textbook, casebook, and real-life models for managing large-scale enterprises. Among the obvious ones are the military command system, the Roman Catholic hierarchy, and the General Motors method. The success of military organizations through history seems essentially to have derived from their ability to parlay the need of a man to demonstrate his virility and his fear of loss of status and of punishment into a force greater than his fear of getting killed in battle. Patriotism, rank, fancy uniforms, material perquisites, hatred of the enemy, moral outrage, and madness also fit into the parlay somewhere. But who would follow the leader if he didn't think he would be worse off running the other way? The Church, of course, has offered even more: "He that believeth in me, though he were dead, yet shall he live."

Modern enterprise has had to make do with incentives less compelling than glory and eternal life (as have the military and the Church recently), usually relying on some combination of temporal power, rank, and money. William C. Durant created General Motors in the early days of automotive history by forming and acquiring an ungainly collection of manufacturers and suppliers, sometimes even using his own money (as Ling did to get Chance Vought). It was a formidable assembly, but it didn't work because, while it was highly decentralized, Durant reserved top-management functions to himself. And his main interest seems to have been financial technology. It remained for Alfred P. Sloan, Jr., to turn the shambling combine into the organizational marvel it became. In his autobiography, *My Years with General Motors*, written with John McDonald, Sloan characterizes his predecessor this way:

> I was of two minds about Mr. Durant. I admired his automotive genius, his imagination, his generous human qualities, and his integrity. His loyalty to the enterprise was absolute. I recognized, as Mr. [John J.] Raskob and Pierre S. du Pont had, that he had created and inspired the dynamic growth of General Motors. But I thought he was too casual in his ways for an administrator, and he overloaded himself. Important decisions had to wait until he was free, and were often made impulsively.

Sloan took the visionary enterprise of Durant and made it into a system, maybe *the* system. It became a kind of federated business nation, with its automotive divisions competing against themselves as well as against aliens, but with a kind of constitution defining their relationships down to price differences among the brands. Through his years,

Sloan was able to forge a corporate patriotism that was most effective. At times, it placed obstacles in the way of "immigrants" who did not come from the traditional General Motors cultural and educational background. The late Roger Kyes was a classic example of a man with a fine mind and executive talent who did not quite make it because he came late to the corporation. By and large, the right men seemed always to rise to their proper levels without unduly rattling the corporate apparatus. At close range, there was evident an awesome amount of politicking in the corporation. Harlow Curtice went against the system when he made Buick the third-largest-selling car in the United States in the mid-1950s, but the end—however damaging it turned out for the Buick division—justified the means, and Curtice became president. There has been increasing indication of hardening of the corporate arteries in recent years as General Motors, along with the rest of the American auto industry, continues, even when it responds, to miss the significance of the influx of foreign cars that began right after World War II. The bloody and personal battle between Edward Cole and Semon Knudsen for the top spot in the corporation, though barely mentioned in print, seems also to indicate that the system, despite the enormous scale of the corporation's activities and profits, does not always accommodate the vagaries of human ambition. And it can be argued that lately the system has been elevating its leaders just one level too late to use their particular abilities to conform policy to current needs.

General Motors is certainly not unique in its cultural lag, and it has done rather well in healing its wounds. The man who fixed Buick after Curtice, for example, would probably have reached the top if he had not died early. But it takes time to build a system that serves an institution by making it able to bend, yet remain powerful and coherent. General Motors survived for half a century before the cracks began showing. The Church, as an organization, existed for half a millennium before it decayed enough to be cracked open by Martin Luther, after having withstood and rooted out earlier reform movements. And though it was diminished greatly in the assault, it survived another half a millennium, losing military and territorial power but remaining a tremendous force in the spiritual marketplace. As the "known world" grew, the Church of Rome, though it had to settle for a lesser share, wound up with far greater numbers than it had had before.

But there is no such thing as picking the right organizational structure off the rack and expecting it to provide proper management for a large-scale enterprise. Alfred Sloan's system might not have worked half so well had General Motors been devoted to making something less remarkable than the automobile. A lot of otherwise well-managed corporations died because they were in the wrong business, but then several thousand automobile manufacturers came and went too. And other churches, even some with excellent middle management and with a "product" as compelling as the Roman, lost their force when they lost their founders, probably because they did not create chief executives with the omnipotence and the omniscience of the Papacy.

A well-oiled machine can survive admirably for a long time even when survival alone becomes its purpose. But bloodless bureaucracy cannot substitute for men. Without Durant and Sloan; without St. Bernard of Clairvaux, St. Dominic, and the other brilliant and resilient men who built the Church and were smart enough to bring on able successors—without men able to temporize, hold together, and regenerate organizations, they don't survive.

It is the rankest cliché that management is an art, not a science. But it is also true. If a system does work, it is because it happens to fit the nature of the enterprise, the markets, the processes, and the character of the people who made it and those they pick to fill the boxes, eventually including their own. Few business enterprises are as vast as the one that Harold S. Geneen has been running at International Telephone & Telegraph since the late 1950s. He has added several diverse acquisitions to ITT since he took over, including Avis Rent-a-Car, Sheraton Hotels, and Continental Baking (though ITT must now divest itself of some of these as the result of that controversial antitrust settlement). And the corporation's primary business—the manufacturing of telephone equipment abroad—has enjoyed a spectacular growth in demand. But, to the extent that it is possible to attribute the corporation's inordinate financial success to any one source, it is attributable to Geneen himself.

ITT has tiers of able managers, but the "system" through which they in turn have been managed has been a monthly meeting which most of them attend and which is chaired by the indefatigable Geneen. Obviously a worldwide organization such as ITT cannot be run by one man. Yet Geneen gives his managers the impression that he could almost do it all himself. No detail of their operations seems too trivial for him to raise at one of these marathon monthly meetings. On one occasion, for example, he cited specific wage rates in South Korea and Taiwan while interrogating the man in charge of a plant in Spain. According to "proper" management procedures, the chief executive of a major corporation should know almost nothing about such details. But Geneen is a man of remarkable intellect and memory and has chosen to run his enterprise as though everyone else were an extension of himself. And though a lot of able men have left rather than submit to the direct hand of the leader, others of apparently equal ability have managed to thrive under the Geneen system. It is both aberrant and effective. And while Geneen says that it is a conscious design, it happens to be one that suits his curious character, his special talents, and therefore his corporation.

When Ling conceived of the idea of splitting up his divisions into separate corporations, the partial autonomy he was creating for them seemed like a sound way to manage the total operation. His corporate staff had studied other companies in LTV's fields, and a plan was put together that considered all aspects of management under Project Redeployment. A summary of the project, written in 1966, used expressions like "specialization with recognition" and "optimum decentralization," dividing up the responsibilities of the "specialized units" and the "parent unit" in a seemingly unexceptionable way. In January, 1965, when Project Redeployment was announced, Ling, in the press release, had said, "Changes in markets, technologies, competition and types of government contracts demand a degree of flexibility that seldom can be commanded by a major defense-oriented company with its tendency to inertia, a highly hazardous characteristic in today's fast-moving environment." The 1966 summary noted that "this single sentence probably best explains the reason for Project Redeployment in its early stages." The summary referred to "ownership instinct" and the "financial carrot" and it remarked on the acceptance of the new system by customers and financial institutions and presented the evidence in terms of the value created in the securities markets by the plan.

No mention was made of real people in the summary, beyond the reference to the January, 1965, Ling statement. And, conceivably, there was no need to say anything about the specifics of who would do what to whom. Corporations, especially those that are the creatures of one man, shrink from any effort to label them as "one-man" companies. Their public-relations people are always talking about the management team, sometimes accurately. But basically what they are trying to avoid is the rarely asked but nevertheless real question: what happens if the one man dies? It scares hell out of investors. And the classic story, applied to several such corporations, usually is put into the mouth of a Wall Street wag who says, "If I were riding in a car with George Golfbag, the one man at XYZ Corporation, and he suddenly clutched the left side of his chest and slumped over, I would tell the driver to stop at the nearest phone booth, where I would make two calls: first to my broker to tell him to sell XYZ shares, then to a doctor."

Nobody was telling stories like that about Ling in those days. And all the top executives of the subsidiaries appeared confident in their new, though not precisely independent, roles. Project Redeployment had apparently created a "system" for motivating and managing the enterprise. What was less apparent was that Ling's own confidence in the efficacy of the financial carrots permitted him to withdraw further from active operating management. He was now turning more and more to the opportunities he saw for using the new "working assets" to make bigger acquisitions farther afield. Okonite was LTV's first major acquisition outside the military-industrial field. But Ling wanted to go even beyond that. His comment about inertia being "a highly hazardous characteristic" of a defense contractor was his way of stating that eventually you could get into trouble betting your marbles on government contracts as LTV had been doing. And now that he was gaining new recognition and respect in the financial community, he wanted to use his springboard to get LTV well away from the risks of contract cancellations. With Project Redeployment in position, he was ready for something bigger and better than ever.

Ling himself "discovered" the company that became known in the late summer of 1966 by the code name of Project Touchdown. He found it by looking for something big and redeployable (that is, breakable into separate corporations) and worth more than it was selling for. Looking for "targets of opportunity" was one of his special hobbies. Much of his reading in the pre-dawn hours, when he usually awakened, was devoted to financial studies of companies that might fit into his plans. He found Wilson & Company, Inc., in a publication of the Value Line investment services long before he was ready to make the move that would turn out to be one of the most beautiful deals in the annals of finance. It was daring in itself, because when he finally went after Wilson in 1966, its sales were close to $1 billion, almost twice the $468 million LTV would rack up that year although, with a big boost from Okonite, LTV's net profit was higher than Wilson's. But more than that, the success of the Wilson operation would demonstrate not only to Ling but to some of the smartest people in Wall Street that there were no limits to what he could do with his new system.

At first glance, Wilson was not what would be considered a hot property. Third largest of the meat packers, it was, like Armour and Swift, able to earn only a small return on its sales, and, like the others, it was caught in the peculiar supply-and-demand squeeze that the farmers who produce the animals and the packers who process them traditionally complain of. The packing business is most profitable, of course, when high farm output cuts livestock prices. But that relationship in turn is affected by weather, feed-crop prices, and government policies. So even the biggest packers have difficulty controlling their destinies. As they used to say in the Chicago stockyards, you had to process and sell everything but the squeal to make out.

But, on closer inspection, if you wanted to buy one of the Big Three, Wilson didn't look too bad. Its management was the first of the majors to close down its ancient Chicago slaughterhouse and disperse its plants closer to the animal supply. That indicated a less tradition-bound outlook. Moreover, its by-product operations looked relatively good. Its sporting-goods business, which had grown out of the processing of gut and hides ("Project Touchdown" out of football out of pigskin), was the biggest in the world. And the chemical and pharmaceutical business that had arisen out of rendering fat and recovering hormones and steroids from animal organs seemed like a nice little business too. That meant that at least three separate companies could be cut out of the original Wilson. Besides, there were only about 2.4 million common shares out, and Wilson's management owned hardly any of them, so it controlled few votes directly.

Once Ling had picked the target and put the code name on it, his plans stalled. The market skidded downward in 1966, and in the credit crunch that followed, the Federal Reserve Board ordered the banks to stop lending money for corporate takeovers. That meant LTV couldn't get the $80 million or so it wanted for the Wilson deal. So Ling put Project Touchdown on the shelf for a few months and tried something else instead. With LTV stock doing well—passing $70 before the market break—a lot of warrants that had been issued at the time of the Chance Vought merger were exercised, boosting outstanding shares by more than 400,000 and bringing in more than $16 million in cash before they expired in August, 1966. (A warrant is a kind of option to buy stock in a corporation. There are many kinds, but a usual one entitles the holder to buy a fixed amount of common stock at a stated price above the market at the time of issue during a stated period. A common reason to issue warrants is to provide an incentive to purchasers of a new offering of nonconvertible debentures or to other lenders enabling them to participate in future increases in the price of the corporation's common stock without actually owning any.) To counteract this dilution, Ling instituted Project Retrieve, swapping about $14 million in cash plus preferred stock for common. That got the outstanding common down to a manageable level, cutting the dilution and boosting per-share earnings.

But he still wanted Wilson, and the only way he could make his move without showing his hand was with a quick private loan that could be refinanced publicly later on. Around Thanksgiving, he was visited by Philip Shelbourne, a partner in N. M. Rothschild & Sons of London, who came out to the Ling house in Dallas. Ling had met him earlier that year in London on a tour that Ling took to introduce himself and his plans to scores of western European bankers. He laid Touchdown out for him, and Shelbourne thought it looked good. Since Ling couldn't borrow from U.S. banks, Shelbourne agreed to get Ling maybe $50 million in Eurodollars (U.S. dollars on deposit in European financial institutions). With that much committed, Osborn of Lehman Brothers thought he could persuade some institutions that were not banks and not restricted by the federal order to lend LTV the other $30 million. Shelbourne got the Eurodollars, and Osborn got some insurance companies, college endowment funds (including Harvard and Stanford), and pension funds to come up with the balance.

In early December, Ling and Skeen were still at work lining up the money. Though Rothschild would act as agent for the Eurodollar loan, a lot of it would come from the London branches of U.S. banks, which were prohibited from lending through their domestic banks. In fact, two of the biggest lenders, for $10 million each, turned out to be the London offices of First National City Bank of New York and Bank of America. Others included Morgan Guaranty,

Continental Illinois, Marine Midland Grace, American Express plus a string of the most prestigious banking houses in Europe. And though none actually put up cash—or had to—before they knew the identity of the Touchdown target, incredible as it may seem, they made their initial commitments blind. The security precautions surrounding the code name seemed airtight, avoiding even a hint of a leak to Wilson's management and preventing anybody along the line of communication from profiting personally. Anybody who knew about the offer could have bought Wilson stock in anticipation of the inevitable rise in the price of its shares in the market, once the terms of the tender were announced. There has never been any evidence that anybody did any premature trading in the stock, nor were there any rumors in Wall Street about LTV's plans before they were disclosed. When Ling and Skeen presented Project Touchdown during the planning and financial commitment stages, they disguised the identity of the target well enough to include scores of major companies listed on the New York Stock Exchange.

Ling got the go-ahead from his executive committee to borrow the money on December 13. The plan to take Wilson & Company before its management could retaliate began six days later, on Monday, December 19, when two LTV planes left Dallas for New York. One carried Ling and some of the supporting staff of legal, financial, and public-relations people who would be involved in the tender arrangements and announcement, and the other carried Clyde Skeen and the rest of the staff group. The two planes arrived in New York in mid-afternoon for a series of meetings at the offices of Lehman Brothers and in the suite at the Hotel Pierre that was chosen as the communications center for the operation.

Next day, Ling and Skeen visited the New York banks whose London branches would be putting up the bulk of the money and Lehman Brothers' offices downtown, where LTV people were working on the details of the tender-offer terms and announcement to the Wilson shareholders. Two men remained at the Pierre to man the phones. That evening, Skeen and some of the supporting cast took off for

Chicago. Skeen had been chosen as the man to make the contact with Wilson management.

The following morning, Ling and his people went back to Lehman Brothers to confer with Robert Lehman and General Lucius Clay, a Lehman partner, and with Wall Street people who were on Wilson's board. Meanwhile, in Chicago, Skeen arranged an appointment with Roscoe Haynie, Wilson's president, for 2:00 P.M. Lehman Brothers' Chicago-office partner arranged meetings between other LTV people and Wilson directors. And in Dallas, the LTV board scheduled a meeting for the same hour to stamp their approval on the plan.

Haynie had no idea why Skeen wanted to see him, and for the first few minutes of their brief first encounter it seemed as though Skeen had come to discuss Wilson golf clubs with him. Then Skeen told him why he had asked for the meeting, and Haynie was furious, as any man would be when first told a plan was in the works to take over his company. Skeen told him that LTV would offer $62.50 a share for 750,000 Wilson shares, about 30 percent of the total outstanding. The day before, the stock had closed at $49.50, and it had never sold for more than $57.875, so it appeared likely that LTV would get its control of Wilson through the tender offer.

An hour after the Skeen-Haynie meeting began, the LTV public-relations people called the newspapers in New York, Chicago, and Dallas and announced the offer. The next day, Lehman Brothers began buying Wilson stock in the open market for LTV, and Ling and his people flew out to Chicago. That afternoon, Ling and Skeen saw Haynie to tell him what they had in mind and to reassure him that LTV was a sound outfit that would leave Wilson's management intact. Then the two planes flew back to Dallas.

If Ling had got his financial commitments that summer, he would undoubtedly have made his Touchdown play then. But the delay caused by the federal ruling actually smoothed the takeover process. The Sunday after the Haynie confrontation and the tender announcement was Christmas Day, and the holiday week surely hampered Wilson's management and directors in any efforts they might have made to thwart LTV's bid. In fact, one Wilson man recalls that the precision of the LTV operation greatly impressed and disarmed Wilson people in Chicago, especially the interposition of Christmas into the schedule, which they assumed was part of the plan.

The LTV tender offer was set to expire on January 5, 1967. Two days before the deadline, Wilson's management made a feeble countermove. In a letter to stockholders over Haynie's name published in a newspaper ad, the company announced a 50-percent (three-for-two-shares) stock dividend and an increase in the cash dividend. The letter also noted that the company's officers and directors would not tender any of their Wilson shares to LTV (but they owned hardly any). But since the premium LTV was offering for the shares was well above the market price, Wilson's management could not advise strongly against acceptance. Such a position might be construed as acting against the shareholders' best interests, which might well be to take the admittedly high offer.

When the offer expired, LTV had received tenders of close to 950,000 and it bought the 750,000 it had asked for. The corporation's open-market buying had brought in another 545,000 Wilson shares during those hectic days. LTV now held 53.4 percent of the voting shares of Wilson, so Ling was now in control of enterprises doing nearly $1.5 billion in sales. When the 1967 *Fortune* 500 list came out, LTV would vault to No. 38.

In 1966, an article in *Fortune* defined a conglomerate as a corporation in at least eight different businesses. Ironically, LTV, which would one day become the best known of all the conglomerates, did not yet qualify. But with Wilson & Company in the house, LTV finally made the grade.

Control of Wilson cost LTV $81,504,653, which it raised mainly through the 7.5-percent Eurodollar and the 6.75-percent U.S. nonbank loans, secured by shares of Wilson and other LTV subsidiaries. Another $5 million was to come through the sale of a note to LTV's own pension fund, a procedure that did not sit well with the fund's trustee, the Republic National Bank of Dallas. (That bank was later replaced as trustee, although it continued to act as custodian of the fund's securities.)

To that point, Project Touchdown was right on schedule. There were some scary moments when some of the Euro-dollar lenders backed out and were replaced by others. And no matter how big a premium you offer stockholders and how much assurance you get from institutional holders, there is always a little breath-holding about whether they will tender their shares or turn their backs on your offer at the last minute. None of that happened, and LTV got voting control for $19.5 million more than what the market value had been in the days just before the offer. Next, LTV brought in the rest of the Wilson shares with an exchange offer that swapped a $5 LTV preferred stock at a very favorable rate. On paper, that exchange cost the corporation another premium of about $61 million, but since it was a trade of one security for another, no cash was spent.

When LTV held all of Wilson, the redeployment phase of Project Touchdown went into operation. It worked something like the original plan two years earlier, but better. LTV created three new corporations: a meat-packing company named, like the original, Wilson & Company; another called Wilson Sporting Goods Company; and a third known as Wilson Pharmaceutical & Chemical Corporation. In exchange for blocks of their common shares, LTV transferred assets to each of them plus about $50 million worth of debt. LTV also kept four meat-packing and -processing plants, which it leased back to the new Wilson & Company. Then the three subsidiaries sold additional shares in public offerings and raised more than $44 million in new money, most of which was used to pay off the debt that LTV had transferred to them, debt LTV had incurred to buy Wilson in the first place.

In the early days after the three new subsidiaries came on the market and were still being heavily traded by the professionals, they picked up the traders' nicknames of "Meatball," "Golfball," and "Goofball." The market responded to these new Ling financial products as though it never had heard that the old Wilson & Company had been in the same businesses with the same executives and facilities. Giving investors a chance to own stock in the world's biggest manufacturer of sporting goods certainly was an important part of the success of the Wilson deal. Sports put you into the center of the leisure boom everybody was talking about then. The stock had the sort of appeal for adults that bubble-gum baseball cards had for kids. And a nice little pharmaceutical company put you into the big new health industry. But that didn't explain the relatively good performance of the meat-packing subsidiary, which ought to have taken a nosedive once it had been shorn of its glamorous divisions. The market was doing well generally, and it was embracing anything with a trace of magic. And Ling was now loaded with magic again. The value of LTV's majority interest in the three Wilson subsidiaries soared, and by the fall of 1967 that interest had a market value of around $250 million, for which the corporation had paid $81 million cash plus $115.8 million par value of preferred stock.

LTV's stock broke $100 a share early in 1967 on the news that the corporation had won control of Wilson, and the price kept on climbing. In July, LTV split its own stock three-for-two, and the new stock ran up to $169½, at which point Ling's own holdings were worth close to $70 million.

It was as though the market were applauding his success rather than reflecting any fundamental change in the nature of Ling-Temco-Vought. And Ling now had a big new supply of loan collateral if he decided to go after something else.

11

THE investment bankers and the financial and legal people were still working on the last details of Project Touchdown when Ling turned to another "target of opportunity." Sorting out his complex new organization, a fullfledged conglomerate by anybody's definition, might have deterred another man. What had until recently been almost entirely a military contractor selling to one customer was now becoming in 1967 a $1.8-billion structure with more than 70 percent of its volume in nondefense sales in many new markets. The subsidiaries themselves were also making acquisitions, presumably in anticipation of the day they too could deploy their own subsidiaries into publicly held corporations. Okonite picked up another maker of wire and cable and then paid more than $53 million in borrowed cash and notes for General Felt Industries, Inc., a floorcovering manufacturer. Ling Altec bought Allied Radio Corporation, a big retailer of electronics parts and equipment through catalogs. And the other subs were also adding product lines and divisions.

Project Redeployment seemed almost to be running itself. And with the reorganization of Wilson & Company, Ling had a new group of executives at the LTV Tower. Roscoe Haynie of Wilson moved down to Dallas to serve as chairman of LTV's executive committee as well as board chairman of the three new Wilson companies, each of which

had its own operating president. Haynie brought with him
some bright, experienced financial people from Chicago to
help carry the load at LTV headquarters. Haynie became, in
addition to overseer of the Wilson companies, a sort of chief
of staff to Ling. He apparently felt no personal rancor against
Ling for taking his company away from him. Ling figured
that the men Haynie had brought with him would eventually be able to take on operating management duties as
he brought in other acquisitions. There seemed little to
worry about when it came to running the burgeoning machine. Whatever problems there might be in digesting the
Wilson operations could be handled by others. Ling was
hunting again.

The success of the Wilson move indicated to Ling that
any corporation, no matter how established and venerable,
could be considered a redeployment target if its shareholdings were widely dispersed and it were in a diverse group
of industries and markets. In fact, if it met those requirements, it almost didn't have to be a very good company.
That was why his next target turned out to be Allis-Chalmers
Manufacturing Company.

Allis-Chalmers had been on Ling's list for years, he once
said. But not until he had taken Wilson did he have the
financial muscle to try to get it. With "working assets" in
the form of rapidly climbing market values of subsidiary
shares—more than $600 million worth if LTV could sell them
at current market prices—he figured that the big banks
would back him. And a group of major American banks
agreed, though at the last moment, one of them insisted that
if LTV were to acquire Allis-Chalmers the move had to
be a peaceable one. The reason apparently was that a
director and former top executive of one of the New York
banks in the group, who was dying, had been an Allis-
Chalmers director and had personal ties with its management. That meant that, to get the company, Ling would
have to win over its board.

After making a thorough investigation of the company
and the community—G2 military intelligence, he called it—
Ling set up a temporary headquarters in the Hotel Pfister

in Milwaukee, for the purpose, as Ling put it, of "infiltrating the Milwaukee establishment." Since most of the company's directors were outsiders and not employees, that seemed the way to get through to the board. Ling met and golfed with the local community leaders, utility executives, lawyers, bankers, press people, in an effort to persuade them that he was no smalltime hustler intent on raiding the community's most important industrial employer. "Conglomerate" had already become a dirty word in conservative American business circles, and LTV was a conglomerate and Milwaukee was a tight business circle. The specter of the man from Texas coming in and closing down the huge West Allis works of Allis-Chalmers with its gloomy aggregation of ancient, inefficient factories and its bloated headquarters staff scared hell out of half the community and seemed to delight the other half. Irwin Maier, Milwaukee newspaper publisher, told his staff that Ling was a raider, though Maier, it later turned out, was not too sure what that meant. And one of the city's leading investment bankers said that if Ling had made a tender offer to Allis-Chalmers shareholders, they would have been so happy at the chance to unload that they would have "declared a holiday." But there is no question that, whatever the company's indifferent management might have been costing its shareholders, it was certainly helping the community by making work. And anybody who wanted to make something of the company, as a management reorganization amply demonstrated later, would have had to chop off a lot of heads.

Ling brought Roscoe Haynie to Milwaukee to demonstrate that he had not damaged Wilson in that takeover, and he appeared in the newsroom of one of Maier's papers to let the local press people have a look at him. He won a lot of allies in the city, mostly among people outside the old guard. But whether he had enough support from the Allis-Chalmers board to win the required "favorable expression" for a tender offer was still not clear.

If he got the company, it was fairly certain what he would eventually do with it. Despite a decidedly unimpressive earnings record over more than a decade, Allis-Chalmers looked likely for Project Redeployment. It was a major producer of tractors and farm equipment, of earth-moving machinery, of electrical-power generation and transmission equipment (including New York City's ill-starred power generator Big Allis), and of a lot of other kinds of heavy capital goods, such as paper-making machinery. With all of LTV's diversity, it still was not a producer of capital goods, the building blocks of American industry. More than that, Allis-Chalmers' major divisions were largely independent of each other in terms of processes, products, and markets, and they would make readily separable subsidiary corporations. Ling knew that the company was pretty much a mess and that it would demand bloodletting that would create difficult public and employee relations. But for him the appeal outweighed these admitted problems. So he prepared to approach the board.

But before he got to that point, a visitor from Dallas came to the hotel in Milwaukee. It was E. Grant Fitts, then president of Greatamerica Corporation, the Dallas company put together by Troy Post to hold investments in a California bank, some insurance companies, Braniff Airways, and soon also National Car Rental. Fitts came to Ling to bemoan that Post, after backing down in an effort to take over the Glidden Company, was losing his drive. Fitts proposed that Ling make an offer to Post, Greatamerica's controlling stockholder, and take over the holding company. The prospect of acquiring Greatamerica was not exactly new to Ling. He and Post had done business together over the years, and Greatamerica was certainly a redeployment candidate, with its already quite separate corporate holdings. Ling probably would have preferred to make the move at a more leisurely moment. But he was certain that he could persuade his board to accept whatever deal he worked out, and he agreed on the spot. He and Fitts quickly worked out a tentative offer that Post accepted in early August, a week before Ling announced his first bid for Allis-Chalmers.

LTV's first offer for Allis-Chalmers' shares would have been $45 apiece in cash for half of the company's stock. Until Ling came onto the scene, the stock had been selling for around $25 and had a book value of about $35. By offering so much more than the stock was worth, Ling hoped to accomplish two purposes: For one thing, he wanted to emphasize that he was a fair man and not somebody trying to take advantage of the situation. For another, by paying what was clearly more than necessary to buy control, he would be communicating the idea that his system could indeed produce new value and justify the high premium. The Allis-Chalmers board held a special meeting and refused to make the "favorable expression" Ling had promised his bankers he would seek before making the actual offer. The company also announced that it had been discussing merger via a stock swap with General Dynamics Corporation "for some time," which hardly anybody quite believed. That sounded more like a defensive reaction hastily rigged to stave off another bid. But Ling made one anyway: $55 in securities and cash for each of the Allis-Chalmers shares. The board turned down that one too.

So Ling and his staff retreated to Dallas and waited, saying that no tender offer would be made but that the door was still open. Nothing happened. General Dynamics said it would not pay more than the equivalent of $32.50 a share, and Ling's higher offers made the General Dynamics price impossible for Allis-Chalmers to accept. During the next couple of years, in the wake of LTV's interest, others bought blocks of Allis-Chalmers and played with the idea of takeover. But Ling dropped the quest. Had he chosen to make a tender offer without the board's blessing, he almost certainly would have got every share he bid for. But he would also have bought great resistance from the community, without getting a bargain. Besides, he had assured his bankers he would avoid a fight, and he didn't want their enmity.

At the time, a lot of people in and out of LTV thought it was just as well that Ling had backed out, even though the attempt scored as a failure. Whatever potential he saw in the company had been there for years. And while he was preparing his bid, he learned that the company had been doing even worse than his intelligence sources had indicated. If Ling had "won" Allis-Chalmers, he would have been under great public pressure to go slowly in his initial efforts to cut the central-office payroll and unload a string of losing divisions. Unless Ling complied, he would have forfeited any claim to being what Milwaukee thinks of as "a good corporate citizen" and would have risked being labelled "raider."

However badly LTV might have fared if it had taken over Allis-Chalmers, that acquisition would at least have foreclosed the chance to make an even worse move. For, once Project Redeployment had "worked" with a company in meat, sporting goods, and pharmaceuticals, it became difficult for Ling to exclude from his view almost any other company, no matter what its business, no matter what its problems, as long as it seemed separable into marketable parts.

Though Ling was in the midst of Allis-Chalmers planning when Fitts came to him with the idea of acquiring Greatamerica, he grabbed at it. The deal he finally worked out for Troy Post and the other Greatamerica shareholders involved no outlay of cash or stock. Instead Ling arranged an exchange offer with Greatamerica stockholders through which they would receive $300 worth of new LTV debentures paying 5 percent and payable in 1988, plus a warrant to buy a share of LTV common stock, for every ten shares of Greatamerica common they turned in. The terms of the deal involved some interesting and complicated relationships among the securities in the offer, but the underlying fact was that LTV was issuing nearly $500 million worth of new debt to buy Greatamerica shares. In twenty years, LTV would have to pay back those debenture holders nearly $500 million as well as nearly $25 million every year in the meantime. The scale of the deal was so big that it would have almost certainly caused anybody else to back away from any other major acquisition for a while. For one thing, just sorting out the pieces of Greatamerica and trying to figure out what to do with them to improve their earnings looked like a major challenge. Greatamerica was not earning enough to provide LTV with the money it would need to cover the interest it would have to pay on its debentures. In other words, Greatamerica would not pay its way as an acquisition at the start, though it had a lot of parts that could be redeployed in one way or another.

Admittedly, there were certain appealing aspects to the deal. Braniff, after all, was an airline that had been attracting a lot of attention lately with its fancy paint jobs and stewardess costumes, and it was an old-time, nationally known Dallas company. Controlling Braniff was worth a lot of money, and it had cost a lot. Another effect of the deal was that it seemed to end once and for all a kind of unconscious rivalry that had grown up between the enterprises of Post and those of Ling. Though Ling at various times had been in Post's debt or at least in the debt of one of the insurance companies he controlled, he was in no sense a protégé of the insurance operator. Both men had arrived on the fringes of the Dallas business establishment at about the same time, but they were dissimilar in many ways. Ling was far-ranging and adventurous in his acquisition program and financing methods. Post, though skillful in parlaying assets, built his financial enterprise by diligent and exhaustive study of one business—life insurance. He first made money in the business during World War II when the company he owned a piece of decided to sell life insurance to soldiers without medical examinations, something that most other insurance companies wouldn't do then. After the war, Post began poring through volumes of a publication called *Best's Life Insurance Reports* that provides financial surveys of life-insurance companies. In the course of these studies, Post decided that life-insurance-company stocks were selling for less than they were worth, because few people knew how to put values on insurance revenues and assets. He bought control of a life-insurance company in Alabama, one of the few states that permit life-insurance companies to invest in the stock of other life-insurance companies. That allowed him to buy a lot of shares in companies that were selling cheap but would soon be discovered by investors. He turned out to be quite right, and he made a lot of money. But Post was, in a way, like the oil men: he made his money from persistence in one

business. Among his most prized possessions is a complete
set of *Best's Reports*.

Because Post was nearly twenty years older than Ling
and because he had lent money to Ling and had been in
ventures with him, people assumed that Post was somehow
coaching Ling in the fundamentals of financial wizardry.
That was in no sense the case. The two were often thrown
together socially, were on each other's party lists, played
golf together, traveled together, and invested together, but
they were not particularly close friends. Post is not an easy
talker, and for years a lot of people in Dallas took that as
a sign of great wisdom in matters of business. Ling, on the
other hand, is superficially affable and can hold forth at
length on subjects that interest or bother him. But it is
doubtful that either communicated much about himself to
the other in their social contacts, because neither seemed
in later years to understand the other. Though both were
small-town boys, Post remained more country than Ling,
at least in dress and speech. Post dresses in the more colorful style of Dallas, while Ling chose a horn-rimmed Ivy-
League look for many years, though he has lately turned a bit
more modish—still in an Eastern version, however.

Ling had come to resent the false view in Dallas that Post
had "taught Ling all he knew." Buying out Post, if it did
nothing else, cast considerable doubt on that idea. It also
gave Troy Post about $100 million face value of LTV's new
5-percent debentures due in 1988 in exchange for the 20
percent of Greatamerica's shares that he owned. Post had
been running Greatamerica in a leisurely manner. It was a
holding company with few executives and almost no headquarters overhead except for lavish offices for the brass. There
was plenty of time for golf and travel. But by selling out,
Post could go further into retirement. After all, his debentures would bring him nearly $5 million a year in interest.
That would be more than enough, it seemed, for the Posts
to maintain an active social life in the world they had recently entered, the international set based in Acapulco. It
is a world that held little interest for the Lings.

Whether the Greatamerica acquisition turned out to be a

good thing for Ling-Temco-Vought would depend a lot on how Ling's financial people handled many aspects of the deal. LTV was in effect paying $500 million for the shares of a corporation that held stock in insurance companies, an airline, a bank, a car-rental company, and some real-estate developments. But how much of that total would be assigned to the various pieces had to be decided against a background of decisions about what was to be done with each one. Whether a holding would be liquidated for cash or retained, spun off to shareholders as a stock dividend, sold now or later to show a gain or a loss, held as a subsidiary, or handled some other way had much to do with how it ought to go onto LTV's books. Such plans and decisions would have major effects on taxes and earnings of LTV for a long time to come. But there seemed to be plenty of time to work out the right moves, because it was unlikely that Ling would get his people involved in another, even bigger deal before they were finished with this one. But he did.

12

MAYBE somebody else would have stopped at
that point to see what he was making, but Ling did not. He
was caught up in the momentum. With the Wilson deal
just completed, he moved on Allis-Chalmers in Milwaukee,
worked out the Greatamerica exchange in the middle of that,
and began looking around for something else. Meanwhile,
despite some skidding in the price of LTV's stock when the
Allis-Chalmers and Greatamerica offers were announced, the
stock was still doing well. So Ling decided that the corporation ought to raise some more money in the stock market,
and LTV sold 600,000 more of its shares to the public in
1967 at a price of $100 a share, which brought in $60 million
of new capital.

Late in the year, Ling made a try at American Broadcast-
ing Companies, Inc. But after an all-night vigil in a New
York hotel room, ABC's management turned him down.
There were other candidates, phone calls, offers, but nothing came of any of them. Then in early 1968, in the casual,
accidental way that even the biggest deals begin, Ling
started toward his next candidate. In a deposition he gave
in LTV's antitrust case the following year, Ling described
it this way:

> We were attending Pat Haggerty's [a founder and
> top executive of Texas Instruments] thirty-fifth wed-

ding anniversary one evening at the Brook Hollow Country Club. And we were in the buffet line. And I knew the man [Fred Mayer of Youngstown Sheet & Tube Company] just very casually. And he commented about some activity in his company's stock. And I have a very bad ear, and I can't hear too well. And I asked him, I said I missed the company's name. And he said Youngstown. There has been activity or something to that effect. I said, well, no, we haven't purchased any of the company stock. And so as fate would have it, we sat down together and began to chat about Youngstown. . . . And I told him we would certainly take a look at it. . . .

Fate did indeed have it, but not quite yet. Mayer arranged a meeting between Ling and Youngstown's president, Robert Williams. Ling told him that LTV was interested in buying control of his company. Later, Williams and Ling spoke on the phone, and Williams said he was not interested in being acquired by Ling-Temco-Vought. Ling was no longer interested in fighting for control of anything, so he gave up on Youngstown. But, by then, he seems to have been bitten by the idea of owning a steel company. It wasn't that he thought that steel making was likely to be a particularly lucrative business or even that a steel producer would be especially attractive, broken into parts, to the stock market. In fact, it is difficult to determine from Ling's public statements about the industry precisely what it was that had moved him. His associates and advisers indicate that they were either neutral or negative about the prospect when he began seriously to consider it. But Ling, some have noted, was no longer listening to any other voices. If the big Allis-Chalmers machines that plowed the fields and carved the land and generated the power and moved the materials of the nation stirred him, the idea of producing the basic raw material of the world must have grabbed him even more. Gaining control of one of Chicago's renowned hog butchers to the world and making it perform for him was surely a source of great excitement and satisfaction to Ling. Infiltrating the Milwaukee establishment was another one. But when he got his first taste of steel, westernmost bastion of the Eastern Establishment, its awesome power became an inexorable challenge to him. When Ling has reflected on the acquisition of Jones & Laughlin Steel Corporation, he has always adhered to statistics and never to emotion. And, to a degree, the figures could be made to support the deal. After all, steel companies tend to have a higher ratio of assets to sales than other manufacturers, so it could be argued that if their assets could be converted to other businesses, they might perform relatively better.

But diversifying out of steel is a lot easier to talk about than to accomplish. And finding lines along which to divide a steel maker into marketable and viable components is not a simple matter either. The complex cost-and-production relationships among raw materials, iron ore and scrap metal, coal to make coke to turn ore into iron to make steel, create enormous difficulties even for the best-managed companies. And the fact that the two largest markets for steel are automobiles and heavy construction ties sales to factors largely out of the hands of management. Then too, foreign competition, particularly from Germany and Japan, has lately increased the industry's problems. In a sense, the fact that the American steel industry suffered no damage during World War II hurt it. Foreign producers rebuilding their industry were able to incorporate innovations such as the basic oxygen process and continuous casting well ahead of their American counterparts, so it was not simply lower wages that gave them an edge in U.S. markets. In these circumstances, the most aggressive management would have had its hands full. But American steel people, for the most part, did not manage their industry, they watched it. Brilliant refinancing in the style of Project Redeployment would help as aspirin helps a cancer.

But once Ling made his abortive move toward Youngstown, he was hooked. His next step was to find another Youngstown, and that turned out to be Jones & Laughlin. It was a little bigger and had a little better recent earnings record, though it was not a star performer by any means. But Ling had been poring over lists of directors, executives, and bankers of the steel companies, and he found a link to J&L. Jack W. Reavis, senior partner of a major Cleveland law firm and a member of several boards including Westinghouse and J&L, also was on the board of the Lehman Corporation, a Lehman Brothers investment company. Ling called Bill Osborn and asked him to arrange a meeting with the J&L brass through Reavis. Hardly anybody at LTV headquarters knew what was going on when Ling and Skeen took off from Dallas one day in April, 1968. As far as the financial staff was concerned, the big job at hand was restructuring the components of Greatamerica. They were laying plans for a public offering of the stock of First Western Bank & Trust Company. Though it was a good property, it would have been imprudent for LTV to be in the banking business in California, home state of Bank of America, its principal commercial lender. Braniff, of course, was Greatamerica's prize holding. As for the insurance companies owned by Greatamerica, they were to be redeployed much as the earlier components had been. Moreover, there was plenty of LTV business they were writing and more that they could write, including several million dollars' worth of group life on its employees as well as the hull insurance on Braniff's aircraft. There were obvious advantages to maintaining control of them, even after Greatamerica itself was eliminated as an entity. Compared with other components of LTV, they were relatively simple to manage. And National Car Rental seemed likely to stay too. The business of renting and leasing cars is largely a financing operation, and that was surely something LTV people knew well.

Ling and Skeen met Reavis and Charles M. Beeghly, then J&L chairman and chief executive officer, in a Cleveland hotel room. The presence of Ling and Beeghly together in Pittsburgh might have been noticed. Ling came quickly to the point: he wanted to make a tender for control of J&L. Beeghly apparently did not take Ling seriously at first. You can be a pretty smart and aggressive fellow from Texas, but you don't make tenders for steel companies. But Ling persisted, making it clear that he meant to offer cash for enough stock to control the company, and he demonstrated that he had a lot of the money and could get the rest. He also tried to convince Beeghly that he would not make an unfriendly assault and in fact wanted the support of J&L and would do anything to gain it.

When the terms were finally agreed on, Beeghly accepted Ling's offer of $85 a share, the book value of the stock, compared to a market price of about $50, provided that Ling would seek considerably more than 51 percent of the shares. Ling agreed to tender for 63 percent, which would cost $425 million in cash, not securities. In addition, to show his respect for this venerable enterprise, Ling agreed to put the J&L stock that LTV bought into a voting trust, the majority of whose members would be J&L people for the first three years. If anybody on LTV's board thought Ling was paying too much money for a middling company in a third-rate industry, he didn't raise a fuss, because the deal was approved by the board almost routinely.

The announcement of the LTV tender offer for Jones & Laughlin may have struck fear in the hearts of old men in old companies, but it should not have. Ling was paying a high premium for J&L's stock, and he had agreed to let the company's management continue to run the company as before, literally making it impossible for LTV to take anybody's job away or otherwise shake up the operation. So anyone who assumed that the Ling machine was going to chew up good gray Jones & Laughlin, established in 1853, was mistaken. The real question, of course, was why did Ling want J&L. And it has never been answered satisfactorily by Ling or anybody else.

A man who grows up in a flat, new, brown place like Texas or Oklahoma sees a different world when he gets to Pittsburgh and the surrounding foothill country where its powerful people live and play. There are those who say that what wrecked David J. McDonald as president of the United Steel Workers union was getting inside the Duquesne Club in downtown Pittsburgh and sitting with the industry establishment. By Dallas standards, Ling was certainly no parvenu when he got to Pittsburgh. He could get into just about any club in Dallas, he was a member of Brook Hollow, the best if not the oldest, and he was on the board of the First National Bank, the second biggest in town. He had all the credentials he needed for acceptance in Dallas. But whatever the wealth and power of the men he consorted with there, it was not like the world around the Duquesne and Rolling Rock and Laurel Valley clubs. And nobody down home could match the wealth, power, and elegance of the Mellons, the unquestioned rulers of Pittsburgh and much more.

Ling devoted a lot of time to preparing himself for Jones & Laughlin, reading, among other sources, a three-part article in *Fortune* on the history of the Mellon family and its fortune. Written by Charles J. V. Murphy, himself a stylish man who had also written the Duke of Windsor's story, the article laid heavy emphasis on the way of life of the family, its baronies, its traditions, and its business satellites. Though shares in Jones & Laughlin did not represent a major holding of the Mellons, at least not significant enough to be mentioned in listings of the family fortune, important connections between the Mellons and the steel company did exist. Two of J&L's board members were involved with the Mellon National Bank & Trust Company. Charles Beeghly, J&L's chairman, was a Mellon Bank director, and after LTV bought its J&L stock, he announced his retirement to take a position with the Mellons. Frank Denton, another J&L director, had been a Mellon retainer and close associate of Richard King Mellon for nearly forty years. The Mellon Bank was J&L's bank, and First Boston Corporation, in which the Mellons hold a substantial interest, was J&L's investment banker. The Mellons could have much to say about what became of J&L.

Months after the J&L deal was completed, Ling met, golfed, and shot with Mellons and their associates. When one of Richard K. Mellon's sons wanted to give Ling a handsome hand-tooled shotgun, Ling insisted that he have it appraised and pay the fair value for the gift, which he did. But rather than use the gun, Ling had it mounted for display in his office.

There are many ways to look at the acquisition by LTV

of J&L. Some have said that Ling's willingness to pay so much for it actually created a suspicion among the J&L people that he somehow had discovered more value in their steel company than they could find and, therefore, that he had made them look bad as businessmen. Others have suggested that once Ling had gained some casual contact with the Mellons and their retainers, he was so awed by their life style that his doubts about the value of the company were overshadowed. Ling considers such speculations ridiculous and asserts that the climate of Pittsburgh does not compare with that of Dallas or the California desert, a favorite recreation spot.

Ling's perceptions about social and ethnic barriers have been slow to approach realistic proportions. He once observed wryly, "I come from Oklahoma, and it was a while after I lived in Texas before I knew there was anything wrong with Indians and Mexicans. My best friend at home was a Mexican kid, and I never thought about it at all until one day when we were standing in front of a mirror wondering whether the girls would like us, and I said that my nose was too big and he said his skin was too dark."

Ling's first deep involvement with country-club politics in Dallas held surprises for him too. As president of a country club with few ethnic barriers—roughly 20 percent of its membership was Jewish—Ling was floored by the proposal from a Jewish member that maybe the club ought to institute a quota system lest it become too strongly identified as a Jewish club. The fact that Stanley Marcus and Fred Florence might have experienced difficulty—even though they might not have been turned down—in trying to join one of Dallas' foremost white Christian golf clubs—to which Ling belongs—dismays him. (They both joined the all-Jewish Columbia Country Club.) So does the fact that one important club excluded members of a renowned local business family because, though Christian, they were of Middle Eastern origin—Semitic, in other words.

Ling has also been frequently surprised by the lines drawn in Wall Street, where, at first glance from outside, the Jews and the Irish seem to operate as freely as members of the old Anglo-Saxon firms and where the distinctions between old and new money even among the Jewish firms were not at first apparent to him. In any place where money is the power and the product, a man from Dallas might think that nothing else mattered as much, certainly not more.

Though no more difficult for some people to grasp than the complexities of Ling's corporate technology, these aspects of human behavior eluded Ling long after he was immersed in them. Until very recently, he had no knowledge of the word "Wasp" as a sociological slang acronym for White Anglo-Saxon Protestant. Clearly Ling is in some crucial ways a naïve man not consistent with the public image that his financial activities have created. Attempting to explain such a man and make him consistent with an image or set of principles is a popular pastime of journalists who figure that if a man is so smart in one field or at one time, he must always know what he is doing.

It is curious, however, and probably even more illogical that at precisely the moment of the J&L tender Ling chose to speak publicly about corporate managers in a way that was certainly not likely to endear him to Pittsburgh or any other entrenched business community he might later choose to confront or, for that matter, to the audience he was addressing—a convention of Southern bankers. He was referring to LTV and its subsidiaries when he said:

> The common chemistry and the physical make-up is that of the entrepreneur, as opposed to the professional "caretaker." Caretakers are quite content to live with precedent and tradition, hopefully to survive and perhaps even to grow in relation to the general increase in gross national product. Caretakers are content in their "country club" atmosphere and unlikely to welcome any new ideas or approaches that would be to the benefit of their shareholders, and, ultimately, to their companies.

Later in the same speech he returned to the subject:

> Today, in the United States there are essentially two types of corporate management: (a) the professional caretakers who seek prestige, job security,

a weekly paycheck, and good fellowship with their cohorts in other companies, overspending time and other corporate resources, and (b) the entrepreneurial innovators who seek challenges, increasing values for their shareholders, and who are willing to put their futures on the line through equity participation in their companies. Should the tender offer be severely restricted in its use and application, the professional caretakers would secure an additional shield behind which to relax smugly and confidently in their corporate fortresses.

Those comments failed to exclude men who were very good at operating companies and subsidiaries but had no taste or talent for Ling's kind of corporate technology. There were many such men at LTV and in its subsidiaries, as Ling well knew, and in the past he had recognized how much he needed them. He certainly had no intention of including them in his indictment. But this and other attacks on the "caretakers" and on the businessmen he had begun to characterize as losers were beginning to antagonize even some of his staff people. The truth is that Ling was right and that the ranks of business are full of time-servers who contribute nothing much and even detract from the value of their corporations. To fault Ling or other major conglomerators for firing such men is preposterous. Some competent executives have lost their jobs for the sole reason that mergers of their companies produced duplication of management. But most conglomerates can probably be criticized more for keeping deadwood in place than for risking bad publicity by wholesale firings. Ling rarely fired executives of acquired companies, even when he felt that he should. Sometimes his failure to act seems to have stemmed from his own feeling that he was an upstart who had no right to tamper. Other times it grew out of concern for public and investor opinion. Men who manage to rise higher than their limitations warrant are feeding unfairly off shareholders. However, Ling was pointing the finger at a lot of people he was likely to be doing acquisition business with, including a layer of top brass at Jones &

Laughlin. They were known around Pittsburgh as the "J&L Club," a term of derogation used by ambitious young executives who felt they were being held down. Ling's disdain for such men was on the record. A rather large slice of American management, therefore, was not likely to shed tears over any problems of Jim Ling and LTV.

Ling's $425-million bid for Jones & Laughlin was the largest cash tender ever made up to that point, and maybe since then. It was greeted with a mixed reaction. LTV's stock at first rose and then, after the controlling interest was sewed up, fell sharply. One of the leading brokerage firms for institutional investors such as mutual funds and insurance companies is Donaldson, Lufkin & Jenrette, Inc., which also happens to manage about $1 billion worth of other people's money. DL&J is a house that has presented itself as a group of bright young securities people who produce superior research on investment opportunities for their customers. Their first comment on LTV's acquisition of J&L was an "action recommendation" that concluded: "We recommend the current purchase of LTV common shares." The stock was selling at about $120 at the time. It climbed above $135 briefly, and then it tumbled, never to recover.

Other firms were less sanguine. In early 1968, while the Greatamerica tender was in process, a report on LTV by the firm of Spencer Trask & Company noted that "the outlook for 1968 is promising." The report referred to "substantial financial leverage" and expressed some concern about "certain pressures on the parent company" and on the importance of Braniff as a contributor to earnings. It also spoke of "what we term the 'James J. Ling risk.' Mr. Ling has put together a good management team, but we believe that a loss of vitality would be apparent in the event that Mr. Ling is made unavailable in some manner." In July, when the J&L deal was an accomplished fact and the Greatamerica acquisition and reorganization had been completed, the firm put out another report on LTV. It noted the problem of the corporation meeting its interest obligations and stated that things would get better when the remaining 37 percent of J&L stock was acquired and LTV could transfer some of the debt to J&L. And it concluded with this comment:

While we cannot rule out completely a display of the agile financial footwork the company has exhibited in the past, as we see it, the company's options are fairly limited at this stage. The difficulties stem, we believe, from paying too much for Braniff [as part of the Greatamerica acquisition], which then forced them into the position whereby they had to pay too much for Jones & Laughlin.

It was an interesting formulation of the situation and one that was apparently shared by others in Wall Street. Shortly after the J&L deal was completed, several large institutional investors in LTV sold their holdings, which contributed to the sharp decline in the corporation's market price. Actually, however, the relationship between the Braniff-and-Greatamerica deal and the J&L purchase price was not quite as the report stated. It seems, in fact, to have worked the other way. In its efforts to raise the money to pay off its loans from the bankers who financed the J&L purchase, LTV seems to have changed its plans for handling the dissolution of Greatamerica and the disposal of its holdings. That change of plans revalued Braniff to a much higher book value than had been anticipated when LTV first began the acquisition of Greatamerica. And that seems to have been a *result* of the J&L offer, not the cause of it.

To make its historic offer for J&L, Ling-Temco-Vought borrowed more than $200 million of the $425 million from U.S. and foreign bankers. Ling had made a whirlwind flying tour of European financial centers after he correctly figured that the abortive revolt in France in May, 1968, would send francs out of the country, looking for a safe refuge. That smart move had brought LTV about $60 million at an abnormally low interest rate of 5 percent, about half the going rate a year later. The rest came mainly from borrowings from U.S. banks, which would have to be paid back in less than two years, and from changing the plans for Greatamerica and selling off its bank and its insurance companies in a hurry. The First Western Bank, which had been slated for a public offering at $80 million, went to a private buyer for about $62 million. And E. Grant Fitts set up Gulf Life

Holding Company and was permitted to buy all of LTV's holdings in Greatamerica's insurance companies for $37 million in cash and paper. Whatever plans there had once been for redeploying these pieces of Greatamerica into partly public companies were abandoned with the need for cash for J&L.

When the Greatamerica company itself was finally dissolved, its components were taken into and then out of LTV. The hasty unloading of some meant that what stayed—mainly Braniff—wound up, when the total price was allocated among the pieces, with a larger price tag than it was worth, in order not to show losses on what was sold cheap. In fact, the price set for Braniff, as a result of the raising of money to pay for J&L, ran to about $200 million more than the market value of its shares. A company is relatively free to set book prices for what it acquires to take into consideration such values as long-term earnings growth prospects and the fact that it owns the controlling shares. And it could well be that the value of a major airline is bound to increase. So the fact that Braniff was priced high was permissible in the never-never land of acquisition accounting, even if the cause happened to be that other things had to be priced low for quick sale.

But with some $200 million of surplus value, known in accounting parlance as "goodwill," Braniff could not readily be consolidated—that is, "fused" into LTV's operations for accounting purposes—because the $200 million would have had to have been written off eventually. And even over the maximum permissible period of forty years, that would have meant a charge against earnings of $5 million a year, which would have wiped out a lot of Braniff's earnings in some years, all of them in a few. Until the J&L acquisition caused these changes in plans, Ling had been looking forward to playing an active role in Braniff's management. He spoke of becoming a "big daddy" to Harding Lawrence, Braniff's boss. But somewhere in the process, Ling seems to have backed off. One LTV executive even suggests there was some sort of unwritten agreement between Ling and the Braniff people that caused him to leave them alone.

Ling just sat back and watched as a member of a board of directors that LTV never assumed control of, even though it owned control of the airline. Ling's principal business contacts with Lawrence, aside from formal meetings, seem to have been the occasions when Lawrence came to him asking for enormous raises and fringe benefits. The public reason for LTV's hands-off policy on Braniff was that, since it was a business regulated by a federal agency, it ought not to be consolidated with the rest of LTV's subsidiaries. Accounting rules permit such a subsidiary to remain unconsolidated, but they do not require it.

As cash-shortage problems became critical and LTV earnings started sliding later in 1968, Ling devised a string of complex transactions—exchanges, sales, and whatnot—aimed at bringing in more money, raising the value of LTV's holdings in some subsidiaries, liquidating holdings in others, and increasing per-share earnings by bringing in LTV parent shares. Somehow, to Ling and to his associates, it all seemed manageable, and for a while it was.

Ling's creation of Computer Technology, Inc., in the late summer of 1968 was another in his series of master strokes. Inspired partly by the success of another Dallas man, H. Ross Perot, Computer Tech was to be, like Perot's Electronic Data Systems, a computer service and software company that would take over and operate the computer systems of other companies. It was set up in what had become the classic Ling manner, by acquiring first of all the computer operations of LTV and its Aerospace subsidiary. That made it a sizable company to begin with, though at the start it was wholly owned by Aerospace and LTV. But Ling saw it as much more than just a spin-off of LTV's own accounting and computer operations. He envisioned "the biggest software company" in the United States, and he got a man to run it who thought in the same big ways—G. W. Woerner, Jr. Like Perot and University Computing's Sam Wyly, Bill Woerner had come up through IBM. When Ling recruited him, he was IBM's Data Processing Division vice president and Midwestern sales manager. A handsome, blue-eyed, tennis-playing, hard-selling man, Woerner not only sold himself on Ling's plan but brought with him some other top IBM salesmen. All of them were to get big incentives in the form of options on CT shares and, later, on shares of subsidiaries CT itself would set up. LTV and Aerospace owned all the stock at the beginning, but through a later exchange offer a block of LTV's shares of CT would become publicly owned. When these shares hit the market, they were expected to rise sharply (which they did) and LTV would get a new "working asset" through the increase in value of whatever shares it held and, even more, from the increase in value of LTV's holdings of Aerospace, whose holdings of CT's shares were much greater than LTV's.

At this point, despite some peripheral concern about paying for J&L and some changes in plans to manage it, Ling was still as ebullient as ever or maybe a little more so. He was talking about further redeploying of LTV and its subsidiaries into a $10-billion complex, maybe even ranking as No. 2, just behind General Motors, someday. It was all said almost deadpan, and maybe sometimes he believed that it was at least theoretically possible, if you could pay the interest. But mostly it was stuff he knew the press liked to hear and print.

What Ling had demonstrated beyond any doubt was that, with few exceptions, just about every widely held company in America was vulnerable to a takeover. And that made a lot of businessmen very uneasy and caused them increasingly to turn to their contacts in Washington looking for some kind of relief. The word "conglomerate" was engendering not only irrational fear but a lot of concern that nobody's job in the executive suite was secure as long as people like Jim Ling, Laurence Tisch of Loew's, Charles Bluhdorn of Gulf & Western, Ben Heineman of Northwest Industries, and a growing list of conglomerators were allowed to run loose.

That may have affected Ling's political habits during 1968. He had been an independent whose political activities were restricted to financial support of candidates of either party. But in 1968 he took a more active interest than usual. First of all, he was concerned about the presidential aspirations of his old enemy Bobby Kennedy. Ling's hostility toward the former Attorney General stemmed, of course, from the days in 1961 when the Justice Department took up Chance Vought's action against Ling and filed its own untenable suit against him. There was a strong feeling in Texas in those days, supported by Texans in Washington, that the Kennedys were systematically attempting to wreak as much havoc as they could among the backers of Lyndon Johnson. Ling's support of Johnson against John Kennedy in 1960 apparently put him in that category.

For that reason, when it came to taking sides in 1968, Ling elected to support Hubert Humphrey, and his name appeared in an ad in May along with Dean Acheson, Eric Hoffer, Frank Sinatra, and Isaac Stern, among other Citizens for Humphrey. Though he was still listed as a Humphrey-Muskie supporter in a September ad, without his consent, along with Henry Ford II, Jackie Robinson, Edgar Kaiser, Mary Wells Lawrence, and others, he had actually gone over to the Nixon camp. After the murder of Bobby Kennedy, Ling had begun drifting away from the Democrats. One of the two Texas Senators, John Tower, was Republican, and so was much of proper Dallas, including Ling's friend, neighbor, and Congressman, James Collins. Besides, Ling's biggest acquisitions—Wilson and Jones & Laughlin—had put him in close touch with top business executives who were, as most top business executives are, Republicans. Ling's political convictions were not unlike those of many other businessmen of Texas and of most other places. He was an admirer of Texas-style Democrats, of whom Lyndon Johnson and Governor and later Treasury Secretary John Connally are typical in that they manage to mingle politics and personal wealth in a blatant way without incurring much comment from anybody but the liberals. Texas has been characterized by at least as many business-political scandals as other states, sometimes including governors among the participants. Yet one former governor who was deeply involved in a much-publicized government-land scandal remains a highly respected member of the financial community.

A more recent scandal touched most of the top politicians

in the Texas state government, including Governor Preston Smith, the lieutenant governor, the speaker of the house, and a United States Assistant Attorney General from Texas. (Among the participants in the complicated financial and legislative operations was the now-defunct firm of Ling & Company, a Dallas brokerage house headed by Michael Ling, one of Jim Ling's brothers. Jim Ling had been a customer of the firm, his oldest son had been one of its salesmen, and the family name had certainly been useful to the firm. But Jim Ling has never been connected in any way with the revelations, and his brother Michael has been described by *Fortune* as "a rather passive collaborator," with the active participation being attributed to an employee of the firm.) In the process, an important supporter of Governor Smith passed what may well be a characteristic judgment on the blending of politics and free enterprise in Texas: "Of course I'll keep backing him. What he did was unethical, not actually illegal."

Since Ling had often supported Republicans, he would have no problem switching affiliation. He insists that his move to the Nixon party and his raising of about $120,000 for the Republican presidential campaign were purely the results of his desire to back the best man for the country. The sincerity of that view seems unassailable. Even with the mounting hostility toward the conglomerates, of which LTV had by now become a sort of prototype, the antitrust chief in the Democratic Administration had made clear his conviction that there was no legal basis for attacking the conglomerates as such. The kind of bigness the conglomerates represented, diverse as it was, simply could not be construed as constituting restraint of trade and lessening of competition as these offenses were then defined in the statutes.

A Texas Republican recently recalled his astonishment at seeing Ling at a Nixon dinner in Dallas, especially since Ling's name had only a few weeks before appeared in the Humphrey-Muskie ad. But despite the support of Ling and others who had switched to Nixon, Humphrey still managed to squeak through in Texas. In fact, it was the first time since the election of 1924 that Texas was not on the winning side in a presidential election, a fact that Nixon could hardly be expected to ignore. But by the time the President chose John Connally as Secretary of the Treasury, presumably in part to bring Texas to his side next time, all the damage the Nixon Administration could work on Ling and LTV had long since been done.

It has never been clear precisely what prompted the anti-trust action against Ling-Temco-Vought. It was at best a dubious action with no strong legal basis. The most obvious conclusion is that a fat file on the corporation and its acquisitions had been put together under the Democrats. When the new Assistant Attorney General in charge of the Justice Department's Antitrust Division—Richard W. McLaren—moved into the office, that file may have been the handiest way for him to make a forthright move against the great threat to the established order. In a way, Ling had been asking for it, especially with his dramatic acquisitions and with his occasional comments against "caretaker" managements and in defense of conglomerates. When McLaren, in office only a few weeks, started saying he was going to do something to stop the conglomerates, which, as such, were in no sense illegal, Ling fought back. He ordered the preparation of a provocative two-page advertisement headlined "Plain Talk from LTV" defending LTV against the thrusts of McLaren, of House Judiciary Committee Chairman Emanuel Celler, and of the new SEC Chairman, Hamer Budge, among others. Though they wouldn't tell Ling, some of his staff people thought it was ill-advised. That ad ran in *The New York Times* and the *Wall Street Journal* in early March, 1969. During the next couple of weeks, Ling, Skeen, Haynie, and other LTV and subsidiary executives with contacts in Washington held a series of meetings there with the Texas congressional delegation, with Senators Dirksen and Hruska, as well as with members of congressional committees that might be involved in probes and actions against LTV and other conglomerates.

These trips and meetings indicate that Ling, or his advisers at least, were expecting trouble from the government, probably including Congress. The late Congressman John C.

Watts of Kentucky, a high-ranking member of Wilbur Mills's Ways and Means Committee, had told Ling that Mills's main interest in conglomerates seemed to center on stopping Ben Heineman of Northwest Industries from acquiring B. F. Goodrich of Akron, as a favor to the incumbents at Goodrich. "Did he get him?" Watts reportedly asked Ling at the end of their meeting. (He did indeed, as Watts well knew.) These meetings seemed to assure Ling that his enterprise was safe from government action, or at least that it was assured of assistance by influential members of Congress if it did get into trouble. That is why, when the new Administration made its move against Ling-Temco-Vought, Ling was not expecting either the timing or the shape of the attack.

13

BEING James Ling in the early months of 1969 may have been unsettling, but it was not dull. Because his corporation had become the biggest of the conglomerates, and because he reacted to government and press criticism of these companies as though he were being attacked personally even when neither he nor LTV was mentioned specifically, Ling had become identified as their spokesman. That was no easy role, because the term "conglomerate" itself was difficult to define, and the criticisms of the conglomerates frequently had little relation to reality. They were based largely on fear of the unknown and on residual distrust of Big Business and High Finance that came out of the 1930s but traced its origins to the populism of the nineteenth century. There were, of course, conglomerates. No two definitions or lists would be quite the same, but the term had grown up during the 1960s to refer to those corporations that had achieved recent and generally rapid growth by acquiring other companies in fields different from their own, largely because the antitrust laws prevented them from expanding within their own industries and markets. A company did not have to be new to qualify, but its diverse growth had to be recent. Hardly anybody called General Electric or Allis-Chalmers a conglomerate, except as a defense against critics, because they had been in diverse businesses for decades. ITT, on the other hand, had been a collection of telephone, cable, and manufacturing companies for more than a generation before Harold Geneen turned it into a recognizable conglomerate.

The word itself probably was first used by some security analyst in an investment firm to cover companies that no longer fitted into their original categories. Textron, to cite a classic example, had abandoned the textile and apparel fields and had to be fitted into some new pigeonhole. Diversifying by acquiring also created financial complexity and confusion. Consider the case of ITT: Among its several issues of securities, there are no less than eleven different preferred stocks. Even without regard to the soundness of these securities as investments, they are hard to understand. And since it is easier to fear than to fathom, the belief among investors that conglomerates had magical powers began giving way as soon as an outstanding one seemed no longer to have any. The process of disenchantment actually began back in 1968, when Litton Industries reported a drop in its quarterly earnings for the first time in fourteen years.

Until then, everything that Litton acquired seemed to produce higher and higher profits. Hardly anybody had noticed that Litton had begun buying outfits that were not very good earners, in shipbuilding, business machines, and office furniture among other fields. Litton's way was to group everything in "systems," as it called its subdivisions. The word in those days implied a special kind of intelligence and seemed to turn rag-tag old companies into glossy new ones. But when Litton finally announced a decline in earnings, though not an actual loss, its stock and the shares of just about every other corporation that had come to be called a conglomerate plunged.

LTV's stock fell along with the rest, dropping below 90 in early 1968. But the market in general recovered, and then the announcement of the Jones & Laughlin deal pushed LTV's stock back up almost to 136 before it started down again. By that time, however, "conglomerate" had become a dirty word in Washington, and all the formulas from "systems" to Project Redeployment lost their special powers.

The second half of 1968 had been a bad time for J&L. That was the first time that LTV could claim any of the steel company's earnings as its own, and there were almost none to claim. Ling was now pressed for cash to pay LTV's interest charges and reduce its debt, so he turned to a planned method of relief. Shares of stock in Braniff, National Car Rental, and the newly created Computer Technology were offered to LTV security holders in exchange for LTV common stock, notes, and debentures at the end of 1968. That exchange reduced interest and dividend obligations and improved per-share earnings by reducing the number of common shares outstanding. But when word came out in early 1969 that the corporation's consolidated earnings for 1968 would be down for the first time since 1963, the stock tumbled from around 100 in early January to below 65 by the end of February.

A statement by Richard W. McLaren, the incoming Assistant Attorney General in charge of antitrust, that he intended to crack down on conglomerate mergers did not help matters. Neither, of course, did the enormous increase in LTV's debt and interest expense. In February, LTV sold some more of its Braniff shares for $33 million in cash. But in its 1968 annual report, dated March 21, 1969, the corporation reported that its consolidated long-term debt amounted to more than $1.2 billion, compared with a relatively manageable $200 million the year before, plus an increase in bank debt of more than $200 million, repayment of which was to begin soon. These increases in debt included the $500 million of debentures issued in exchange for the stock of Greatamerica and a lot of the cash used to buy J&L, but it also covered large borrowings by subsidiaries for which the parent was ultimately responsible. In 1967, interest expense for the consolidated enterprise had come to a mere $18 million, but during 1968 it climbed to more than $67 million.

LTV would need a lot of earnings from its subsidiaries in 1969, but the way the steel company was performing indicated that it was going to take some fancy redeploying by Ling and his financial people to get the debt-ridden machine running properly again. Though LTV owned the majority of J&L's stock, the trust that had been established to vote those shares after the acquisition kept voting control in the hands of the steel company's management. Therefore, if they chose to,

J&L's three members of the five-member trust could ignore Ling's plans for restructuring the company. What he had in mind, though his plans were still rather vague, was the formation of at least two steel subsidiaries from the components of J&L. One possibility was a division of the company along geographic lines into an eastern unit based in Pittsburgh and a western one based in Illinois, where J&L had just completed a huge rolling mill. Another possibility was to divide the company along product lines, with so-called specialty steel in one company and basic steel facilities in another. Neither of these preliminary ideas took into consideration the fact that the components of this steel-making concern were not readily separable into companies that could operate on their own. For one thing, the new rolling mill at Hennepin, Illinois, did not have any basic steel-making capacity and would have to get its steel from J&L mills in Ohio or Pennsylvania, which led him to consider selling it to Bethlehem or some other steel maker with a plant nearby. It would be a while before Ling learned enough about the realities of the steel industry in general and of J&L in particular to understand the enormous management problems LTV had bought.

Ling still seemed undaunted by the scale of his problems. In fact, he actually appeared enthusiastic as he contemplated the future. His excursions to Washington in mid-March had persuaded him that the bark of the government watchdogs would not be followed by any serious bites. The worst that seemed likely was that McLaren would try to limit acquisitions by and of major corporations. Though Ling bridled at the prospect of such restraints on his dreams, their actual effect on LTV would be negligible, because the corporation had neither the money nor the credit to acquire anything else. In fact, LTV was selling off some of its holdings to raise money and reduce debt. McLaren, Congressman Emanuel Celler, and Hamer Budge of the SEC could make threats that could affect the stock market, but it didn't seem that they would do much more.

At about this time, Ling agreed to work on a tape-recorded journal of his activities. He had plenty to keep him occupied

without talking to a machine every day, so he did not pursue
the project on a regular basis. During the next six months,
however, he did work periodically with the recorder. What
came of his efforts was a mixture of sporadic diary and random monologue. The segments of the transcripts that appear
here cover events in the spring and summer of 1969. They
represent only a fraction of the total he recorded during those
days, and they have been edited to tighten the inevitable
loose syntax of an oral record. Even so, the style and most of
the words are Ling's. When Ling undertook the project, his
major concern was the redeployment of Jones & Laughlin.
But by the time he began talking into the microphone, the
course of his history had veered sharply in a new direction.

March 22, 1969

Even before I picked up the phone this afternoon, I
knew something big had happened. I was at Brook Hollow
Country Club, in the clubhouse, playing gin rummy. We've
got a rule around the company that I'm not to be disturbed
at the club, especially on Saturday, unless it can't wait. This
call couldn't wait. It was Dan Burney, LTV's general counsel.
He had just got a call from Washington, from Norman Diamond, a partner in Arnold & Porter, the law firm we retain
in Washington. Norm told Dan he had just received a call
from Richard McLaren. We were about to have an antitrust
suit filed against us. They were going to try to get LTV to
divest itself of Jones & Laughlin.

My immediate reaction was absolute, utter disbelief. We
had had no warning, and there had been plenty of time to
alert us if they had been planning this sort of move. I don't
mean we never thought of the possibility of antitrust action.
You have to. The antitrust laws are part of the rules of the
game. You consult your attorneys before you make any move
that might involve those laws, and unless they think you're
in the clear, you don't make the move. There are innumerable
companies we would not consider acquiring or merging with
in countless fields we would not attempt to enter because of

antitrust problems.

But our acquisition of Jones & Laughlin was not one of them. We bought 63 percent of the stock of J&L back in June of 1968, fully confident that nothing on the law books prevented us from doing that. And now we were in the midst of acquiring the rest of J&L's stock through a tender offer to the other shareholders. This could not have been a surprise to the Justice Department. We had announced our intention of making the offer back in December, and they didn't try to stop us. We had registered our tender offer with the SEC on February 5, and we had not been notified that any action was planned against the move. We had formally begun the offer more than a week ago. Still no word. Now that we are right in the middle of the thing, they want us to stop.

I went back to the table, but couldn't keep my mind on the game. I lost $135. But I wasn't just sitting there at the gin table feeling sorry for myself or the company or all the people whose money was invested in what we were doing. I was already beginning to develop a game plan about what we would do if they went ahead with this thing. By the time I left the table, I had a pretty good idea of what our course of action would be, at least as far as we had any real choices to make.

When I got home this evening, I talked to Dan Burney a couple more times. He said we would be hearing from Mc-Laren again tomorrow. I alerted our top executives and staff men to be ready for a meeting in the morning. Meanwhile we just had to sweat it out.

March 23

Dorothy and I went to early Mass and were back at the house in time to get the latest word from Washington. Overnight the situation had escalated. Yesterday McLaren was saying that he would *recommend* to the Attorney General that a suit be filled against LTV. This morning the word was that the Justice Department would *definitely* file one and would announce its intention later today. And unless we

agreed to withdraw our tender offer for the rest of the Jones
& Laughlin stock, they were going to get an injunction to
stop us.

I asked our people to come to the house for an eleven-
o'clock meeting. We had Clyde Skeen, LTV's president;
Roscoe Haynie, chairman of LTV's executive committee;
Bill Tinsley, my neighbor and a partner in our Dallas law
firm; Dan Burney; George Griffin, our financial-planning vice
president; Johnny Johnson, our public-relations vice president;
and some other staff people, because we weren't sure exactly
who and what we would need.

Our chain of communication goes through Dan Burney in
Dallas to Norm Diamond in Washington to McLaren at the
the Justice Department. The word comes down that McLaren
is going to make a statement to the press at three o'clock
Washington time, period. Then we get a copy of the text
of his release. It's just a single paragraph saying Justice told
us last night that they are going to sue us, but not saying
when or on what grounds. They also say they are going to
get an injunction to stop us from going through with the
J&L tender, unless we call it off.

We asked McLaren for a meeting in Washington to discuss the tender offer. He told our people he didn't think anything constructive could come of the meeting. But I told Dan
to get across to him that there were a lot of factors involved
and at least he ought to know them before he went into court
for his injunction. Finally he agreed to see us in Washington
tomorrow afternoon at 2:30.

Our people wrote a statement pointing out that we had
checked carefully on the antitrust aspects of the J&L deal
before we ever began it. We also said that we thought that
our entry into the steel industry was "the most pro-competi-
tive development in that industry since the government itself
supported the formation of Kaiser Steel and Lone Star Steel."
We figured that if the government was so eager to promote
competition in these old-line closed industries, they would
be glad to see us acquire J&L.

I tried to figure out why McLaren had picked a Sunday
afternoon to make his announcement. After all, he had not

actually filed a suit against us or even said when he would or on what grounds. Word had come back to us that he was concerned that the stock market might overreact if he announced his plan when the exchange was open. But you don't have to be a public-relations expert to know that not very much happens in Washington on Sundays and if you put a story out that day you'll very likely get a lot more newspaper space and radio and TV time than on any other day. I began getting calls that evening. We were the lead story on the front page of *The New York Times* and the first item on CBS-TV news, plus a lot of local coverage.

March 24

We were wheels up out of Grand Prairie, where we keep our jet at the LTV Aerospace plant, at six this morning. My calendar showed a haircut and a doctor's appointment that had to be canceled. When we landed at Dulles International, Ted Mann of our Washington office was waiting to brief us and drive us into the city. We were headed straight for Arnold & Porter for a strategy meeting. The *Wall Street Journal* and the *Washington Post* were full of the story. I read them in the car. I'm not used to reading the *Post* and I was shocked by the tone of their editorial, a real pile of crap mostly. The conglomerate fear was spreading all over the country, and damned few writers seemed to understand what we and the other companies they were tarring as conglomerates really were all about. They say there is supposed to be a presumption of innocence for anyone accused of anything. I hope the courts operate that way, because it was apparent to me that the press didn't.

As we drove, I was thinking, "My God, every time we get our head up, somebody tries to knock it off." And I thought how hard it had been to sell the Jones & Laughlin people—their ultra-conservative board of directors, members of the so-called Pittsburgh Establishment—on our concept. It was going to be a real radical departure for them. And I was beginning to wonder if it would come about at all now.

We arrived at Arnold & Porter's offices at 19th and N streets sometime after eleven, and their planning meeting was already going on. What we wanted to do was get McLaren to agree to hold off on his injunction so that we could continue to acquire J&L shares. We all agreed that we wanted to bring this thing to trial as quickly as possible rather than have it drag through the courts for years. There was no question in our minds that McLaren would go ahead and file the suit. There was no point in thinking politically about the case. McLaren would certainly consider any attempt on our part to delay the case, for whatever reason, as an attempt to bring political pressure to bear.

We agreed that we would avoid any dilatory tactics, stipulate as many facts as possible to eliminate time-consuming investigations and depositions, appeal any adverse trial-court judgment, and generally recognize the desirability of clarifying existing law. That way we hoped to get the case over and done with so we could end the paralysis to our business that this had to produce.

There were a lot of reporters hanging around when we arrived at the Justice Department, so we were taken up in the private elevator of the Attorney General. Johnny Johnson had told the press we might make a statement after the meeting. McLaren's office was what you would expect for an Assistant Attorney General—big, with paneling, massive furniture, that sort of thing, and with a lot of chairs and sofas arranged in a kind of semicircle. McLaren was there with Paul Owens, his senior staff assistant, and three young lawyers. And we arrived with Dan Burney, Bill Tinsley, Norm Diamond and other Arnold & Porter lawyers, Bill Stephens, who had become chairman and chief executive of Jones & Laughlin after we took over, Robert Peabody of J&L, and Richard Pogue of J&L's law firm. We shook hands all around, and Norm and the other Arnold & Porter lawyers were very cordial with Paul Owens and the government lawyers. I realized that what was war to me was just their profession to all of them.

Norm made the statement that we were eager to get the case into court as quickly as possible. His point was that we were as interested in getting a decision on the case as they were, but we had to have the stock tender offer in order to go ahead in an orderly way while we were awaiting the judgment. McLaren said, "I'm not sold on that at all. No, sir, we're not going to let you get any more of the securities. You have 63 percent. I don't want you to get any more."

Norm said that it would be illegal for us to withdraw the offer even if we wanted to; it was irrevocable. McLaren and Owens looked at each other, startled. "What do you mean by that?" McLaren asked. Norm referred them to the prospectus we had registered with the SEC covering the terms of the offer. At first nobody on the government's side seemed to know what we were talking about. I was incredulous: it looked as though they didn't even have a copy of the prospectus. Finally Owens dug one out of a slim file of papers.

While they were looking for it, I asked one of the Arnold & Porter lawyers what you call an Assistant Attorney General—I didn't reckon you called them Attorney General. He whispered, "General." "General McLaren," I said, "aside from the legal question of whether it's irrevocable, we've got a moral obligation to literally thousands of shareholders to continue this tender. And if we stopped it, even with your backing, we'd have millions of dollars' worth of lawsuits on our hands from people who didn't get a chance to tender their shares for the premium we were offering before we withdrew it. If I can't sleep tonight, I don't want it to be because I didn't try to persuade you of our obligation to these stockholders. I predict to you that our shares in the stock market will be bombed all over the lot tomorrow and the next day. We already gave up some four points today with millions of dollars' worth of losses because of this action, to say nothing of at least $20 million through not getting a tax consolidation, for which we have to have at least 80 percent of the shares."

McLaren said that he was afraid that if we got more stock, we would claim that it was a financial hardship to dispose of such a large block at one time in case we lost the suit. I assured him that we could unload the stock if we had to. I mentioned Howard Hughes's sale of 75 percent of TWA, the public sale of Ford Motor Company by the Ford Foundation, and the du Pont divestiture of its General Motors shares. I assured him we could manage it.

McLaren still expressed doubt that we could and would. "I'll tell you this," he said. "I intend to get the best financial advice from Wall Street." I wondered if that was an admission that he had not got financial advice *before* he proceeded with this action against LTV, but I didn't say anything. We were trying to be conciliatory. But by then I had got the impression that these antitrust people had not been doing their homework. So the next time I addressed McLaren, I demoted him: Instead of calling him General, I dropped him down to the rank of Mister, which was as near as I could get to Private.

We summed up our positions and worked out a press release that LTV would put out covering the meeting. McLaren made seven changes before he would OK it. He insisted that there be no other publicity whatsoever on the case. We agreed. We took the private elevator down, and Bill Stephens and I got into a limousine waiting at the back door of the building. Since McLaren had said no leaks, we weren't about to say anything to the press, even though Johnny had told them that we might. The newsmen spotted us and one shoved a microphone at me. I was straining my neck out the window to see who was talking to me, and I started to say something. I guess this guy thought I was making an unfriendly gesture. Anyway, he said, "Just wait until you see ABC tonight."

When I got back to Dallas tonight, I saw the ABC news, and this guy really ripped me about being in a big limousine and avoiding the press and looking distressed. I'm not used to being notorious yet.

March 25

They bombed us again today for more than six points. I make it a point in situations like this to get very quiet, don't really say too much, be quite precise and not get carried away. That's how I got through the board meeting of Wilson Pharmaceutical this afternoon. I'm not really "mad" or "sad" or anything else. I'm thinking: Where do we go from here? But I kept thinking to myself, really play it cool. We have enough people in our company who get upset, terribly depressed about things. The market drops and these guys' faces drop. I've long since gotten over letting myself react to these things. I just kept thinking about the situation all day, and I felt the odds were that we're going to beat this guy.

[Ling returned to Washington later in the week to work out an agreement with the Justice Department that permitted LTV to continue its exchange offer to take in and hold up 81 percent of J&L's shares. That, in turn, would permit LTV to consolidate J&L's operations with its own when it filed its federal corporate income-tax return. Since J&L had changed the method by which it computed its depreciation for tax purposes, it had in effect increased its 1968 pre-tax income by more than $20 million. By getting 81 percent of J&L's stock, LTV was thus able to report 81 percent of that increase as an addition to its own pre-tax income. As part of the agreement, LTV had to withdraw its representatives from the steel company's board of directors and from the stock-voting trust and not participate in the company's management. That meant that LTV had nothing to say about the operation of its largest single investment and its biggest management problem. When he returned to Dallas, Ling met with security analysts from several brokerage firms to reassure them that he had plans for solving LTV's problems. But LTV's stock kept dropping.]

April 9

I have a meeting this afternoon in New York with our investment bankers, Bill Osborn and Gus Levy, to consider some of the options we have for getting out from under. Dorothy and I left the house around seven, and we got to the Aerospace field just as everybody else on the trip was pulling in. The plane we were taking, the one I usually fly, the jet Falcon 570L, was parked against the fence. We were in and buttoned up in minutes, with me in the captain's seat and Ray Balwierczak, our chief pilot, on my right.

We checked out the aircraft, and I taxied through the gate onto the field, and with no traffic to wait behind, I took it up minutes later. A perfect flying day all the way to La Guardia, and I had the controls pretty near all the way.

In the last three years, I've been spending at least 600 hours a year in the air. That means I am airborne roughly fifteen forty-hour weeks a year. Or try it this way: I spend the equivalent of only a bit less than a third of my regular working time in the air. I can do only so much work on an airplane. I do a lot of my thinking early in the morning when I get up, so I get bored in the back end of an airplane. I get bored playing gin rummy all the time, particularly if I get beat, which happens occasionally. And I don't want to relieve my associates of too much of their money, which has happened a lot more frequently.

I get annoyed when people crackle and snap Fritos or potato chips, and I can't stand people cracking ice or chewing gum. I guess that comes from a time in 1945, coming back from the Philippines. I spent nearly six weeks cramped in the hold of an aircraft carrier with a little bastard who never stopped chewing gum, and I couldn't duck him all that time.

I had also got into the habit of drinking in the back end. Not excessively, but still, when you take a couple of drinks, even when it's an evening flight, you get to your destination a little groggy, and the first thing you know, you have a lot of calories aboard that you have to get rid of. Also, monkey see, monkey do: if I have a couple of drinks, a lot of people will follow suit.

So I decided to go up front to see what was going on there. I had a jump seat specially built so that I had a good view of what the pilot and copilot were doing. It was only a matter of time before the senior guy would invite me to get into the right-hand seat and play with the controls. I got to the point where I had a pretty good feel and an elementary knowledge of the systems. So, about a year ago, I decided that I wanted to take lessons as an official student. As instructors, I had Ray Balwierczak along with Ed Black, another of our pilots.

We had some pretty bumpy rides, and I got—for lack of a better word—the thrill of bouncing a big jet aircraft doing 140 mph back into the air and seemingly losing control of it. It scared the living crap out of me the first couple of times. After a few trips to the West Coast, where I took instruction in the right-hand seat, I had about fifteen or twenty hours in. I was assisting in takeoffs and landings.

By early June, I was headed for Europe to borrow some money for the J&L tender. The Falcon had been flown over earlier for me, and I was to fly commercial from New York to London to meet our people there. When I got to London, my associates had the itinerary and the routes all worked out. We were going from London to Geneva, Zurich, Milan, Frankfurt, Paris, and Nice before we headed home. We were seeing bankers mostly and Dessault, the aircraft manufacturer, in Nice. After Nice, the plan was to fly to Shannon, spend the night, and then fly the Atlantic. I had got a lot of flying time in on the tour, and when we were ready to leave Europe, our pilots, Ray Balwierczak and Blair Whitelaw, decided that I would fly the Atlantic and they would be the navigators.

We took off from Shannon bright and early. It was fantastic to pass over the various radio ships, the glaciers, and the little outposts of civilization in places like Greenland. It was cold and windy when we came down in Iceland. The next leg was rough. Coming into Greenland, I made my first GCA [ground-controlled approach], under rain, thunderstorms, snow, a little bit of everything. Today that would be a cakewalk. But at that time, what with trying to follow the direction of the controller who talks you into the slot and having Blair and Ray both second-guessing me, I was a goddam nervous wreck by the time I set the airplane down. Thank God it was a 9,000-foot runway. It worked out all right, even though I made some mistakes. At Iceland, I think it was, I accidentally cut off one of the engines as I was taxiing on the runway.

I got pretty tired, so I finally turned the controls over after

Greenland, so they could take it the last 2½-hour leg of the trip to New York. Except for that stretch, I had flown the Atlantic, and it was one of the biggest thrills of my life.

Since then, I have logged maybe 500 hours of jet aircraft flying, but I have never flown a conventional reciprocating-engine aircraft. Of course I don't have a regular pilot's license, just the one that allows me to take instruction. I've got to the point now where I have enough feeling and understanding so that I am no danger to anyone, and of course, with one of the pilots always with me, I never really was anyway. Since last June, I have probably made 90 percent of all my landings. The pilots, of course, log my flying time, and they have a rating system for my landings too: When it's a good one, it's an AB landing, which stands for Atta Boy. And when it's bad, it's an AS—Aw Shit—landing. My AS landings are quite rare.

But aside from my own flying, flying our corporate private jet has given us tremendous quick-reaction capability. It may be great for my recreation, but it is far more important for our operation. The trip I took last year, the time I flew the Atlantic, was to raise funds to repay some of our bank borrowing for the Jones & Laughlin acquisition. The student strikes in Paris made me think we better go quickly if we were going to get European money. Lehman Brothers, Goldman, Sachs, and Rothschild helped us line up the bankers along the route. We were able to borrow at 5 percent. Today it is doubtful that we could borrow at less than 9 or 10 percent, if we could get money at all.

So the airplane, I am convinced, had a lot to do with our success in financing that deal. I think the bankers who flew along with us—I didn't give them any bad landings—were impressed by the fact that we were a real aggressive, hard-nosed corporation that would make money, because we used a jet aircraft as our prime method of transportation. If we had waited to play the game this year, or even later last year, we would be paying $7 million a year in interest instead of about $3.5 million. The whole atmosphere, politically and businesswise, has changed dramatically since then. And thank God we were able to react to it in time.

Today as we came in on the approach at La Guardia, Ray grabbed the controls because I was coming in too steep. We hit kind of hard anyway, but nobody in the back thought anything was wrong. Or at least they didn't say anything. But I think maybe Ray would have rated that one as something less than an AB. But we had a guest in the jump seat today, and Ray reminds me that I sometimes don't do well when I've got somebody watching.

The cars were waiting, and we headed for the Regency Hotel, where we keep a suite for our people. That's where I had the meeting with Bill Osborn and Gus Levy to plan our overall strategy as a result of the lawsuit.

We talked about possible ways of reducing our debt. If we can increase our holdings of Aerospace to 81 percent and if our current offer of debentures and warrants for the J&L stock brings in more than the 81 percent McLaren is allowing us and also if we can get in 81 percent of Wilson Sporting Goods, we will be able to consolidate them and be in a better cash-flow position and also be able to sell off the excess over 81 percent of J&L we get, for cash. I also heard from them that Household Finance has a strong interest in buying our holdings in National Car Rental. Since National Car has a contract to use and advertise General Motors cars and since General Motors is a big customer of Jones & Laughlin, we have to sell National now anyway to get rid of that potential reciprocity conflict.

We talked about the possibility of reducing our holdings in the steel company, and while they thought it was an attractive idea from the standpoint of our short-term debt problems, they said let's retain the 81 percent for a while. Their rationale ran this way: The steel industry is on the upswing again. Every day in the paper you read about new steel requirements, etc., and they feel that steel stocks will be relatively strong. Thus, retaining our position in J&L is not bad, simply from an economic point of view. I pointed out that there's got to be a serious morale deterioration among the J&L people as a result of the lawsuit, but I assume that we should be able to handle it effectively. I was also thinking about our plans to set up a Computer Tech of Pennsylvania, a CT subsidiary to take over the computer operations of J&L as a start.

We also talked about the prospect of selling J&L to somebody else. But whoever would buy it—unless they were very small, which is unlikely—would have the same antitrust problems we have. Or maybe we could exchange our J&L stock for the stock of a smaller company and we might even have stock left over. Then we could have a series of secondary offerings over a period of time when the economy was more favorable. So we can get out from under our problems.

These are things that occurred to me as they were outlining their brief for our staying in the steel business. Then of course, based on everything they've heard, they feel strongly that we should win our lawsuit. But I don't think that is so easily predictable. The Justice Department has won 71 out of 72 antitrust cases taken to the Supreme Court. So we would really have to break some sort of record to win if it came to that.

It was also suggested that Aerospace might exchange its Computer Tech stock for its own stock outstanding. That way, without LTV doing anything, our ownership of Aerospace could be increased to 81 percent so we could consolidate it. Or we could acquire all outstanding shares of Aerospace, and once it was wholly owned, we would have control of Computer Tech. Then we could redeploy the divisions of Aerospace later. By swapping Aerospace's CT for its own shares, we would be using a high-multiple share—maybe 100 times earnings—to bring in Aerospace—about 16 times earnings.

At one point, Gus Levy said that the idea of creating Computer Tech was a stroke of genius and that it had only recently dawned on him that we have made about $150 million for Aerospace and LTV with essentially no cost at all.

We talked about a lot of possibilities such as these, and it was a very good meeting. After they left, I had more ideas, but I kept coming back to the idea of using Aerospace's Computer Tech stock to reduce the outstanding shares of Aerospace. That's the best one I can come up with so far that makes sense from everybody's point of view.

I phoned George Griffin and outlined all these things to him so that he can start studying how they will work out from the technical standpoint.

[LTV might well have saved itself from its future desperate problems if Ling had elected to unload the corporation's Jones & Laughlin shares or even part of them. LTV had paid $85 a share for them. By this time, they had been split two-for-one, and those still publicly held—something less than 20 percent of them after the March tender offer—were priced at around $30 (or about $60 for the old unsplit shares). Had the corporation got out of the steel industry then, even at the loss it would have sustained, it would have been able to reduce its debt substantially. The decision to hold on turned out to be a major error. Of course, an announcement by LTV that it planned to sell its J&L shares might have lowered their market value just because of the vastly increased supply that would hit the market. Instead, Ling focused on Computer Technology, Inc., the computer service company he had created out of the accounting and computer operations of LTV and LTV Aerospace Corporation, which still owned 71 percent of CT's shares, most of the rest by now being in public hands and trading at extremely high prices compared with the value of the underlying properties that were put into the company at its inception. Ling was now ruminating on the prospect of Aerospace offering its CT shares to Aerospace stockholders in exchange for Aerospace stock. The Aerospace subsidiary would thus have cut the number of its shares in public hands, which would automatically have increased the percentage of its shares in LTV's hands. If that share had reached 81 percent, LTV could consolidate Aerospace for tax purposes. That plan did not go into effect, however, because Ling decided instead to have Aerospace sell its CT shares rather than trade them for its own.]

April 10

This morning I got a call from Gus Levy to tell me that Charlie Bluhdorn [head of Gulf & Western, another major conglomerate] had placed an order for 10,000 shares of LTV "to help old Jimmy." Gus also told me that one of his partners had met a former law partner of President Nixon who had said that one of the reasons Justice filed the suit was because of some documents they had found in J&L's files, a master list of suppliers as well as customers.

Before we decide what we are going to do, I have to go over George Griffin's studies and find out from Bill Stephens whether or not his game plan for J&L's 1969 earnings is still on. It would appear that they can earn their minimum projection of $38 million. I would like to hear Bill say that their more positive plan of $50 million is attainable. I need to have another meeting with the LTV people—Haynie, Skeen, Burney, Griffin, and maybe John Dixon. I also need to find out the status of our bank loans. Also I'll probably need to check back with Gus on Household Finance's interest in buying National Car Rental. So probably between now and Monday we'll decide specifically what programs we'll undertake to best serve the shareholders of LTV.

April 11

Back to Dallas this morning. This happens to be our tenth wedding anniversary.

I spent the rest of the morning briefing the other members of the LTV staff on my meeting with Gus Levy and Bill Osborn. We were informed later that the Justice Department had notified Arnold & Porter that they intend to bring the lawsuit bright and early Monday morning, April 14. That's Dorothy's birthday. I called the public-relations and legal staff together to develop a position paper and news release on the lawsuit.

April 14

The day began typically enough with me working out at 6:15 in the Spa, our gym on the twenty-ninth floor of our

LTV Tower. I was at my desk an hour later, waiting. Today was the day, according to our Washington lawyers, that the Department of Justice was finally going to file its antitrust suit against us in Pittsburgh. Clyde Skeen, Roscoe Haynie, Dan Burney, and George Griffin came in, waiting to see if there would be any surprises. I could tell that everybody was a little apprehensive, but as we thought about it, we couldn't see how there could be any surprises. Well, we were wrong. Of all the goddam things that could happen, that miserable lawyer representing Justice missed the plane from Washington to Pittsburgh, so they weren't going to be able to file the suit until noon. It's unbelievable that for one of the great landmark cases of all time the Justice Department couldn't at least be on time to file.

That created a problem because I just had to attend the surprise party some friends of Dorothy were giving for her birthday at the new Fairmount Hotel in Dallas. The surprise was that the men were invited too, which is unique for Dallas, Texas. But I shoved all my business problems aside and stopped in at the party.

The lawyer finally got to Pittsburgh and filed the suit. We got a report on the contents of the complaint, which deals mostly with a lot of things that *might* happen as a result of LTV acquiring Jones & Laughlin, all hypothetical. So there's nothing new in the lawsuit and nothing we're concerned about, and that's a relief.

Now I am anticipating a real problem between Paul Thayer and Bill Woerner over Computer Technology, Inc.

[Thayer, as president of LTV Aerospace Corporation, was involved because Aerospace at that time was CT's principal shareholder and Thayer was, in effect, Woerner's boss.]

April 15

The Spa bright and early and in the office by 7:20. I had breakfast at the telephone and began the day with calls to the East, first to Gus Levy. My secretary called Paul Thayer's office to confirm that he and Woerner were having their meeting. It had been going on since 7:00 and was still in progress, so I left word for Paul to call me as soon as it was over.

Paul called at around 9:45 and said he wanted to talk to us right away, so I had Clyde Skeen and Roscoe Haynie come in too. Paul gave us a quick synopsis of what happened at the latest confrontation with Bill Woerner. Without going into what he referred to as all the gory details, he said they had arrived at a game plan of operations that would seem compatible. Bill, it seems, made some very telling arguments. He was so damned persuasive about the things Computer Tech was doing that, even though he has not closed any major new accounts, he has convinced Paul that he will.

I've been anxious to see exactly how Paul handles this, because if Paul had walked in and told me that the deal was off and Woerner was leaving, that would not, to my way of thinking, have been a "body blow" but rather just the equivalent of a bloody nose for us. It would cause some reorientation of people and create problems for us with some of the people that Woerner has recruited, and who are loyal to him. I think that Paul has calmed down and accepted the fact that Woerner will be a problem child, and in all probability Paul has given in on some major points. The whole problem is that Woerner reacts like a bull to a red cape any time he has to report to Paul on any matter. And of course Paul is constantly egged on by his staff to have Woerner's Computer Tech people submit to his staff. I've told Paul over and over and over that if that happened to me I would be just as antagonistic as Bill Woerner is. Paul keeps reassuring me that it doesn't happen. But in looking over the recent memorandums, one especially, there is no question that it is an antagonistic situation. On the other hand, they're all very able people, and basically it's just a personality problem.

As I told Woerner in my last meeting with him, I would just rip his butt up and down about three different times and fire him if he were working for me and didn't obey me and conform to the system. The way it was left between them, according to Paul, was that Woerner would go back to CT headquarters in Chicago and put down on paper their agreement as he understood it. Paul said it had some real rough edges but of course it would probably be acceptable. So apparently we're beyond the critical point.

It would be a hell of a note to blow a deal that might involve $250 million for us simply because of our inability to handle a guy like Woerner.

April 16

We flew up to Chicago this afternoon. I have to make a speech here tomorrow at a luncheon meeting of the National Industrial Conference Board. I left Dallas today principally to get away from the phone calls. I had two or three drafts that I personally worked on with the staff, so I wanted to lock myself in the hotel room and work on the speech tonight and start thinking about my agenda for tomorrow morning too. I asked Bill Stephens to come over from Pittsburgh and have breakfast with me tomorrow. I want to talk to him about redeployment and also about the feeling we have been getting about the people at J&L, that all of a sudden they think they might be out on their own again without having us as major stockholders, so they don't have to pay any attention to us.

April 17

Bill Stephens came into our apartment at the Drake Hotel at about 7:30 A.M. The first thing on the agenda was the earnings prospect for the year. As developed in my discussion the other day with Bill Osborn and Gus Levy, people are suddenly realizing that this steel industry will be around for a long time and they are probably now cycling into a new productive phase. They now have an earnings estimate of $38 million at J&L with an objective of $50 million. But on the other hand, being prudent men, in our game plan presented to our directors we have cut it back to $27 million to be on the conservative side. Bill confirmed that they shouldn't have any trouble meeting the $38 million. He's not optimistic about the $50 million, but he was solid on his $38 million, which makes our game plan good at $27 million.

The next item was to discuss a study of the potential redeployment of two or three of his divisions into publicly held subsidiaries. They were hopeful they could make their stainless-steel division public and thus, with a major acquisition in certain areas, give some glamour to it. They need some—in his terminology—super alloy and exotic technology through a merger that they don't have in the house at the moment. And then there is the wire rope, cable, and chain division, but he is not optimistic about doing anything with it at the present time. So I told him—that is, I recommended—that he should continue his investigation.

And then we got to our concept of Computer Tech Pennsylvania, of organizing a number of high-powered Computer Tech service centers that would use J&L's computer services as a base. The idea would be that J&L would own 25 percent of the company, and our Computer Tech, which has the know-how, would be the parent and would own 75 percent. I'm not sure Bill understands it, but he knows the end results are good.

Next on the agenda is what I call my "philosophy of cooperation." I outlined to him very frankly the real or imagined problems that exist between his operational people and our people—there's a coolness, and so far as I'm concerned I might as well get it on the table. And Bill confirmed that some of his secondary people, but, more important, some of his directors, without naming them, were concerned about me being at the J&L annual shareholders' meeting, since we are no longer allowed to be members of their board. I reviewed our involvement with their company. They did not protest the tender offer. To the contrary, they tendered their securities. I think the Mellon Bank tendered about 300,000 J&L shares. J&L shared the legal opinion that there were no antitrust problems, and I feel we ought to have a shoulder-to-shoulder posture in defense against the lawsuit. They have looked up our innards as individuals for the past nine months. They've gotten to see every aspect of our business. They've gotten to know me personally and our people, and they shouldn't take a different position publicly than they have privately with us. That is what I call integrity. So Bill said that as far as he is concerned, they will file with us against the Justice Department and that we will have a position of unanimity, if that's the word for it.

My speech at the Conference Board went over well. A lot of people came over afterward to express their support. But we were supposed to be in Oklahoma City at 4:30 P.M. for a big reception. They had declared it LTV-Wilson Week in Oklahoma. So I rushed like hell to get to the airport, and the weather had socked us in. We hit the deck running, got to the plane, taxied out, and sure enough, there were forty or fifty planes ahead of us. Thunderstorms all over the area and the weather's coming in and they rotated us around two or three times and several guys, I could hear on the intercom, were having to get out of line because they were running short of fuel. We waited an hour and ten minutes and took off into the weather. Coming in, it was bad. Right before we hit the deck, I told Ray, "You got it." So he made the final part of the landing. He wondered later why I did that, so I told him, "I couldn't afford the embarrassment of blowing a landing in front of all those people." There was no way to make up the lost time, so the Governor couldn't wait to meet us, but the Mayor and a lot of other dignitaries were there.

Tomorrow, Clyde and I, who were both born in Oklahoma, are going to get honorary Doctor of Law degrees at Oklahoma Christian College. That will be my first degree of any kind. On Saturday, we go over to Arkansas to meet with Governor Winthrop Rockefeller and then I'll get another degree at the College of the Ozarks.

April 30

Wheels up from Grand Prairie at 8:00 for a hectic trip of meetings and speeches in New York, Boston, and Washington. Dorothy was along as far as New York to check on the progress of the decoration of the apartment we bought in New York to replace the suite we had been renting in the Regency Hotel. Also on board were Al Brill, a former pilot who is our corporate chief of transportation, and Chan Chandler, who is heading the new educational-systems program in which LTV Aerospace is acquiring business and technical schools. Chandler is slightly perturbed at the bureaucracy he's run into in Paul Thayer's office. I was a bit sympathetic. Incidentally, he was terribly guarded about it. It was strictly a matter of reading little clues in his manner; there was no open criticism, but I reviewed the way things take place and what you have to do to get at the heart of it, knowing that Paul Thayer is reachable. I gave him some good advice. He and Al Brill were headed to New York to take a look at one of the air-safety flight schools that we might add to the Aerospace division that Chan is running.

First work of the day in New York was a fund-raising meeting for the National Jewish Hospital downtown at the Bankers Club. I am on the national committee this year, and I got Gus Levy, who is one of the world's greatest fundraisers, to accept the chairmanship of the Wall Street division. I had agreed to serve because I could see the need for it: people who give money are more likely to support a local hospital in their own community, and here's an institution that needs extra help because it doesn't have a local community in that sense. Andrew Goodman of Bergdorf Goodman was the m.c. who introduced Gus. There was an exceptionally good turnout, partly out of respect for Gus, partly I think out of curiosity to take a look at me. Gus went through a stack of cards of those present, starting off with the announcement that Goldman, Sachs and Lehman Brothers, each of which had already pledged $25,000, would give another $5,000 apiece. Gus's timing was great: he called on me next, faking me out in a good sense, and I gave $25,000, half from LTV and half from me personally. I hadn't done as much for the drive as I had wanted to, but then I hadn't anticipated our antitrust problems when I accepted the assignment.

I got back to the Regency around 5:30 to meet Dead-Eye

Henry, an executive of a big company here, whom we're thinking of hiring to represent us in New York. He's hesitant about coming to work for us now, because his wife is gravely ill and he wants to be around New York all the time. I told him to take his time about making up his mind. Then I went to work on the two speeches I have to give tomorrow in Boston, one to the Harvard Business School alumni and the other to a group at Boston University. I worked on the Harvard speech for a couple of hours, cutting it, trying to score all my points and grind all my antitrust axes.

Finished that speech and tried to relax a bit. I decided to have just one drink and shot the breeze with Rich Thomas, my administrative assistant, and Ray Balwierczak. Then I went downstairs to eat, and there was Chuck Beeghly, chairman of the Jones & Laughlin executive committee, whom I had seen the day before in Dallas at LTV's shareholders' meeting. I made small talk with Chuck and his wife: "How's Dorothy?" "Fine." Then I went back to my own table and ate my lamb chops and mint jelly too fast because I figured I ought to take a look at the other speech. I reminded Kathy, the elevator operator, that I wanted the morning papers as soon as they came in and I also told her that I still owed her a dollar from our last trip to town. She seemed grateful that I had remembered and mentioned it. I don't think she would ever have asked for it if I hadn't brought it up.

May 1

Off to Boston this morning. Johnny Johnson, our p.r. vice president, was there waiting. After the bad time they gave me in Washington about jumping into a limousine to hide from the press, we're not using limousines for a while, especially not in Boston with all those Harvard Business School people, those Eastern Establishment types, watching. So we rode in an Oldsmobile sedan.

We stopped at John Hancock Life to talk to Bob Slater, the president, about being on the board of LTV Development Corporation, a company we are thinking about setting up with a broader representation of directors than we have had before, including a West Coast banker and John Murchison, who is from Dallas but is regarded as a national figure in the investment community. Slater thought he would be unable to serve on the board because of a conflict of interest, but he suggested another man. We'll check him out.

I rehearsed the Harvard speech at the Ritz-Carlton, and I cut it some more. Good turnout, and the audience seemed very sympathetic to our situation, and I got almost a standing ovation several times at references to the Nixon Administration and Assistant Attorney General McLaren in particular.

Next we had a meeting with the economics department of Harvard, and among the participants was Donald Turner, who had been a predecessor of McLaren and who had given us a hard time in past encounters that we won hands down. Now back at Harvard, Turner has, I discovered today, said some very favorable things about conglomerates. Then came the Boston University events, some cocktail parties and the dinner with me speaking. I shook at least a hundred hands and met lots of people, but one person stands out. A man named Schwartz—I'm not even sure what he does—came over and told me he thought my eyeglasses were too small. He said I ought to wear a size-49 frame, that I would look much better. I get all kinds of advice and comments all the time, but nobody has ever said anything about my glasses. So I made a mental note to take a look at a size 49 first chance I get.

There was a packed house for dinner, somebody said it was the biggest crowd they'd ever had in the room. The BU people were ecstatic at the sell-out. I kept wondering if what I had to say would meet the expectations of this crowd. I was seated on the dais, and as I went through the first course of dinner, I noticed a guy who looked vaguely familiar coming up on the platform toward me. Turns out he is Vincent Wolfington of an outfit in Chicago that had been interested in buying our holding in National Car Rental. He had called several times, but their bid had not been as good as some others. He had even called this afternoon, but I just didn't have time to get back to him, and anyway, we are just about committed to selling the company to Household Finance. Anyway, Vince says he has to see me, but I couldn't leave the table then, so he made me promise to set up a date for breakfast tomorrow.

The speech went over well, including my ad-lib jokes. At least, the audience laughed at the right times. I skipped the hospitality suites after the dinner, but I still didn't get back to the Ritz-Carlton until around 10:30. I stopped in to see Eli Goldston, our host for the dinner, who is head of Eastern Gas & Fuel. Finally, back in the Ritz suite, I managed to put my feet up and have a glass of the special aged akvavit I like to have as I review the day. Johnny and Rich are near collapse, but I am starting to get my second wind or something. I guess the adrenaline is still flowing, because now it's after midnight, everybody has gone to bed, and I've been sitting up reading. Vince Wolfington is going to be up at 7:00 A.M. for breakfast, so I called down to have them send it up.

May 2

Awake about 5:30 A.M. Started to pack. Ray was up too, and he started to make coffee. We carry our own coffee pot wherever we go. The breakfast arrived on time and so did Vince. He was talking about a bid for National Car of $10 a share. I told him, "In the event that the other thing we're working on does not work out, we'd want $10.50 a share." Wolfington said he could get a cashier's check for sure from Chase Manhattan and insisted that I call the bank and verify that they had the money so I would not think, as he put it, that he was bullshitting me about it.

I had called George Griffin last night and he said that we were about to close with Household Finance, that we had made a definite commitment and we would be closing this morning. So I called Gus Levy down in Washington. He assured me that his client, Household Finance, would be closing. So I am in a kind of sticky position, because they are only paying $9.50 a share. If we wanted to cut out the

Household Finance people, we could pick up another dollar a share or $3.3 million altogether. But we had made a commitment, George and Gus both assured me, to sell at $9.50, so I didn't have much of an argument with my conscience, but would have to stick with it. If, on the other hand, Household Finance backed out of the deal, I could have sold it to Vince.

As it turned out, Household Finance did settle, though Vince made a hell of an effort. He even came down to Dallas. I told him that it ought to be a good lesson to him not to screw around when you want something. We'd have been delighted to sell him the company provided that the National Car people would accept him. At the last minute, our people were waiting to see if I would renege. But I couldn't. We're stuck with it, I thought. If we pulled out now, we would certainly be breaking our word to our investment bankers who set up the deal. So that decision cost LTV $3.3 million, but we would hope that the management of our company would place more value on integrity than on making a one-shot deal.

[It is possible that there were other reasons for Ling to pass up the extra $3.3 million that could have been obtained from selling the National Car shares to Wolfington's Chevway Corporation instead of Household Finance. By that time, backing out might have been a breach of contract that could have cost LTV as much in time, legal fees, and bad publicity as it would have gained in cash. Or Gus Levy may have been more enthusiastic about a deal in which his firm stood to make a good commission—according to Ling, Household Finance was Levy's client—than he would be about one that would merely benefit LTV. (To suggest the possibility of such a conflict of interest does not mean that it existed or was acted upon.) None of this is meant to imply any questioning of Ling's sincerity in citing business ethics as the reason for his forgoing the extra money. Ling knew that his words might be published, so they may well have been self-serving. But more likely they are another example of the naïve Boy Scout pieties he brought to his business life and really believed were shared by the good guys who ran the respectable corporations.]

We flew down to Washington, where I had a lunch date with Ted Mann and Admirals Tom Walker and Tom Connally, who are among our biggest customers at the Pentagon, both great guys, the epitome of what military people ought to be. We met them at Burning Tree, talked awhile over lunch, then played golf. Dorothy came down from New York and we had dinner at the Manns' house. I fell asleep in the car going back to our apartment at the Shoreham.

May 3

Today Ted and I played golf with Judge Hamer Budge, new chairman of the SEC. I had a very good first nine for me, but I blew that back side. I shot an 84. I probably should have done a little more putting and a little more thought process, and I could have broken 80 comfortably. Judge Budge is a very consistent golfer and hit the ball real well.

Met Dorothy at 3:00 P.M. to take a tour of the city. First time I've been sightseeing anywhere in maybe eight or nine years. That evening I was the guest of *Newsweek* at the White House Correspondents' Dinner. When I got there I found that I was the only one not wearing black tie. I got out the invitation and a couple of letters: no mention of black tie, so what the hell. Jim Bishop, my *Newsweek* host, introduced me to Senator George McGovern, who sat at our table. McGovern is a terribly impressive guy. I got to thinking that there's no way you can condemn people or think of them at all from what you read about them in the press.

In about twenty minutes, Bishop covered the whole Washington scene with me, including Judge Budge, McLaren, and all the rest. The President arrived, pretty much on time. LBJ would never get any place on time.

Later that night, I learned from Dave Fleming, who was at the dinner and spoke to McLaren, that Attorney General Mitchell had turned down our request that our antitrust case be expedited under a statutory procedure that brings it before a three-judge panel. Our earlier information had been that the request would be approved. This thing is not working out well at all. But it wasn't all bad. At least McLaren, according to Fleming, turned out to be talkative and approachable at a party, which somehow isn't the picture I had had of him. But I think we have lost something. Fleming made a good suggestion: he said I ought to use my one shot with the White House. If I can do it, I'll say that we want the right to vote our J&L securities and go on the J&L board again so that at least we can operate the company while this thing is going on. Otherwise, especially if they won't expedite, we are in a terribly bad field position.

May 5

I'm back in Dallas finally, and Bill Stephens called me from Pittsburgh to tell me he was worried about our extending the Jones & Laughlin tender offer. He said he thought we might get a lot more shares in. I told him I couldn't understand his concern, because, as I had told him before, we have a number of ways of disposing of any more than the 81 percent the Justice Department has agreed to let us own. For instance, if we got a million more shares than the maximum, we would sell them for cash. That wouldn't be a bad move and would get us more than $30 million cash.

Then I mentioned what we had in mind as a response to Attorney General Mitchell's turndown of our expediting request. I told him that our lawyers were upset because we were completely voiceless in the management of J&L now and were open to shareholders' suits. I said that, from a fiduciary-responsibility standpoint, we had to participate, at least through the board of directors.

I said that since we had shown great trust in them for all this time, they had to reciprocate. What did I have in mind? he wanted to know. Simply that if Mitchell would not reconsider, we would explain to him that we would suffer great economic damage if we could not get back onto the J&L board, and that we wanted to eliminate completely the voting trust we had agreed to set up when we first bought the company.

We would agree, I said, not to consolidate the companies now or acquire any more stock in J&L. And I told Stephens that even though we were backing him 100 percent from an operational point of view, there was always a chance that some of his more cantankerous directors might take exception to what we think would be sound creative ideas for the company and could vote against us and we wouldn't have any say-so.

Bill said fine, he understood our position. He didn't give me any strong feeling of support, but I didn't detect anything negative in his voice either.

What I have done is throw him a bombshell, telling him that we may try to eliminate the voting trust which gives them control until 1971 under the terms of our original acquisition. It will be interesting to hear the reaction from Pittsburgh.

I can't understand this business about Louis Wolfson and Justice Fortas. What an incomprehensible thing for him to have done, to accept that check under those circumstances. I can't believe Abe Fortas would do that. There must be an unusual story behind it. Maybe I'll ask his former law partners, when they come to lunch tomorrow.

[If Ling asked and got answers about Supreme Court Justice Abe Fortas from members of the law firm that had originally been known as Arnold, Fortas & Porter, he did not mention the fact. But, like most people, Ling found it difficult to accept a simple explanation: that in addition to his brilliant mind and his powerful connections, Fortas liked money and, if he ever thought about it, was convinced he could handle any conflict of interest that might arise from the fact that Wolfson was serving time for securities-law violations.]

The main purpose of meeting them tomorrow is to figure out what we are going to do now that Mitchell has turned down our request to expedite. Certainly we'll ask him to reconsider. Also we will get to all the top Republicans we can reach.

I've already told my neighbor Jim Collins, who is the Congressman from this district now, that Mitchell has turned us down, and he seemed upset. Roy Edwards of Wilson was in touch with Senator Hruska from Nebraska, and Roy thought Hruska had expected Mitchell to go along with our request. I gather Hruska had got the feeling from Dirksen that Mitchell had considered ours a reasonable request. But apparently Mitchell has been persuaded by McLaren or his staff not to go along.

When Mitchell replied to me, he sent me a copy of his letter to Arnold & Porter, and also he referred to that letter as an answer to the one I wrote to the President. Which means, of course, that the President has decided to ignore the issue and let the Attorney General handle it.

If Mitchell won't reconsider, then we have to take some other kind of action. After all, it is the government's position that they are right and we are going to lose. If that's how they feel, we at least ought to have the right to build up the value of the property a little before we have to sell it. So Mitchell ought to let us get back on the J&L board and into its active management so we can get it moving again. The question is: should we level with Mitchell that we have a little bit of unrest among the natives in Pittsburgh, and that some of the directors don't want us in there at all? He might use that against us instead of for us. What we don't want is to be absentee owners with no vote.

May 6

Up at 5:30, read the papers and some material in my briefcase. I came down to the Spa bright and early and worked out. I had a meeting scheduled for 7:30 with Clyde Skeen and Jim Weldon [chairman of the board of LTV Electrosystems and founder and president of its Continental Electronics subsidiary]. We had a very unpleasant duty to perform this morning. This was the time we had to tell Jim, who is nearing retirement, that we are considering certain changes in the management of Electrosystems.

We briefed Jim on the changes that would be taking place. Jim had been a very good and loyal friend and supporter of mine for many years and a brilliant engineer, and doing this did not come easily for me. But Jim is a great gentleman and took it well, and agreed that some changes at the top had to be made. He made a couple of very good suggestions.

It went off as well as those things can go. Electrosystems has had some special difficulties recently. Top security matters are involved, and I cannot talk about very much that goes on out there. But I can say that Electrosystems was responsible for all the intricate electronic gear aboard the *Pueblo*. We knew all the people there, and had trained some of them. [The *Pueblo*, a U.S. intelligence surveillance vessel operating off North Korea, was captured by the North Koreans before it could be scuttled. The result was a minor international scandal.]

Though that kind of technology is mostly beyond me, I have been involved occasionally with some of the details of Electrosystems. A few years ago, when I went to Europe, I had some contacts with representatives of a European government's security agencies. I remember how when we were working on a classified electronics contract there I met these people in a hotel that had been a castle outside Frankfurt and then rode down the Rhine to Bonn to meet someone on the train. It seemed straight out of a Grade-B movie, but of course it is deadly serious business.

Anyway, this had been a bad year for Electrosystems, and it is part of the system to make these changes, though you don't do that lightly. We'll see what happens in the next few months. I think they'll turn the corner, although I must say their problems are enormous.

Norm Diamond and Dennis Lyons from Arnold & Porter, Bill Tinsley, Dan Burney, and I met for lunch upstairs and then began an antitrust strategy meeting that was scheduled to last the rest of the day and into the evening. Tonight, Harold Schmidt, a lawyer we have retained in Pittsburgh, will join us.

We spent a great deal of time dissecting and analyzing the approach we should take. We decided to release to the public the fact that the Justice Department has refused to cooperate with us in this landmark case by putting into operation the expediting procedure provided for by law. Johnny

Johnson and the lawyers worked the better part of two hours drafting that release tonight. We wanted to state the situation fairly, without condemning Attorney General Mitchell overly. We blasted them about as strongly as we could, and I used the word "incredible" and some other adjectives that the lawyers thought would not be in bad taste.

We learned from Harold Schmidt that the federal judges in Pittsburgh usually lunch together and that, like judges generally, they are in touch with public opinion on cases of this sort. So, from a strategy point of view, it would be important for me to maintain a good Pittsburgh image with the press and make clear the fact that we recognize that J&L is a major Pittsburgh company—I think it may actually be the largest employer within the city limits—and that our past record on acquisitions is solid as far as not firing people or moving facilities is concerned.

We also spent a fair amount of time discussing the problems of our relations with the J&L lawyers. There seems to be an internal power struggle there that is affecting our conduct of the lawsuit preparations. We discussed tactics and strategies on the case as well as on our problem in trying to run the steel company without having any representation on the board. One of the things I will do is see that we have a frequent Pittsburgh presence. But there are plenty of other things we can and will do, even though we are in an especially difficult position, not being able to participate in running this huge investment of ours.

May 7

I was supposed to go to Southampton yesterday, but the meeting with the lawyers caused cancellation of the trip, and that left me with a whole day free of appointments. So I've got a chance to work on some speeches and operational reports and reviews. Unless I get a day like this once in a while, I don't seem able to keep up with the operational work since we have got bogged down in this lawsuit. I am setting up a monthly CEO [chief executive officer] briefing that will be held after each company's report is in. I simply haven't been able to attend all the board meetings and important operating meetings of all the subsidiaries. A lot of them would be redundant anyway.

At the same time, though, I want to be damned sure that I stay abreast of what's going on in our companies. So I have instructed Clyde to give me briefings on the exceptions—that is, what is happening that is better or worse than expected and projected. Also I want a synopsis of monthly budget comparisons. I figure this will take the better part of a full day each month.

There have been problems, ranging from a deterioration in the ability of some of our people to forecast cash flow to our failure to lean on the Electrosystems people a little bit harder. But we finally made changes, or at least they will be made officially at a special Electrosystems board meeting we have called for Friday, May 9.

May 8

We are changing some of the reshuffling at Electrosystems, because one of the people involved came to see me to talk about his downward move. He had had some second thoughts. We discussed his record, which has been very good until the past eighteen months. He understood the need to make the move and he knows we consider him a valuable man. So he asked that, in the reworking of the top-management structure, he be made vice chairman of the board, which I think is a reasonable request. Anything that will help the morale of the people who have the job of turning the company around I'm all for.

The other change from our original move is that Jim Weldon will stay on as president until he turns sixty-five, which will be sometime this year, I think.

I spent a good part of today working on the papers piled on my desk and also planning the presentations we will be making to the banks.

[The rest of the entry for this day has been heavily edited

in the hope that the major implications of the deal Ling is ruminating over will be apparent. In a sense, the exchange offer he is contemplating here, though it did not actually take place, illustrates what interests Ling most in corporate management and gives him the greatest pleasure, if that's the word, in business. It is an example of a singular talent, which, however fascinating it may be in the abstract, could be irrelevant and harmful when actually pursued. Almost a year later, during the congressional investigation of conglomerates, Congressman Emanuel Celler, himself an adept in business matters, and the subcommittee's chief counsel, Kenneth Harkins, an able public servant, had no success in dislodging Ling from his insistence on the relevance of this special financial dynamics: that if a holder of your promissory note is willing, either because of lack of faith in your ability to pay or because he will not wait till maturity, to sell the note for far less than its face value, that fact can be considered an asset to you. Valid or not, it is certainly an unconventional and, to investors, a disturbing way for an executive to view the financial state of his corporation. From an esthetic point of view, however, it can be exciting, like the working of a lever or some other law of physics.]

I have been thinking about a master plan to reduce our long-term debt outstanding and decrease the interest we have to pay, and so on. I have been playing with one set of ideas for a while, and I had one of our fellows in financial planning take a look at what I have worked out, and he says it looks favorable.

Since one of our biggest long-term creditors is Troy Post, who owns roughly $80 million worth of our 5-percent of 1988 debentures, which he got when we bought Greatamerica Corporation from him, I stopped by to visit with him for a few minutes this evening. I went over the plan I had in mind to show him that I think it would be a damn good deal for him and any of the other bondholders who would want to take it, and a damn good deal for us too.

The plan is a unique one. It is based on the fact that our 5-percent debt is selling in the market for only $55. That is, you can buy a $100 bond that earns $5 a year in interest for only $55. And the point is, of course, that in 1988, when they come due and have to be paid off if they are still outstanding, we will have to pay them off at par, $100.

Now here is how the plan would work: We would offer the bondholders an exchange. Let's say you have a million dollars of these bonds. In return for your million in bonds at face value but with a market value of only $550,000, you could get $600,000 worth of new debentures that would carry a 6.5-percent interest rate, and they would be eight-year debentures, maybe with 25 percent of them amortized in each of the last four years. Now we would also have to give out some warrants to buy LTV stock, maybe 60,000 warrants for each million of debentures turned in, and the new bonds could be cashed in at face value to exercise the warrants in the future.

From our standpoint, we would be eliminating $400,000 worth of long-term debt for every million that was exchanged. Now the interest cost on the new $600,000 worth of notes would be only $39,000 a year, compared with $50,000 on the million of 5-percent. So the company would reduce its interest costs by $11,000 for every million that came in, and all that we would have to give up would be some warrants.

Now I've gone through an exercise using $200 million that we might call in. Assuming that Troy would submit his, I think we might get that amount in. And if we did, we would eliminate $80 million of long-term debt from the liabilities side—because we would be giving out only $60 worth of new debentures for every $100 worth of the old ones, at par, that we took in—which would be a nonrecurring gain, and would reduce our interest cost by $2.2 million a year, which is the same as saying that we would increase our pre-tax earnings by that amount.

It's almost like doing it with mirrors. And the attraction for the bondholders would be that they would get a chance to translate part of their bonds into equity, if they exchange their warrants for stock. Now if we give out 60,000 warrants per million of debentures exchanged, we'll be giving up 1.2 million warrants. Say that at today's market price for LTV shares of about $50, we would make the warrants exercisable at $60. We would in effect be selling those warrants at a price of $80 million, which would be our gain from the exchange of the bonds. But if the warrants were all exercised at some future date, we would be getting $60 apiece for the new shares, which would mean another $72 million we would realize from the warrants. Add that to the $80 million we, in effect, got when we made the exchange in the first place and that means that we will be selling those new LTV shares for around $126 apiece total for shares that are $50 on the market now. That's not too bad.

May 9

I put in a call to Chuck Beeghly in Pittsburgh this morning. I got a letter from him yesterday in which he said he was disturbed at the story we had released on Tuesday, which got a pretty good play in the *Wall Street Journal* and maybe in Pittsburgh too. He said in his letter that he was concerned about my remarks that LTV had been knocked out of the box as directors and members of the Jones & Laughlin voting trust. I told him that I simply had to say those things, that it was my responsibility. I explained that I always qualified my statements about this matter with the observation that we have a great deal of confidence in the management of J&L but nevertheless we had been deprived of our shareholders' voting rights by the Department of Justice.

He said that such statements might cause concern among some of his employees. I told him that I understood that he was concerned about *his* public up there in Pittsburgh but that I had publics in all fifty states, people who were LTV shareholders and who ought to be informed that we had been knocked out of the box.

We're also having some new problems with Bill Woerner at Computer Tech. As I understand it from Legal, he has executed some sort of letter of intent down in Florida that they tell me might be in violation of the Robinson-Patman Act [requiring that all customers get comparable treatment]. Also he apparently has gone so far with my idea for redeployment of Computer Tech into a group of companies that a disclosure problem seems to have developed; that is, apparently some new moves he has made since we filed our registration statement with the SEC might require amendments. He is running wild again and not acting like a proper chief executive.

I talked to Paul Thayer about this, but I couldn't do much with him on the phone, because it was a ship-to-shore call. He is on a boat called the *Forty-five* out of Oakland, and anyone on the frequency could audit the call. So instead of going into detail so he could handle it, I just told him that I would take care of his Computer Tech problem. But I had to put him into the communications loop, because it is really his responsibility.

I just got word that a pre-trial conference has been arranged in Pittsburgh for next Tuesday, May 13. I am not superstitious at all, but it occurred to me that I didn't want the conference jinxed by that date. I am not sure if the government will respond that quickly anyway, but I hope they can react as fast as we do. If they don't, we'll try to go back in again under the expediting statute and demand a three-judge tribunal even though Mitchell has already turned us down once.

June 10

This morning I signed a note to First National for $5.2 million that I'm using to buy out Jim Bond and A. D. Martin, who have been partners with me for two or three years in Alpha-Omega, my personal holding company. [Both were then LTV directors and had been longtime backers of Ling. Bond was a real-estate man and a regional official of the federal government, and Martin was an oil man.] That gives me a bigger stake than I ever had before in LTV. And I have been thinking a lot about our lawsuit. I sit here trying to analyze our ability to project the next twenty-four months and second-guess the outcome of the lawsuit and what we could do with the dollars if we sell the steel-company stock. Then maybe second-guess what our own egos would suffer in case we threw in the sponge, if that's the proper word, by selling the company. That would make the suit academic. Is it really important for me to fight McLaren, or is it more important to be a good businessman for myself and our stockholders? Those are two different issues. I'll come out all right anyway. But what about using a lot of other people, especially the stockholders, just to win a point? I think I can beat McLaren if I stick with it. But that could be just to satisfy my ego. Is it—trying to look at it from a historic point of view like in Vietnam—a matter of getting so engaged in it to win my point that I might hurt many other people, when there is really no other point in staying in the fight?

This afternoon, I played golf at Brook Hollow in a fivesome with some of the regulars. They play a complicated gambling game called Hammer; it's a local thing, where you keep hammering, that is, doubling up, starting at a dollar and then it keeps building. Once a Hammer game here got up to $3,200 a shot, and the guy who was on the green, and who probably could have afforded it as well as anybody, just picked up his ball and said that it wasn't worth it in friendship. We didn't get very high up today. I didn't putt too well, but we were lucky, and I managed to win a few dollars.

June 27–28

I was invited to a two-day golf outing at Arnold Palmer's home course, Laurel Valley, in Latrobe, Pennsylvania, as the guest of the Mellon Bank. They had invited maybe forty or fifty top executives of American industry to play in a golf tournament. Among the guests that come to mind at the moment were Gardiner Symonds, chairman of Tenneco; Bob Anderson of North American Rockwell; Charles Beeghly of our Jones & Laughlin; Fletcher Byram, president of Koppers Company; Frank Forster, chairman and president of Sperry Rand; Ed Gott, chairman of U.S. Steel; George Jenkins, vice chairman of Metropolitan Life; and George Love, chairman of Consolidation Coal, who helped put Chrysler on its feet again recently.

The idea was to have a two-day golf tournament, with full handicaps applied, to give net prizes as well as gross prizes. I came out here with a 14 handicap, because I have not been playing much lately. But I did not want to embarrass myself, so I worked real hard on my game in whatever free time I could find.

I shot two 84s on Arnold Palmer's home course. I must say it was a man-eating course. Fortunately I won both days, so I ended up with a lot of golf balls with the Mellon insignia on them. But that was all right, because they were our Wilson balls.

Friday night, after dinner, Johnny Mayer, the president of the Mellon Bank, introduced Charlie Walker, the Undersecretary of the Treasury. He gave us a briefing on some of the current policies of the Nixon Administration. Charlie is from Texas; I remember playing golf with him back in the early 1950s when I first took up the game. He's a Ph.D. and a damned interesting and attractive guy. He said that Nixon's policy was very deliberate and that he would go forward slowly but surely, and then he looked over at me and said, "Except in Ling's area," meaning the antitrust area.

In general, this description of the Nixon policy did not sit well with most people present, and they said so. They seemed to think most of Nixon's moves were anti-business. After a number of drinks, they were quite loose with their comments. The general impression I got was that they were all disappointed as hell in Nixon.

On one of the days I played with George Love, and on the tenth hole I hit one of my best shots in several months. He told me that, even as much as he played with Palmer, I had hit the longest tee shot he had ever seen on that particular hole. It was thirty steps from the edge of the green, and the card said it was around 360 yards. Something just happened, and I caught it dead-letter flush and it was an amazing shot. I damned near bogied the hole anyway on a simple thirty-yard wedge shot; I knocked it clear over the edge of the green, but I got it back down.

My friend Frank Denton, who is a J&L director and chairman of the executive committee of the Mellon Bank, had a locker right near mine. He was cordial enough, but he didn't exactly go overboard being nice.

George Love said that I ought to become a member of the club. I asked him how much it would cost to join, and he said $6,000. I might very well do it. It's a great golf course, though I need another country club like a hole in the head. But obviously I saw a lot of American industry there that I don't get involved with too often. This seems to be their place, so I might very well join the club.

July 8–12

Off to Alexandria, Minnesota, with Dorothy and the Wilson Schoellkopfs. For the last several years, we have been houseguests here of either the Jim Chambers or the Joe Cowdreys. Jim is my friend, a director of LTV and publisher of the Dallas *Times Herald,* and Joe is the senior man in Dallas with Merrill Lynch. They usually take off for the better part of the summer in this little area. It's a beautiful part of the country, and it's an old watering hole for the old Dallas families that probably dates from the early part of the century, from the days before air-conditioning.

It has a lot of homes that the moneyed people built then, and there are still plenty of them around. The fishing is great. And they have a single golf course, which cannot be compared to our Texas courses, because of seasonal problems.

The entire environment seems to be Scandinavian, and there are a lot of Thors and Jorgensons and Dahlbergs. The atmosphere is conducive to relaxing. Probably the principal thing you do here, if you aren't playing golf or fishing, is stand on a street corner and watch the people go by. It's a fine, small, good-looking Minnesota town. Everybody seems to know everybody else, and you're likely to be playing golf with the haberdashery salesman or the math teacher from the high school.

My idea in accepting the invitation this year was, aside from having a few days off, to spend some time in preparation and background study for the antitrust suit. I am slated to make a deposition on the case the end of next week in Washington. So I packed up all the material that the Justice Department had indicated they would cover in their interrogation.

Aside from the antitrust case, I also wanted to review some of our LTV financial statements. I am still toying with some ideas for a game plan that reflects the total environment in which we and all our underlying companies operate financially. I want to consider all the factors in that environment, to be sure that I have not overlooked any possibilities or opportunities. The number of options is enormous, and I want to be sure that I recommend the best of all combinations to our management group and then, ultimately, to the board of directors.

I'd get up bright and early in the morning and do some reading. When I finished, I would go out on the highway, where I had stepped off a 440-yard track and walk, jog, or run a mile and a half.

I still had a lot of time to kill, because my host and the rest of the Dallas contingent wouldn't ordinarily show up at the golf course until 10:30 or 11:00. So I decided that I would get in some extra flying time. The days were beautiful, no weather at all. It was absolutely perfect for touch-and-go's and some low, slow flying around the area. I invited a boy named George, very articulate and sales-oriented, who kept the clubs and the range balls in the back of the pro shop and supervised the polishing of the shoes. He's about twelve or thirteen. I asked him to take the trip with us, which he did.

Next day I wound up with three or four more of the caddies. By the time we had landed the airplane, their families were all out against the fence that separates the parking area of this little airport, which is basically just an FAA control center and two very nice landing strips. We had a lot of company and a lot of attention, and I enjoyed it. I got some good experience in those few days, and I told Dave Keys, our pilot for the trip, to record the number of hours so I could turn them in, because that is personal expenses and it is definitely not negligible. I think that just for gas and oil and normal depreciation on certain parts of the aircraft, it runs several hundred dollars an hour. Under the practice of being absolutely honest about the use of company facilities and conveniences, I wanted to be sure I was not overlooking any expense involved.

Anyway, we'd fly for forty-five minutes to an hour each morning. I'd get back to the club and hit a few shots on the practice range, then wind up on the putting green, chipping and putting. Incidentally, the weather has been hot and humid for Minnesota, and I'd be drenched and dead tired by the time the golfers showed up to play. This showed up in my game.

Though I didn't get much reading done, Minnesota was good for me. It cleared my mind up and gave me a different perspective, and I am prepared to do a good job in Washington next week.

July 13

Wheels up this afternoon from Alexandria, Minnesota, to Dallas. Tomorrow is my only day in the office before I go to Washington for the deposition to the Justice lawyers.

July 14

George Griffin is due back from vacation today, according to a note on my calendar. First order of business was a brief meeting in Clyde Skeen's office with Bernie Brown, our treasurer, and Roscoe on some financing matters. I got into my own office to look at some of the mail that had piled up and then went for a haircut.

We had a meeting of the Wilson & Company executive committee this morning with Clyde, Roscoe, Bert Eitel, and Roy Edwards, who is president of Wilson. Roy made a persuasive argument for moving the company's headquarters from Chicago to Oklahoma City. He says that it is a better place for his executives to live, that Chicago has become a tough place to live in and commute to. Of course Roy comes from Oklahoma, so it might be a bit more attractive for him than for some of his people. But I can understand his feeling. He is a very capable executive and almost fanatical in his support of Project Redeployment.

July 15

Arrived in Washington this morning and went straight to the offices of Arnold & Porter. Their main office is in an old mansion at 19th and N streets which used to be the home of a Supreme Court Justice. But they also have offices in some old houses across the street that are connected by little passageways and odd stairways.

First off, I got a briefing on what had been going on during the previous few weeks of depositions. The Justice Department lawyers had interrogated about a dozen of our people. I had been selected as the last one to give a deposition. They had also seen a number of Jones & Laughlin people during the last two weeks, so the government was about a month into it, and there was already a lot of material, a lot of information they had that was still Greek to me.

I came into a conference room where there must have been a dozen thick black volumes of documents and background material. Our lawyers briefed me in general about the proper attitude of a witness—he should be cooperative and responsive, but not volunteer any information that is not asked for, and not get rattled. In other words, I am to give specific answers to specific questions.

Jerry Stern, one of the firm's bright, young, aggressive partners, began as a sort of devil's advocate. He took all the material that the government had subpoenaed and played the part of a Justice Department lawyer and queried me on everything that they had. He asked me hundreds of questions about memos, letters, reports, about mergers and acquisitions, about my attitudes, my intentions, interpretations, meanings. It was a helluva comprehensive job.

When Jerry got tired, Norm Diamond took over. He made it quite clear that they would not let me have the advantage of knowing any of the testimony of any of the other witnesses. He felt it would be just as well for me not to know what had been said by others. The strategy was that I'd go in cold and let the facts speak for themselves. I said that I wasn't sure that was the right thing to do. I thought it would be better if I had some of the specifics. But he feels that what we ought to do is take the questions as they come and let my answers arise from my own recollections. That way I would be natural and honest.

Norm made quite an impression on me. He's a tough fighter, a real professional. I have no idea what a trial lawyer ought to be or what his capabilities are, but I could see that he would acquit himself well in a courtroom.

The review took the rest of the day. Then we went back to the Shoreham apartment and had a few drinks. There was Dan Burney, Dave Fleming, who has taken over our Washington intelligence operation from Ted Mann, and Rich Thomas. We talked about political contributions of some of our executives and how we didn't want them to give money now to anyone they hadn't given to before, because that could make it look like we were trying to buy somebody. We went out to dinner to a nice little place around the corner called Arbaugh's where we had martinis and spareribs.

July 16

Back to Arnold & Porter for more interrogation. Later we drove over to the deposition hearing room in a building the government now uses which used to be the office of the *Evening Star.*

Norm and our other lawyers sat at one long table and Paul Owens, the Justice Department's chief lawyer on the case, sat at another table with his associates. There were maybe a couple of dozen other chairs in the room behind those tables, for whoever wanted to come and watch the proceedings. I am told that the spectators were mostly Arnold & Porter's young lawyers who wanted to take a look (Norm reassured me that we wouldn't be charged for their time), maybe some other government people, and possibly some reporters. But depositions are not very interesting spectator sports, I wouldn't imagine, so I really don't know what anyone without an interest would be doing there.

I sat at a chair in the front, facing everybody. It was like a little courtroom, but without a judge. And back in the corner to my left was a stenotype operator. Every half-hour or so they would change these stenotypers so they could have their material transcribed. That way we could see what was going on pretty quickly.

We started a little after 2:00 P.M. I guess I was a bit tense at first and somewhat impatient. Maybe I was trying too hard to get to the point, but I couldn't really see any point to a lot of the questioning. Of course, being a novice in these matters, what I probably didn't appreciate was that if I was intense for the full three days, then this thing could degenerate into verbal fencing matches. The first hour and a half was spent in sort of getting organized, and I guess I had a normal amount of apprehension about doing a creditable job. The questions seemed very repetitious, over and over again, with just a little change in phrasing, and I tried very hard to remain alert.

At the first coffee break, Norm Diamond mentioned to me that I was a bit aggressive and a bit unfriendly and here's what I ought to do: be a good witness and be friendly to Paul Owens. Norm pointed out that Owens was a very nice guy just trying to do his job and that he had been working for the better part of a month taking depositions and there was no point in offending him.

I still find it difficult to accept the proposition that I should be friendly to him. As far as I am concerned, he's the guy across the line, and my objective is certainly not to be friends with him. Incidentally, during the coffee break, Owens and Diamond went into the men's room at the same time, and one of our people, who happened to be there, said they just stood there talking about fishing and things like that, like a couple of old friends who happened to meet on the street.

After the break, I began to detect what I guess you could call real professional characteristics to Owens' questions. I felt he was really trying to get somewhere, that he was working to frame questions, groping sometimes to put it right. I had a better feeling about him then.

One of his tactics seems to be to start very intensely and carefully, kind of leaning across the table with his hands folded, and begin a question. Then, as the question began to develop, he would lean back casually in his chair and his eyes —he wears horn-rimmed glasses like I do—would go ceilingward and he would pause, sometimes for a long period. Then he would pick up on the question, start it in another direction, or start a whole new question. I didn't time it, but there would be times when a full two minutes seemed to elapse from the moment he started a question to the moment he finished asking it.

So, to keep from being bored stiff, I would try to follow him very closely with my eyes. But that was just killing me and it didn't seem to help, so in the late afternoon I found that during his long, staring-at-the-ceiling pauses, if I averted my gaze, maybe looking over my shoulder at what the court reporter was doing, he'd return right away to the question.

We ended the session about 4:30 and drove back to the main building at Arnold & Porter, and had a drink. It was a very friendly atmosphere, with all the lawyers who were on the case, plus some who had dropped in to watch, plus others, including Paul Porter himself. In fact, he was sort of the host. The impromptu cocktail party took place in his huge corner office with a lot of old carved woodwork. I guess it must have been a study when the building was still a private house. Paul is a member of the Braniff board of directors, so we chatted about a lot of things including the airline.

At one point, Paul showed me a copy of a letter that Thurman Arnold had written. I believe it was in reply to one written to Arnold by a professor who complained that the law firm had assisted the tobacco industry in some proceeding before some government agency on the harmful effects of cigarette smoking. Arnold, the famous trustbuster of the New Deal days and a very distinguished man [Arnold was still alive at this time, though not active in the firm], explained patiently that everybody has a right to a legal defense, irrespective of guilt or innocence. Then Arnold went on to tell a story in the letter about Paul. It seems that Paul had been accosted at the Burning Tree Club by an angry member. The man said to Paul, who is a big, imposing, dignified man, "I hear that your firm is now defending Communists and homosexuals." Paul looked at him without batting an eye and said, "Yes, indeed! What's your problem?"

You can see that these people have a helluva sense of humor, which I guess you have to have in this town and in this field.

July 17

The morning started with an early meeting at Arnold & Porter, and then over to the hearing room for the depositions. We had a chance to review the transcript of yesterday's session briefly before we had to go back to meet the government.

When I tried this time to avert my gaze the minute I saw Owens' head start to rear backward and turn toward the ceiling, it didn't work quite as well. Frequently it seemed to disorganize him to the point where he would start all over again.

At one point this morning, Owens was questioning me about some preliminary talks we had with Youngstown Sheet & Tube before we went to Jones & Laughlin. I had mentioned how the whole thing began back in early 1968 with a casual remark by a man next to me in a buffet line at Brook Hollow Country Club. Owens asked something about how long it took from the time we first started talking to them until, as I recalled his words were, "you fell out of bed, as I understand from Mr. Griffin the expression is." Well, Norm Diamond objected to the question on the grounds that George Griffin had used that expression about a totally different situation. Then Norm insisted that they go off the record for a discussion of the issue of whether I knew what George had said in his deposition. Norm pointed out that I did not have access to what George had said, and that the expression "fell out of bed" did not necessarily describe the situation we were now discussing, and it went on and on, and would Owens please rephrase the question without that particular vernacular expression in it. And so he asked the question this time very nicely and smoothly about how much time elapsed until the discussions between Youngstown and LTV ended. And I said, "It fell out of bed after about three weeks." And it brought down the house. You can use all the laughs you can get at times like that.

July 18

In reviewing the transcript, it seemed to me that Owens' alertness would fall off dramatically as the days wore on. I would grade him 100 percent in his work in the morning, but by late afternoon he was barely making a passing grade of maybe 66⅔ percent with his questions. Norm pointed out that Owens is a bachelor and that he is about to be called up for a tour of military-reserve duty in a few weeks and that he was working twelve to sixteen hours a day on the case, so I guess he was just wearing out quicker these days.

In any event, it has been quite an experience for me. The logistics is fantastic—the army of people doing research, digging up the materials, handling the transcripts, and on and on. I might add that our monthly legal bills are running as if we do have an army that we are supporting at Arnold & Porter.

It was an experience that would lead me to believe we're wasting quite a few million dollars of taxpayers' money if this is typical of all antitrust suits. But it's been a good experience for me, valuable training in discipline and composure.

[The depositions in the J&L antitrust case were now completed, and the "discovery" phase of the government's action was just about finished. While the Justice Department lawyers were at work preparing their case, LTV's lawyers would be developing their defense and, at the same time, trying to anticipate what the climate in Pittsburgh and especially in the courthouse would be. It was still generally assumed that the trial would begin in the fall. While Ling believed that the corporation was not guilty of any violation of the antitrust statutes in its acquisition of the steel company, he was also aware that the government generally won such cases if they were not settled out of court. Still he was hopeful that by speeding the process rather than delaying it, LTV would soon be free to begin the enormous job of restructuring Jones & Laughlin in some way that would permit it to be divided eventually into companies attractive to outside shareholders. That had worked with LTV's original corporate divisions and with the three companies he made out of the divisions of Wilson & Company. At the same time, he knew that his parent corporation was under mounting pressure to repay loans and meet interest payments. That was why he was beginning to consider the possibility of selling off more of LTV's assets. Typically, Ling was impatient to get moving again, though he did not view any of his corporations' problems as crises. And, if it came to that, he could probably unload all or part of LTV's holdings in J&L, which would relieve financial problems as well as get the government off his back.]

July 19

I was supposed to fly to Lubbock this morning for a meeting of the Board of Regents of Texas Tech, of which I am proud to say I am a member. But I had to cancel my appearance because we had too much work to do. Monday morning I'm going to New York for a series of meetings with our commercial bankers there. Actually Clyde and I are covering the country to reach all twenty-five, I guess it is, who are participating in the $110-million loan. The loan is due the end of this month, and we want it extended. So I was in the office most of the day today.

August 18

A couple of weeks ago, I read that Howard Hughes seemed to have abandoned his effort to take over Air West. As I recall, the little airline had had some very substantial losses, and its net worth had fallen to a point where he had a right to withdraw his offer. It occurred to me then, and several times afterward, that Hughes might well have an interest in buying Braniff instead. I thought that if we ever came to the point of selling our Braniff holdings, Hughes would be a leading candidate to buy the shares.

So when my secretary told me on the intercom that there was a gentleman on the phone calling from Las Vegas, I immediately thought it might be a Hughes representative. It turned out to be Parry Thomas of the Bank of Las Vegas, who I knew was at times an intermediary for Hughes. We had met before, and we exchanged a few pleasantries, and he finally said, "Of course you know what my call is about." I told him that I did, though neither of us had mentioned the airline or his principal. "My party has a very sincere interest in the possibility of buying Braniff," he said.

I wanted to be sure who his party was, so I said, "Let's be sure we understand each other. Your party is Howard Hughes."

"That's right," he said.

I told him that we could go on from there. "We'd be delighted to chat with you, but we have no real desire to sell the company. We have a cost on our books of $23-plus a share, and if that's the area you are thinking about, we'd be glad to talk about it."

He said that he wanted to keep the thing confidential, and I agreed completely. We didn't want anyone at Braniff to think we were shopping around to sell the airline, which we certainly are not. So I said I would keep the thing from everyone here except a couple of my key associates. He asked about my traveling schedule, and I had some things set up here I couldn't get out of easily. He said that he and the man he wanted to bring with him could probably come to Dallas. "Fine," I said. "Give me a call when you're ready."

August 19

Up at 5:25, so I read awhile. I have an advance paper from the Hudson Institute, Herman Kahn's think tank, on which I'm privileged to serve as a public trustee. Its title is *Greece, the New Vietnam*. I've only skimmed the paper, but the author says Nixon should condemn the junta, delay the appointment of a new ambassador to Athens, and join with our NATO allies to terminate military aid. He thinks the present Greek situation contains the seeds of another Vietnam. It was provocative reading.

I got downtown to the Tower about 6:45 and went through the exercise routine at the Spa. Then I came up to the office, had breakfast, and went over some material that's involved in an SEC registration statement covering one of our securities offerings. I also spent a little time looking over some material of the Rolamite Corporation. I've agreed to go on their board. They're having an offering to raise several million dollars and, according to the hoopla, it could conceivably be one of the most important new technological processes. It is a mechanical system, two rollers inside parallel guide surfaces, a kind of free-rolling cluster with an entwined flexible metallic strip. It can be miniaturized, requires little lubrication, and seems to have a lot of consumer and industrial applications including that of a swing, a fuse, a switch, or a latch. A single Rolamite system can be substituted for many parts. I remember years ago in Ling Electronics, when we needed a certain strain gauge, there was only one, and it cost maybe $200. Recently I saw a demonstration where $3 worth of Rolamite parts will replace one of those gauges. It doesn't seem to be just a stock promotion. They've got some distinguished people on the board, including M. J. Rathbone, who used to be chairman of Standard Oil of New Jersey.

I had an early-morning appointment with Dr. Levy, my dentist, for a checkup. Then *Business Week* magazine interviewed me. I had a meeting with Al Brill about whether we should lease another Falcon jet. And then I got a call from Parry Thomas in Las Vegas. He said they were interested in going ahead with our talks within the guidelines I had set, meaning the general area of my price. But he said he didn't want to come to our offices on the thirty-first floor of the Tower, because that would be a giveaway. Hughes, of course, would not be there, but one of his top men would come with

Thomas. I asked him where he wanted to meet, and he suggested Bill Tinsley's office because Bill has worked with him. He's our LTV outside counsel too. I said fine. He told me they were coming in by private jet and wanted to make it tomorrow, Wednesday.

Now I have not played golf once in the last nine or ten Wednesdays, and I was hoping to sneak out to the course tomorrow and recharge my batteries, so I had been keeping the afternoon free. But this was something else. I said, "The afternoon is fine. Call me when you get to Bill's office. I'm just a couple of minutes away."

Sure enough, ten minutes later I got a call from Joe Cowdrey, who was working up a golf game with Jim Chambers and a couple of other fellows. I told him, "Sorry, Joe, but I've got to work tomorrow afternoon on behalf of the shareholders, of whom I am the largest."

August 20

Parry Thomas called me a little after 2:00 this afternoon to tell me they were ready for the meeting. I came down to the conference room of Bill Tinsley's law offices, which are on the tenth floor of our Tower. I was introduced to Robert A. Maheu, the representative of Howard Hughes, and a man named Morgan, a senior man in a Washington law firm that represents Howard Hughes's interests. I thought, as I looked at Maheu, that here's a man who is right next to one of the most fabulous figures and one of the greatest businessmen of our century, yet hardly anybody knows him by sight. Even looking at him struck me as like looking at a shadow. In fact, that's the name I have given Maheu in our internal communications, for security reasons.

[These talks, of course, took place more than a year before Hughes made his mysterious retreat from his Las Vegas penthouse that set off the great struggles over who was empowered to speak and act for that strange man. Maheu, the former FBI agent, was then accepted as the Hughes satrap in Las Vegas, and it was he who negotiated the deals for all the casinos and real estate around the city. The warring among the factions, the stories of Hughes's illnesses, the strange band of Mormon male nurses, the phony autobiography were all to come. So Ling had no reason to doubt that when he was dealing with Bob Maheu, he was dealing with Hughes's agent.]

A little bit of a ritual developed after the introductions. Maheu stepped out of the room while Parry Thomas and Morgan advised me of the purpose of the meeting. They thought, for reasons of their own, that Maheu shouldn't be present, or maybe he did. They said they wanted to be sure that this would be an informal meeting and that we were to discuss the possibility of LTV wanting to sell one of its companies and maybe more than one.

That's not exactly true, of course, but if that's the way they wanted to start the meeting, that was perfectly all right with me. Before he was ready to call Maheu back in, Thomas asked if it was possible that LTV might have an interest in acquiring any of the Hughes properties, such as the Hughes Tool Company. I said it was possible. And such as the Hughes Aircraft Company. I said yes. And such as the aircraft division of the tool company. I said I certainly had an interest, although our appetite is not for acquisitions at the moment simply because we're lacking in wherewithal. But you can't tell till you take a look at them.

At that stage we called Maheu back in. I repeated what I had said. We were certainly flexible. I had no appetite to sell any of the LTV companies, but, under certain circumstances, we might very well. I explained to him that our cost for Braniff was roughly $230 million for the nearly 10 million shares we own, and certainly in today's market it is selling for substantially less than that. On the other hand, the earning capacity of the airline—at least $30 million—would make it worth more in the future. I also told them that Harding Lawrence, Braniff's president, was talking with two or three of the other major airlines concerning a merger. There has been a lot of talk lately that the future of the airline industry may depend on mergers to pay for the big 747 and SST purchases that will be due in the next three to ten years. I said that we had instructed Harding to talk in terms of LTV receiving more than $20 worth of some combination of cash and marketable securities for each Braniff share in any merger. I wanted Maheu to understand that we were not thinking of anything less than that.

Maheu, Morgan, and I chatted for a few minutes about the business, and then Maheu asked me if I had any specific ideas of how we might arrange a deal. I said, "Actually, if I had a piece of paper, I could diagram something that might perhaps be more eloquent than ten minutes of my conversation."

Everybody looked a little surprised for a second, then Morgan said, "I know what you mean. Some of the best deals I've ever seen have been made that way." He reached into his pocket for his airline reservation folder. He took his plane ticket and some other papers out of it. Then he tore it so it came out as a flat sheet about ten by fifteen inches.

Very quickly, I sketched the plan that had already been taking shape in my head. The first step, I said, would be for the Hughes interests to make a tender for LTV shares. Everybody looked shocked, and I could understand why. After all, they had come to talk about buying Braniff, and I was telling them that what they should do was buy into LTV. I explained what I had in mind: They would make a tender at around $50 a share for 2 million of our parent-company shares, and at the same time we would announce that Hughes or his associated enterprises were receiving an option to buy our interest in Braniff for approximately $230 million. We would take the 2 million shares of LTV stock plus another $130 million or so in cash or equivalent at the time that Hughes got Civil Aeronautics Board approval of the Braniff acquisition, which I figured would probably take anywhere from six months to a year. So the plan that I would now classify as "Project Home Run" is in full steam. Whether or not we'll actually execute the program, I don't know, of course. But, oversimplified, it would work like this: The two million shares would represent in excess of 50 percent of our capitalization. By having them tender for half the shares and then turn them back to the corporation as part of the purchase price for Braniff, we would be retiring about half of

LTV stock. You could say that we would be making a reverse acquisition. Let's call that the first base of our home run. When the change of ownership of Braniff was finally approved and we received the $100–$130-million final payment, that would be used to repay our LTV bank loans. That's the second base.

Next, by reducing the number of outstanding LTV shares by half, we would be increasing our earnings per share—nearly doubling them, except that we wouldn't have our share of the Braniff earnings in the pot. That's the third base, and the fourth, the home run, comes when, because we have reduced our shares outstanding and thus raised our earnings, the price of our shares in the market goes up, and assuming we sell at a decent price-earnings multiple, the price may go up to $130 or more, and then we can, in the long run, retire our long-term debt, because once our stock price gets up that high, holders of the warrants will exercise them. The exercise price is now around $103 a share, so once our stock price goes up past that, we will start getting the $103 from warrant holders who convert to stock.

As I told the Shadow, Maheu, maybe Braniff is not worth $230 million now. I explained to him that Harding Lawrence might not want to go along with the deal because he might feel that he should merge with one of the other major airlines he's talking to. But Braniff's long-term earnings capacity, $30 million to $50 million, would certainly make it a steal at our asking price. I also mentioned the fact that we too had been interested in acquiring American Broadcasting at about the same time that Hughes was dealing for it. We all agreed that we're better off for not having got involved.

We got back onto the subject of Braniff when Maheu asked why we were considering selling our holdings, in view of its earnings potential. I told him that we were drastically undervalued in the stock market as a result of the federal antitrust suit and that that had created unexpected financial problems for us.

Maheu said he thought the plan I had proposed was a magnificent, simple plan—those were his words—and that it could be implemented with no major trouble if they decided to go through with it. In fact, he turned to Morgan and said that there didn't seem to be any particular need for legal expertise at that point.

He then asked if we had any interest in buying the tool company, which pretty much dominates the oil-drill-bit business of the world—80 percent of it, I think they have. Or the helicopter company, which is the aircraft division of the Hughes Tool Company. Or the Hughes Aircraft Company, which is in a lot of the same kinds of business as our LTV Electrosystems, what they call the "black box" area, electronic reconnaissance. I knew that they had had some problems with the helicopter business. We thought that at the time they went into it Hughes had taken a $100-million licking building that little quick-reaction helicopter being used in Vietnam. Maheu indicated that the loss was well over $100 million and that Hughes himself had said to keep the production line going. I think his expression was "Get the helicopter to the boys," whatever the hell that means. And we're partners with them on some government electronics programs, so we know about them that way too.

Maheu indicated that if we worked out a deal to buy some of their properties and if the total payment for them exceeded what they were giving us for Braniff, they would work out an arrangement for us to make the deal without cash. That was of interest to me.

Then Parry Thomas suggested that the three of them go off to assemble some information on the companies for me. It was around 4:00 P.M. by then.

I did notice that when I began to ask about sales and earnings of the Hughes companies—which are privately owned and therefore don't issue any financial reports to the public —I drew blanks. I am not sure if they didn't know the answers or if they were under instruction not to give me any information without first checking back with that Man in Las Vegas. They asked me for my private phone numbers and said that, due to the nature of the situation, I could expect all sorts of odd calls. Of course I have heard of the eccentricities of the principal, because it's no secret that Howard Hughes has a habit of calling people at odd hours. So I expect to hear from Maheu or Morgan at any time. They asked me to swear my staff to secrecy and I told them that there would be no staff involved, that I'd be the staff, plus Roscoe Haynie and Clyde Skeen and Bill Tinsley. That was all we would need to work this deal, as far as I could see.

I told them that this was a deal I'd like to do and that I would be available on a quick-reaction basis: we'd either go or no-go. I said I would have no interest in doing it at the turn of the year unless the entire environment was the same then as it is now. The environment is good now to go for what I'm calling Project Home Run.

We've got a lot of things working now: redeployment of Wilson & Company meat packing into five separate public companies, redeployment of LTV Aerospace, and now this Project Home Run in the background. The end game of all the moves we're making would be to reduce LTV's debts substantially, reduce its capitalization substantially, and increase the earnings on a per-share basis. Then, along with all that, there's Project Cutdown, which is a huge reduction of corporate staff and personnel and development of more efficient techniques all through our subsidiary companies. Incidentally, the quick read-back on the results of that program is that we will have total possible savings of some $10 million to $12 million across the full spectrum of the LTV companies. It could go as high as $15 million.

August 21

I met with Clyde Skeen and George Griffin after breakfast about the general status of our financial plans, then went to the board room for a meeting of the parent-company executive committee. Then back to my office for the executive committee of Aerospace. At 10:00 A.M. I was back in Bill Tinsley's conference room. Maheu, Morgan, and Thomas were there, as well as Bill Tinsley this time, and an associate of Parry Thomas' named Sullivan. The meeting was concerned with many alternatives as to how we might possibly arrange for the purchase of Braniff by the Hughes interests. We considered all sorts of combinations of tne Hughes companies. It has become quite clear that they have an interest in selling us not only the drill-bit company and its aircraft division that makes helicopters, but also the aircraft company located in California that is not in aircraft but in electronics.

It appears that Mr. Hughes feels we would be a proper company and apparently I, as an individual, a proper person to take over his group of companies. Incidentally, they've offered to sell the companies for no cash, low-yield convertible preferred stock, and on very favorable terms. So I'm flattered.

Mr. Hughes also sent word, according to Maheu, for me not to be concerned about the controlling interest in case we swap stock and they wind up with a major position in our company. He would apparently consider a voting trust or whatever else would be required to keep control in our hands even if they held enough shares of LTV to control it during the transition period that I had outlined.

We also discussed the possible CAB approval problems that might result from their taking over Braniff, because they seem to have in mind to go ahead with the Air West deal, despite what I had read, even though Air West is bankrupt. Hughes seems to have the idea of combining Braniff and Air West. I guess, after his years with TWA, he still has a strong appetite for controlling an airline.

We left with no specific deal set, but merely a concept. One of the complications that occurred to me later was that there might be a problem with the antitrust people. They might not look favorably upon LTV acquiring a military-electronics company doing a half-billion dollars a year or an oil-drill-bit company that I understand accounts for 80 percent of that business in the country. That's another problem I'll face when the time comes.

I came back to my office and broke out my file on Hughes. An article in *Fortune* last year gave me a feel of what the net worth of all their companies might be. It seems the Hughes Aircraft and Hughes Tool companies together are worth $600 million or $700 million. My Dunn & Bradstreet reports verified those estimates. They've had substantial growth in recent years, from somewhere around $260 million net worth several years ago.

It's quite an exciting concept, and we could very well increase our earnings substantially as a result of these acquisitions, and we might back into a major cash position. As they pointed out, they're cash heavy and asset heavy in some of their underlying companies. Part of the trade would conceivably be that they would take over our bank debt right now and save us the interest we're paying on it. That would free us to acquire more of our own LTV stock out of the market.

Since yesterday, I have already figured out maybe twelve or fifteen possible opportunities and options that we now have in the Hughes situation. But I don't think I've yet figured out anywhere near all of them.

I've alerted Ray Balwierczak to keep Falcon 570L on the ready, because we might have to scramble on an hour's notice when we get the big call from Las Vegas.

I stayed in the office the rest of the afternoon getting caught up, getting almost caught up, on a pile of detail work. But I was still keyed up from waking at 3:00 A.M. plus all that happened. And since there was no further action around the office, nothing in my appointment book, I went out to Brook Hollow around 5:00 P.M. and hit a few practice shots.

[Nothing ever came of the Hughes overtures toward Braniff or of the dozens of permutations of deals that had gone through Ling's mind in those days. Shortly afterward, Braniff began losing heavily, and nobody was about to pay the price LTV needed to get for the airline in order to avoid an enormous loss. Hughes's Las Vegas enterprises were apparently not doing very well either, as it turned out. But that was about the last that Ling ever heard from the mystery men in Nevada.]

August 22

One of the first things I did today was call Gus Levy in New York to discuss the possibility that Prudential Insurance

Company might buy Computer Technology from us. Their people are coming in this morning to discuss the deal. He and I figured that even if we could only get $65 million or $70 million for it, that would cut our bank interest by about $6.5 million, since we'd use the purchase money to pay off bank debt. That would mean our pre-tax earnings would be that much higher. One of the strategies we have to think about now would be what we do if we can't get together on a deal with Prudential. I think we have two basic courses: either fire Woerner or try to sell the company to University Computing, Control Data, or Ross Perot's Electronic Data Systems. I lean toward University Computing because they are located here in Dallas and probably could handle the servicing of our computing business a little better for that reason. I don't think University has a helluva lot of cash around, but I wouldn't mind taking their securities in addition to some cash. It would complicate our lives too much if we fired Woerner right now. So what do we do? I want to make sure we pick the right option.

But before the Prudential meeting, there was a meeting in Roscoe Haynie's office of the Aerospace stock-option committee. The problem today is created by our plan to redeploy Aerospace into several separate companies and send executives from its headquarters to positions in these new companies we will be creating. Since none of these companies exists yet, they have no stock-market values to give us a firm basis for setting up option plans that will provide proper incentives to their new managements.

I was running a bit late when I left Roscoe's office for my appointment with the Prudential people at 9:00 A.M. When I came out into the reception area on the way to my own office, I saw a group of men with briefcases and realized they were waiting for me. We introduced ourselves. There was Frank J. Hoenemeyer, executive vice president of Prudential, which is either the biggest or second biggest insurance company in the world, and two others in the group were lawyers. It occurred to me that with a couple of lawyers present, they were going to make an offer for Computer Tech then and there. You wouldn't ordinarily come loaded with lawyers if you were just making a preliminary investigation of the possibility of a deal.

I had Roscoe and Paul Thayer join us and we went into my office. Hoenemeyer, as spokesman, said that they were considering the purchase of Computer Tech but that there were a lot of problems involved. One was getting the New Jersey insurance commissioner to approve the deal. But he said that they had already done some groundwork to the extent of letting the commissioner know they were considering diversifying into the computer field and that he had indicated it would probably be all right.

Another question was whether Bill Woerner could meld CT with their own computer operation, which is a big one on its own. Payment could also present a problem. If they were to make an offer, Hoenemeyer said, Prudential did not want to borrow any money and have to show bank debt on their balance sheet at the end of this year.

I made it clear that one of the reasons we were interested in selling the company was that we wanted to use the proceeds of the CT securities we held to facilitate our plan for redeploying the Aerospace company, specifically for the exchange offering we had planned to make. But I told him that if we got any kind of commitment from them that would be bankable—that is, that we could use to borrow the necessary funds against—that might work out. I said it would be absolutely essential that we would be able to come out of the deal with somewhere around $35 million in cash before the end of this year and that we could take the rest of the payment after year end with no difficulty. He said he thought that that wouldn't present a problem.

Hoenemeyer made some comments about how Woerner might demonstrate his capability and his performance. I caught Roscoe's eye, because I was thinking that if that was the only thing holding up the deal, then we could bank on it, because we both know that Bill Woerner is the best goddam salesman that ever came down the pike. Woerner can sell anybody anything once he makes up his mind to.

We finally got down to the point where an offer was about to be made. After my talk with Gus this morning, I decided that my own personal choking point—and it was a lot less

than I wanted—would be $70 million. I felt that in my ini-
tial contact with Prudential's people in Paul Thayer's office
nearly two weeks ago, I outlined what we had to have before
we would have any interest at all in selling Computer Tech.
I said then that we were about to make an exchange offer of
CT shares for Aerospace securities when the market price of
CT dropped from around $25 to below $15, so we withdrew
the offer. At the time I first talked to them, I guess the CT
price was around $13. But in the last few days, it has climbed
again, and yesterday it got to around $20. On that basis, I
figured they would offer the equivalent of about $15 or $16
a share, which would be something like $60 million or maybe
$65 million.

I figured that on the basis of what I think the stock really
is worth, I would then counter with $85 million, and we
would settle for somewhere in the range of $75 million to $80
million. The point is that I had crossed the Thayer-Woerner
conflict bridge by deciding to sell Computer Tech.

At this point, I am sitting across the table from Hoenemeyer, with Paul Thayer on my left and my chair turned
slightly to the right. I'm looking at Hoenemeyer, and he is
just about to lay it on the table.

In view of our preceding conversation and subject to the
caveats he had raised, Hoenemeyer announces, Prudential
would be willing to buy Computer Tech for $90 million.

Afterward, Roscoe told me that my face was a complete
mask, that it showed no expression of any kind. He said that
if I portrayed any emotion at all, it had to be that of a man
in complete shock. Roscoe also said that Paul showed nothing, except that his tie was going up and down his Adam's
apple.

I sat there trying to organize my thoughts, because here I
am with an opening bid maybe $30 million higher than I had
expected it to be. Finally I suggested that the bid was less
than we had wanted, at least it was less than the company
would have been worth before the market dropped so sharply.
Then I suggested that Roscoe, Paul, and I should caucus in
Roscoe's office and that they should remain at my conference
table.

I did not smile as we went through the reception area to

Roscoe's office, but I walked fast because I didn't want them to react out there either. When we finally got inside, I said, "For chrissakes, you people, don't scream for joy."

What it all means is that the original concept I had for forming Computer Tech, putting together all of our computer operations and making them into a separate, publicly held corporation, despite all the agony, the trials and tribulations with Woerner and Thayer, and all the rest, what it comes down to is that if the Prudential offer stays glued together and we consummate it, we will have sold Computer Technology for $150 million, including what we have already got from our prior underwriting offer. In other words, to quote Bert Eitel, our controller, who is one of the financial people we got from Wilson, what we really have done is to sell "a goddam glorified bookkeeping department" for $150 million. That is very oversimplified, because there's a helluva lot of computer hardware there and computer service is a lot more than bookkeeping or accounting. But Bert is not so far off, because the bulk of the value is in the processing contracts.

We stayed a proper amount of time in Roscoe's office talking about what I would say. I decided I was going to raise two or three possible problems before I said, "Yes, but hell yes." Roscoe said that we really shouldn't have been so surprised. After all, he said, Prudential is not a rag merchant. In effect, I had told them at that earlier meeting, or at least had indicated, that I wouldn't be satisfied with anything less than about $80 million or better, based on what the market price now stood at. And Roscoe said that they merely took me at my word, at my precise word, that I would not be satisfied.

We returned to my office determined not to appear too eager. I sat down and said, "I recognize that this is a fair offer, though certainly not what we had hoped for. On the other hand, I found a long time ago that if we're going to do something, we ought to make up our mind quickly to do something that's reasonable and fair." I said that under the terms and conditions that would expedite the sale so that we could have the necessary cash to go through with our proposed SEC registration of the Aerospace Corporation exchange offering plus the normal legal caveats and disclaimers, we would accept their offer. We then talked about Woerner's requirements and our need to expedite the deal, as well as our intention to continue using CT for our computer services, and so on. Then we stood up and Hoenemeyer and I shook hands on the deal, and that was the beginning.

Next I called in Fred Ash, who is the LTV secretary, George Griffin, who works directly for me on financial planning, and Sam Downer, who is Paul Thayer's financial man at Aerospace. I briefed them in front of the Prudential people on my understanding of the deal and then had the Prudential people present their view of it. Hoenemeyer and I sent the legal and financial people down to draft a memorandum covering what we had discussed. Then he too left.

Haynie and Thayer stayed in my office after the others left, and I called Gus Levy to tell him what had happened. He congratulated me and called the deal fantastic. I put in a call to Clyde on vacation in Seattle. As I explained it to him, he kept saying, "You're not kidding me, are you?" and Roscoe and Paul were laughing in the background, which Clyde heard, so at the end of the phone call he asked me again, "You're not kidding me?"

I said, "No, this is a genuine opening bid. Whether we close or not is still subject to all sorts of conditions." Now Paul and Roscoe and I got down to our own strategy meeting. I told Paul that at this stage, if anybody blows it from our end, he can damn sure know what to expect from me. I said, "I do not want this deal to go down the drain as a result of some damn nit-picking or personality problems." Paul got the message, and he is going to be very careful what people of his he puts into the negotiations of this CT deal. I made some specific suggestions of which ones I didn't want. We discussed some other points necessary to keep the thing going forward.

If we had not had the Thayer-Woerner problem, if we had had Woerner reporting directly up to me, we could easily have wound up in three or four years with at least $200 million worth of Computer Tech stock and maybe a lot more. With Prudential putting their own people and about $35 million worth of computers and about $35 million of computer service business into it, it could become one of the biggest computer software companies in the world. Hoenemeyer certainly has grasped our concept of how Prudential could get a paper profit of better than $250 million from this deal.

I had an LTV Ling Altec board meeting after lunch. The most important item on the agenda was the sale of one of its divisions to a group of local investors. When the motion to approve the deal was put before the board, it occurred to me that a lot of the directors didn't understand the issue. There was a lot of discussion, and the motion was defeated, probably because the new management of the company was inexperienced about briefing directors, especially outside directors.

I've been running my own show for twenty years now, and I've developed an informal style, my own way of communicating. But I try not to take it for granted that they understand something just because I do. In fact, I try to assume that they don't know anything when they arrive. But of course there are times when you have to prepare them, so I sometimes file a report with board members as much as a week before the meeting if possible. I think I'm going to make it a rule for all the companies that any major item has to be sent to the members three or four days before the meeting.

At 4:30 this afternoon, the people working on the Computer Tech deal brought me a two-page memorandum covering the points we discussed. One of the Prudential lawyers said he was concerned about the possibility of an antitrust action. I told him I couldn't believe that with the Justice Department always on IBM's back, trying to break them up, that they wouldn't welcome a major new company entering the field. But the lawyer insisted on Prudential having the right to withdraw if legal action was threatened by Justice. I kidded him and said, "Hell, what you fellows ought to do is stay in and fight them and not let them get away with irresponsible acts." But we wrote the withdrawal provision into the memorandum. So that's how we stood today.

[But that deal too was not to be. The reason Prudential finally offered for withdrawing two months later, after Ling had indicated a willingness to cut the price if necessary, seems to have had to do with the insurance company being a mutual company—meaning it has no stockholders as such but is "owned" by its policy holders—and therefore not being able to acquire a subsidiary corporation that would have shares owned by the public. Whether that was the real reason is not clear. In any event, even at the outset, Ling had made a mental back-up plan to sell Computer Tech to Sam Wyly's University Computing Company or Ross Perot's EDS. A deal with UCC was closed in late 1969. As part of the agreement, CT's headquarters was to be moved from the Chicago area, Woerner's home, to Dallas, and Woerner was to be demoted. That resulted in his protesting and filing a suit against the deal, which was finally settled out of court. The sale of CT to University Computing also resulted in a dispute over the final price, UCC complaining that it had got less than it had bargained for as CT began crumbling with the departure of Woerner, his associates, and his deals.]

August 23

I went out to the Cotton Bowl tonight and saw the Dallas Cowboys—I'm on their board—break the Green Bay jinx for the first time. Last year, we were going great until Danny Reeves got hurt. He has tremendous agility and a damned good mind. We were dead on our ass tonight until Reeves came in and made one or two plays and carried the ball. He had a recent operation and he's still a bit gingerly about it. He took the ball in one play and started around the right end, and Rentzel worked into the open. The secondary had committed themselves, and I guess the picture they saw was an end run or an end run with a pass right down the right sideline short, but the man who was there wasn't in the clear, but Rentzel was deep and open. Sure enough, Reeves pitched a perfect strike, and Rentzel made a great broken-field run and scored. The Cowboys caught fire then. You could see it. It was strictly a case of leadership and how it works to turn a situation around, the same as in business.

September 5

Tonight I attended a cocktail party and dinner at the Lancer Club on top of the LTV Tower in honor of Senator John Tower. Some of the Republican hierarchy were there besides John. Erik Jonsson of Texas Instruments, who is Mayor of Dallas, Peter O'Donnell, the young fellow who is head of the Republican organization here, and some others were present, as well as people not identified with the Republican party. Bob Vial, a local lawyer, who was a classmate of John's at Georgetown, said that they were trying to raise money to endow a chair in honor of John in political science at Georgetown.

The reaction to the idea was, of course, quite favorable. I think it should be done, and we certainly will participate. But once we began to talk, a lot of people began grilling the Republican leaders along the lines of "What the hell is the party trying to do to Texas?" The issue, of course, was the proposed changes in the oil depletion allowance, which to a lot of Texans is their life's blood.

Jake Hamon, who is probably, after Getty and Hunt, the largest independent oil man in the country and is reputedly worth well over $100 million, said that with Washington disallowing certain kinds of charitable deductions, coupled with the change in the oil depletion allowance, he would just have to take another look at his hole cards.

I found it kind of embarrassing to have to watch John Tower on the defensive. He finally hung his head and said that it was just a damn miserable shame and that they had tried hard to coach the President. In fact, he said that he and George Bush, the young Congressman from Houston [defeated in the 1970 race for the Senate, Bush was appointed Ambassador to the United Nations], had just got back from San Clemente the day before yesterday, and they had tried to make the President aware of just what the hell he was doing. But it appears that he has got caught up by the professional bureaucrats at the Treasury. Apparently it is just not coming through to him, the attitude of oil men and of major businessmen in general.

He has unquestionably reneged on a campaign promise to the oil industry. And apparently he has done the same thing to others. His Administration's attack on the conglomerates would seem to be another example. People in this part of the country seem to be less than enthusiastic about the President these days, and understandably so. [That, of course, was before John Connally was named Secretary of the Treasury and an unofficial contender for the Vice Presidency.]

September 16

I had a meeting this afternoon with Harding Lawrence. Harding gave me a briefing on the status of his new route applications. He reports that August was generally quite good, operationally speaking. September does not appear too good. He was a little bit evasive about meeting his forecast for the year. He also reported that he had had further talks with Pan Am, TWA, and Eastern.

He finally got around to what he was really here about. Oversimplified—although I don't know if it's so oversimplified—he wants to chat about the contract he has sent me. Now, bear in mind that I chatted with him back in the early part of the year and deferred any action on it. So he wrote me a letter—seven or eight pages—stating all his accomplishments at Braniff and the progress they've made under his stewardship. I had of course replied that, yes, he had done a good job, that I was certain that in the long run the profits would flow from the development of new routes, and so forth. But on the other hand, he was damn well paid, in my personal opinion. We had essentially given him a $50,000 raise once we had taken over Braniff from Greatamerica. We financed 100,000 shares of stock for him—which we have never done for anybody else—because of an implied obligation on the part of Greatamerica that they did not honor. I chatted subsequently with Troy Post and Grant Fitts and, as they recall, there was no such agreement to buy shares for him.

He asked what I thought of the contract, and I said it was

very professionally done. "Yes," he said, "Mr. Grant prepared it." Mr. Grant, it turned out, is Arnold Grant, a lawyer for some of the movie stars and for Bob Six of Continental Airlines. Harding asked if I wanted to talk to Grant, and I said, "No, I really have no appetite to talk to him." That was my initial reaction. I felt that Harding was being well paid. Based on what we had paid for Greatamerica and the amount we had more or less paid for Braniff, they were making only a minor contribution to the overall LTV earnings. I just didn't see how we could justify doing anything further for him. The contract he wants calls essentially for a thirteen-year extension. Furthermore, he'd like a ten-year consulting contract, and the numbers are enormous. He's asking for a $100,000-a-year raise. And he's asking for a raise in the event the cost-of-living index goes up as though he was a union man. He's asking us to buy him another 100,000 shares of Braniff. He wants 25-percent incentive compensation, based on earnings increases. The demands are pretty fantastic.

I could see him getting a little uptight, not too uptight, but just enough. He said he wanted to bring a lawyer in. I told him that was fine and maybe he could brief us on the proposed legislation in Congress about deferred compensation, salaries, etc. I also told him that if he worked up a hell of a good merger, then of course he should be rewarded. I suggested deferring the contract until that time. He said he was anxious to get this done pretty quick. The only inference I could make from his asking for such an unusual contract now was that he wanted to be in a top trading position in case there is a merger with another airline. We made an appointment to meet with his lawyer, Grant. I'll review this with Clyde and Roscoe. I can't for the life of me imagine going to the compensation committee and the board of Braniff and having them ratify a contract anything like this. We'll see.

[This is another instance of the curious diffidence and deference with which Ling treated Lawrence. Ling clearly felt, as he indicates here, that Lawrence was asking for a lot more than Ling thought he was worth, though he did feel he was an able operating man. Ling sensed that the airline executive was not making an accurate forecast of Braniff earnings for the rest of the year: there were not going to be any, and Lawrence should have known that. But Ling did not confront him with a direct question. He saw Lawrence clearly as a man very able in the area of promotion of himself and of Braniff—helped of course by his new wife's brilliant plane painting, Pucci costuming, and advertising of the airline. And he said often that one of Lawrence's most important talents was figuring out new routes and applying for and frequently getting them, and Ling didn't want to do anything to disturb Lawrence's efforts. And he needed Lawrence for a merger. But there was something about Lawrence's style that seems to have put Ling off and caused him to back down even after he had determined not to. Once just a country boy in middle management in a provincial airline, Lawrence had become a regular jet-setter, moving easily (after all, he ran an airline) in and out of the movie-star-Europe-Acapulco high society that Troy Post had also sought access to. It may have occurred to Ling, as it did to others, to reflect that one reason Lawrence was coming around again for a big raise was that his wife, Mary Wells, was making potfuls of money out of her publicly held advertising agency and that he wanted to stay at least even with her in the press and the proxy statements. He knew that, as much as Harding and Mary were taking home, they were living a very fancy Dallas-New York-Europe life that cost lots of money—so much, in fact, that they were renting out their Italian villa, when they weren't using it, to top people such as Charlie Bluhdorn of Gulf & Western. Ling knew that he could and ought to, at the very least, lean hard on him. Yet the best he could do was say, "We'll talk about it later." As long as Ling was in the saddle, however, Lawrence did not get his new contract, which must surely have been a reason why Lawrence went over to the other side when there was one to go over to.]

September 18

Bill Stephens [the chairman] and Harvey Haughton [the controller] of Jones & Laughlin were in early this morning. I told them I was frustrated as hell not being able to do anything with J&L. I told them I had half a dozen different outlines of programs they could look into, including redeployment of their company into several components, also the idea of J&L buying its own shares back, of buying shares out of the market, or of just going out and getting $100 million to put in the bank for further acquisitions. Harvey expressed some reluctance and started talking about high money rates.

I said, "Hell, you guys should have raised a lot of money when it was 5 percent. I assure you you'll have no trouble making 10 percent on your money, even if it costs you nearly 10 percent. What the hell is your alternative? You need to do something. If I were running your show, that's what I would do. I'd do any combination of these things."

Harvey left, and I told Bill, "We need to do something, because we can sit around here not doing anything and lose a lot of time." He agreed, and then he told me that the $400 million that J&L has spent in the last four years, including that new mill at Hennepin, Illinois, has not improved their capacity to produce one extra ton of steel.

"Goddam, I can't imagine that, Bill," I said.

"That's right," he said. Harvey came back and confirmed that Hennepin has not done a thing. I asked what we had to do to make it productive. He said that there was no sense in putting in the $350 million or more it would take to make it an integrated operation, at least not now. So it's just a great big lemon sitting out there in the Illinois prairie, when you get down to it. Bill made it clear that the Hennepin decisions were not his. I get the impression that they thought it was Chuck Beeghly's way of building a monument to himself down there on the Illinois River.

September 22

We're getting into high gear for our five-year planning session. I've got preliminary copies of the analyses and summaries of the five-year plans of some of the individual companies. I had a briefing with Clyde on the consolidated picture, and it is damned impressive. Year after year, with the exception of last year, we've hit our projections fairly close. Unquestionably there's a great deal of both enthusiasm and romance in our projections. But on a preliminary basis, if everything went right, LTV could earn $65 million after minority interests and after all costs, which is unbelievable, of course, because J&L has already cut its forecast for the year down from $38 million to $33 million and then down to $30 million, and it seems doubtful that Braniff can come up with their $17 million that they cut down to from $25 million. But we'll see.

[As it turned out, Jones & Laughlin did not earn $30 million in 1969, and Braniff did not earn $17 million. The J&L net was $22 million, of which LTV's share was $15.7 million, and Braniff earned $6.2 million, $3.5 million of which was LTV's share. The reports were full of explanations for these bad performances: wildcat strikes, start-up costs (what would bad managers do without "start-up costs" to blame?), downturn of the economy, all kinds of things that they could not possibly have anticipated in the first week in October.]

September 30

Wheels up at 11:00 A.M. for Kerrville to connect with the Alouette helicopter to take us to the Eagle Ranch. The offsite meeting begins tomorrow.

[Ling was on his way to the offsite meeting with a planeload of friends, directors, and helpers. He was going to hear how the subsidiaries of his corporation were faring and how they might be expected to wind up the year 1969. After all, it ought not to be too difficult to forecast the outcome of a year with three fourths of it already gone. At least, that seemed a reasonable assumption. But, as Ling was to discover, the still relatively rosy presentations of figures and color slides were to alter markedly by year end, especially at Braniff and Jones & Laughlin. Whether these deviations from forecasts were the result of subsidiary managers' sweeping their problems into the fourth quarter and hoping for miracles or whether they stemmed literally from unforeseeable circumstances is unclear. Whatever the reasons, operating earnings would be sharply diminished in 1969. And with this evaporation of profits, Ling's own hold on the empire would suddenly be threatened.]

14

T H E calls are always bad when you lose," Ling explained, in a succinct confusion of cause and effect. Though
sports metaphors are basic to his lexicon, he was not using
one to describe his own business circumstances this time. He
was in fact talking about a sports event, the 1971 Super Bowl,
where the Dallas Cowboys went down to clumsy defeat at the
fumbling hands of the Baltimore Colts. By that time, he was
all done talking about his own defeat in the equally maladroit
game played out during 1970 at LTV in Dallas. He was finished speculating, playing his game of ifsy, over what might
have happened if the market had not become disaffected with
conglomerates after the seemingly infallible Litton turned in
a bad quarter in 1968, and if institutional investors had not
dumped their LTV holdings after the takeover of Jones &
Laughlin, and if the Justice Department had not filed its antitrust suit against LTV, and if J&L and other LTV companies
had not performed so poorly in 1969, and if the stock market
had not continued to knock hell out of LTV along with everything else into 1970.

Not that he didn't still harbor some rue about the messy
and finally fruitless way he had been done in. And they did
get him right through the middle. But he is not a bleeder.
And besides, even toward the end, with the empty titles of
vice chairman of the board and consultant—virtual insults
in the language of corporate organization—he still had too

much of a financial stake in the future of LTV to engage in recriminations and vengeance. For one thing, his words and acts could still be construed as violations of his LTV employment contract, then worth about $300,000 a year.

The way Ling went down must be unbelievable to anyone given to thinking that the men in the upper reaches of corporate enterprise are more perceptive or dispassionate than anybody else. The cabal that moved against Ling had no carefully worked-out plan, despite appearances. Its members didn't even seem to have certain basic facts about their own stake until after they had removed Ling. Even then they did not accomplish any of the purposes that could possibly have explained their move. Except perhaps the simple act of cutting Ling down to size.

If a map or a flow chart of the process by which Ling was taken out were drawn, it would have the form of a lunatic's daisy chain. It would involve a set of conflicting motives, pressure points, animosities, obligations, and tribal customs. Since none of the several principal participants, even now, has a clear sense either of what went on or of why, no such map exists. But one can be pieced together—with holes, to be sure, but describing at least a semblance of what happened during those weird and wild days in Dallas.

What may have been the beginning was a day late in 1969, after the meeting at Eagle Ranch, when E. Grant Fitts came to tell Ling he was unhappy about the drop in the prices of LTV securities. The common shares had fallen to $24 from a high during 1967 of just under $170. The insurance companies Fitts controlled through his Gulf Life Holding Company had more than $30 million invested in LTV. Fitts had some of his own money in the company. And he was a director. He told Ling he didn't think Ling was doing enough to improve the situation. Ling, with an even bigger financial stake in the form of LTV's largest stockholding and large personal bank debts secured by his shares, figured he had motive enough and was doing a lot to solve the company's problems. Something called Project Cutdown, a belt-tightening program, had gone into effect in late summer, and Ling was planning to reorganize executive responsibilities so that Clyde Skeen would be better able to handle day-to-day operations. Ling had already seen his own stock drop in value by around $40 million. But he told Fitts he wasn't really worried because he had plans that would make it all work out. He even pointed out that, since he had started out with only $2,000 and still had a lot more than that, he wasn't really in such bad shape. Fitts is not a man to live happily with that sort of response, even as a joke. Later, Ling would take pains to assure Fitts that he meant that, while he was concerned, he was simply not worried. But by then, the distinction would no longer matter to Fitts. He would be determined to act on his own, if necessary, to protect his investment and make clear, for the record, that he was shouldering his own responsibilities as a corporate director.

Before Fitts began to move against Ling, however, he first seemed to move with him. In fact, at one point later in 1969, Fitts made a curious effort to invest in the holding company through which Ling actually owned his personal shares of LTV. The arrangement would have given Fitts an interest in the holding company and therefore in Ling's roughly 10-percent interest in LTV. It would have given Ling income he could have used to help pay his personal interest charges, which were then running about $900,000 a year. Fitts also hoped to regain for one of the insurance companies he controlled the employee insurance business of LTV. A Fitts company had had that business—worth nearly $3 million a year in premium income—during 1969, but was about to lose it, beginning in 1970, to a lower-bidding John Hancock. Later Fitts would insist that LTV fire the executive who handled the actual bidding that took the business away from Fitts's company. Nothing came of the Fitts proposal to invest with Ling. But in the course of his efforts, Fitts got together with Robert H. Stewart III, chairman of the board of First National Bank in Dallas, where Ling had a loan of about $5 million. That loan, not his only personal debt then, would become a focal point of the successful attempt to force him out. And Bobby Stewart would be a tool in the process.

Shortly afterward, Fitts began pressing Ling to shake up LTV and get rid of Clyde Skeen, the president. He urged that

Stewart be made a member of the board of LTV, and he got Stewart to express concern about the financial plight of the corporation. Fitts also expressed his doubts to other members of the board of directors. Ling apparently underestimated Fitts's determination to play a larger part in the life of LTV. The steely intensity behind the slightly ironic Fitts façade eluded him completely. To Ling, Fitts must surely have seemed a man who could safely be faced down.

But Fitts was not about to back off. On January 6, 1970, at the regular LTV board meeting, Ling presented his "Master Game Plan," an enormously complex scheme, much of it at least plausible, for solving the corporation's pressing cash problems. It discovered "new" assets where none had seemed to be. It envisioned the disposal of subsidiaries, particularly the Okonite Company, in what had become a recognizable pattern, but with a somewhat different twist. The idea was to have LTV bring in the 19.2 percent of Okonite shares still held by the public, through an exchange offer. Then the company would be split into two parts, one that owned the name, the product lines, and other intangibles—in other words, the "going business" aspect of the wire-and-cable company—and the other that owned the land, buildings, and other tangible assets. Both would then be sold. Ling had no idea who would buy either of them, but if he could sell them at the high prices he thought they were worth, LTV's condition would look a lot better.

Ling easily spelled out the details of his Master Game Plan, his cost-cutting activities, and his insistence that LTV was not only solvent but on the verge of a resurrection. He also made clear that Clyde Skeen was not leaving, even though Ling had already concluded that maybe Skeen would have to be reassigned to placate critics. As usual, the plans were beyond the immediate grasp of most of the board, though they understood well enough that earnings—originally projected for $47 million in 1969—would only reach $2.4 million, before deducting losses on sales of securities and subsidiaries totaling more than $10 million. But the board's members seemed willing to continue believing in Ling, even though they could not quite follow his reasoning, which now lacked the buttressing of solid earnings and sanguine investors. At least most of them did. But not Grant Fitts.

That evening, Ling met David Mahoney, president of Norton Simon, Inc., another burgeoning conglomerate, to try to sell him Braniff. Gus Levy had arranged that meeting, and his firm of course would receive a fee if a deal resulted. Both Levy and Mahoney spent that night as the Lings' guests. Next day, Ling put what he hoped would be the finishing touches on the sale of half of Aerospace's stock in Computer Tech to Sam Wyly's University Computing Company when he attended the formal closing at UCC's headquarters. Even as he signed, Ling knew that Bill Woerner, CT's ex-boss, would take legal action trying to unglue the deal. But he figured it would go through in the end.

On Friday, the Lings flew down to Eagle Ranch with James Chambers, publisher of the Dallas *Times Herald*, his wife, and Otis Chandler, of the Times-Mirror Company, the Los Angeles newspaper and book-publishing empire, and his wife. Chandler wanted to buy the Dallas afternoon paper, and Chambers wanted Ling's advice on whether to sell. Chambers' presence on the LTV board of directors had caused considerable embarrassment at the working level of the paper and in LTV's public-relations department, to say nothing of sneers about favored treatment in Dallas' only afternoon paper and on its TV and radio stations. But he would not be on the board much longer.

The party flew back from the ranch on Sunday, and the next day the Lings and the Posts flew to Acapulco to spend a few days at Troy Post's resort club. Tres Vidas, as it was called, would have as much as anything to do with Ling's ouster.

While Ling was relaxing in the tropical sun, Grant Fitts was bearing down in Dallas. In the week following the meeting, Fitts composed a nineteen-page critique of the company and of Ling's management, which he sent off as a letter to Ling in mid-January. Though much of its substance dealt with problems Ling himself recognized and thought he was attacking properly, it also proposed that a committee of the board be set up to monitor Ling's activities. Fitts wanted the committee's members to include himself along with Bobby Stewart and Troy Post, neither of whom was then a member. Fitts also stated that he had shown a draft of his letter to Dennis Lyons, a partner in the law firm of Arnold & Porter.

To Ling, the whole thing was nothing more than a "palace uprising" not to be taken too seriously, since everything would soon work itself out. If he felt that Fitts, together perhaps with Lyons, had any intention of moving against him, he did not indicate it. The prospect that some sort of plot or conspiracy was afoot was still unimaginable. After all, nobody else really understood the whole picture with all its possibilities for creating assets and higher market values for the stock, he must have thought. And, in a sense, that was one of Fitts's major criticisms: the whole structure was just too complicated for anybody else to understand, and directors have a legal obligation to understand and to assume responsibility for management action even if they don't understand.

Fitts had urged, in his letter, that LTV settle its antitrust case with the Justice Department rather than attempt to win the case in the courts. Apparently he did not know that Ling had already begun the process of settlement.

Almost from the beginning, Ling had recognized and stated privately that even though he thought the Justice Department had picked on LTV unjustly and without sound legal basis, he had no intention of jeopardizing the welfare of the corporation to win some empty moral victory in the courts. But he had expected the case to come to trial quickly, sometime in the fall, with a decision early in 1970, so LTV could begin the increasingly difficult process of turning Jones & Laughlin around. That was why he had conceded—"stipulated," in legal terms—so many points and facts in the case without argument.

But the Justice Department did not bring the case to trial in the fall. Instead, the antitrust people asked for a lot more information from LTV, so much in fact that somebody in the corporation figured it would take a couple of hundred man-years and a million dollars' worth of payroll and computer time to come up with the answers. Word from Washington seemed to indicate that the government's lawyers were having trouble establishing a case against LTV based on reciprocal dealings with suppliers and customers and on concentration of "control of manufacturing assets," in the words of the complaint. For its total sales volume, LTV controlled what probably were relatively few "manufacturing assets." Braniff had none, the meat-packing business requires few compared with sales, and as for the subsidiaries engaged in government contract work, many of their assets were owned by the government, which is typical of military suppliers. The steel company admittedly had plenty of manufacturing assets. But Ling's contention that the antitrust people were not finding what they had hoped for and were stalling seems reasonable.

In mid-November, Ling called a meeting of his antitrust lawyers in Dallas. He told Norman Diamond of Arnold & Porter that the firm's forecast of a trial timetable had gone awry. Diamond conceded that the case could not possibly reach the courtroom before the late winter of 1970 and that, allowing for arguments, deliberation, and the summer recess, no decision was likely before the fall of 1970.

With Jones & Laughlin by that time forecasting earnings of less than half of its original prediction of $38 million for 1969, LTV was confronting difficult times. Ling proposed that some way be found to get LTV out of the suit. Diamond argued that this was a landmark case and that McLaren would be unlikely to accept any settlement short of the government's demand that LTV divest itself of Jones & Laughlin. Ling did not agree and stated that he thought that the Justice Department did not seem eager to bring the case to trial and might welcome a settlement, even suggesting terms: getting rid of some other subsidiaries instead of J&L.

Diamond and his associates initially held that such a proposal made no sense and had no chance of working. But Ling argued that the case itself was "so illogical that an equally illogical solution might very well work."

Within a week after that meeting, Ling began moving on his own toward a settlement of the lawsuit. His curious personal war with Assistant Attorney General McLaren made a direct approach virtually useless, so Ling sought instead to make contact through Attorney General Mitchell. That method worked. Mitchell seemed willing to accept the prospect of an escape from the suit for his people, so he passed the word down that LTV wanted to settle. Ling's lawyers soon began meeting with the antitrust people.

Ling was deeply immersed in hammering out an agreement with the Justice Department at the time Fitts's provocative letter reached him. And his certainty that a settlement would solve the corporation's and his own financial problems may have distracted his attention from the personally critical passages of the letter and from its implicit threat. In any case, even then he saw Fitts as nothing more than a hovering gadfly.

The following week, Ling flew up to New York to tell Mahoney that Braniff was in trouble, and Mahoney backed off. He also spent a couple of days talking to LTV's New York bankers: Manufacturers Hanover, First National City, Bankers Trust, Chase Manhattan, Marine Midland Grace, and Franklin National. Meetings with major lenders are a routine part of the life of every big user of credit, and LTV owed these and a score of other banks around the country about $110 million, so it was natural that they should want to know how the corporation was doing and, specifically, where it would get the money to pay them back. Ling explained his plans to them, and though they knew that LTV was having problems because of the huge earnings drops, especially at J&L and Braniff, they seemed satisfied with what Ling told them. And, of course, their loans were still backed by plenty of collateral.

Though LTV's lawyers had been talking settlement with the antitrust people off and on for a month or so, Ling himself was staying away from the actual discussions in Washington. For one thing, the matter was a legal one, and he was not a lawyer. For another, the abrasive relationship between Ling and McLaren would hardly lubricate face-to-face encounters. But Ling was in constant contact with his lawyers as they began their negotiations in early December. His hope was that a settlement would permit LTV to hold on to Jones & Laughlin. At that point, it represented an enormous book loss to the corporation, something like $300 million on paper. He felt that, given time and an opportunity to work his redeployment plans, he could get it back up in value. But that could take years, so he didn't want a judgment hanging over him that required him to unload it at a loss. Instead, his lawyers sought an agreement along the lines Ling had proposed. If LTV were to offer to dispose of subsidiaries other than the steel company, that might permit the McLaren people to assert that LTV was no longer a force destructive of competition, whatever that meant.

Ling had already tried to sell Braniff to Howard Hughes at the August meeting with Robert Maheu. But nothing had come of that. Nor would he be able to sell it to Norton Simon, Inc. An earlier attempt to sell the airline to Charles Bluhdorn's Gulf & Western Industries got Ling nothing more than a cogent analysis from Bluhdorn of what was wrong with airlines in general and with Braniff in particular. Now if Ling could get the Justice Department to accept the divesting of Braniff and Okonite, two companies he had been trying to sell anyway, instead of J&L, he would have brought off a neat coup. Ling's lawyers wanted to avoid a settlement that named specific companies to be unloaded. After all, if the government says you have to sell something by a certain deadline, that in itself will tend to push the price down. But McLaren insisted that the companies to be sold must be listed in the agreement. Another concern of the Ling forces was the government's insistence that the J&L people in Pittsburgh acquiesce to the terms. Ling's people fought this because they felt that since LTV owned 81 percent of the steel company, they ought to be free to make an agreement about it without Pittsburgh even knowing about the deal beforehand. There was some concern that the steel-company management might try to stall the deal. The feeling seemed to be that Pittsburgh was content to allow the situation as it then stood to go on indefinitely, with the principal J&L stockholder unable to exercise any management control over the company. It was a safe assumption that once LTV was free to manage the steel company, it would make a lot of changes, many of them uncomfortable for the incumbents in Pittsburgh.

The public announcement by Jones & Laughlin at the end of January that it had just completed its worst year in a decade increased the pressure for a settlement. J&L earned only a little more than half of what it had said it would early in 1969. In a press release, the steel company's chief executive, William Stephens, cited a string of unanticipated labor-relations and technical problems in explanation. But some people wondered whether Stephens was confusing cause and effect. After all, one of the functions of management is to anticipate. When a Dallas man suggested that perhaps "the Pittsburgh natives are restless," another man corrected him with "maybe they're just resting." Worst of all, there was no indication that 1970 would be any better. The consequence of this poor showing was that dividends from the steel company, a major source of cash for LTV, would dwindle or vanish. During this period, Ling was also scouting prospective buyers for all or parts of J&L, and he made preliminary contacts with representatives of British, German, and Japanese interests.

The talks with the Justice Department were reaching their climax. On any day when LTV's lawyers were slated to meet with the antitrust people, Ling was never out of reach of a telephone. And if a meeting was taking place, he practically held his breath until he got a call from Dan Burney, the corporation's general counsel, telling him how it went. Even at home over dinner, he would jump every time the phone rang, until Burney's report came in.

The antitrust settlement, Ling must have felt by now, would solve much, or at least set the stage for solutions. His preoccupation with what was happening in Washington seemed to shove Fitts and his letters into the background. But the letters and the urgings continued.

Following the LTV board meeting on February 3, the Lings and some friends flew to Palm Springs, California, to see the Bob Hope Golf Classic. Ling was able to relax a bit because he had just worked out a tentative deal with Pepsico, the parent company of Pepsi-Cola among other enterprises, to sell LTV's 75-percent ownership of Wilson Sporting Goods for $63 million in cash. Wilson Sporting Goods was the biggest company in its field, it carried a lot of prestige, and it was a good moneymaker. Why then would Ling sell it? Because LTV needed cash right away to pay interest and retire debt coming due. But Ling could also rationalize that it was an especially good time to sell it: leisure industry companies were selling, relatively speaking, at least as high as they ought to be, and a lot of people would pay top dollar for Wilson just because they wanted to be next to bigtime sports stars, just as other large companies used to pay too much money to buy motion-picture companies and book publishers so their top brass could consort with movie stars and famous writers.

The day after Ling returned from the desert, he met with his finance people to discuss collateral problems on some of the corporation's loans. It seemed that falling prices of the securities of LTV subsidiary companies had reduced the collateral behind a major bank loan to the point where it was below the prescribed minimum level of 250 percent of the loan's face amount. The bankers were willing to reduce the collateral requirement to 225 percent, which would have solved the problem for the moment. But LTV would have had to make a public disclosure of that fact, which Ling emphatically did not want. Such an announcement would probably have upset the financial community and lowered the price of LTV's shares. No corporate executive ever wants that to happen, but Ling was especially vulnerable at that time. LTV shares, then selling at slightly more than 20, were worth just about what he owed at two Dallas banks. Anything that dropped the price below about 20 would put his loans, as they say, underwater. He was not, as it turned out, any closer to drowning than many of his friends and associates. But when he later discovered *that* fact, it offered little consolation. It simply increased the pressure from the others to remove him.

One way of solving the LTV collateral problem was to pay off some other loans and use their collateral to shore up the squeezed bank loan. The sale of the sporting-goods company would accomplish that. But apparently the Ling people themselves liked owning Wilson, so they were looking for alternatives. There was talk around the table of huge private loans from unnamed European sources, long term, no collateral, and relatively low interest, only about 10 percent, not bad in those tight-money days when the prime rate in New York was 7.5

percent. Ling thought these loans were fantasies, but he told his people to pursue them, fully convinced that the sporting-goods sale was the best way out.

Several days later, when word began leaking that LTV was trying to settle its antitrust suit, the Justice Department announced publicly that the negotiations were in fact taking place. As Ling had expected, the European loans never materialized, so LTV went through with its deal with Pepsico and sold the sporting-goods company. Within a few days, the last details of the antitrust settlement fell into place and the J&L people approved it. The terms were made public in March, and LTV stock moved up quickly, almost to 30. The move was based largely on a *Wall Street Journal* story out of Dallas that gave the impression that, in almost no time, LTV would be on its former soaring way again. Despite the fact that LTV came out of the suit without having to do anything except sell Braniff and Okonite—which it would have done anyway—the optimism was premature at the least. Now the corporation would have to sell both those companies at big losses, because their earning power had dwindled. So LTV decided to restate its already disastrous 1969 figures by setting up a $30-million reserve for some of those expected losses. That produced a net loss for LTV for 1969 of $38.2 million, compared with a net profit the year before of $29.4 million. At the same time, LTV stopped paying dividends on its common stock. That announcement came about a week after the post-settlement climb, and the stock again began dropping precipitously. By the end of March it was down from 29⅛—its 1970 high—to 20, and it kept on falling.

Fitts's pressure mounted, and Ling finally agreed to allow Bobby Stewart and Troy Post to fill vacancies on the board, along with LTV's outside counsel and Ling's own lawyer, William H. Tinsley.

Ling was still not visibly dismayed. His next obstacle would be to get the federal district judge in Pittsburgh to approve the antitrust settlement agreement, so he could start to work on the steel company's problems. There were other irritants along the way, but J&L would still offer the big opportunity for a turnaround in the fortunes of the empire. In the midst of all the local turmoil, Ling had to spend the better part of two weeks in April in Washington testifying before Congressman Emanuel Celler's subcommittee investigating the subject of conglomerates and competition, somewhat stale by then. He got back in time to chair LTV's annual shareholders' meeting. The shareholders were far less restless than had been anticipated. In fact, considering that the corporation was reporting on the worst year in its history, the meeting was positively tranquil. Stewart, Post, and Tinsley were elected to seats on the board, and Ling had at that moment, without quite realizing it, already begun to hand over the reins to his successors.

The next few days were filled with golf, playing and watching. First there was the Byron Nelson Classic, named for Ling's old friend and idol, then a quick trip with Nelson and some friends to the Masters' course at Augusta, Georgia, and another flight to Palm Springs, California. Ling returned on Wednesday, May 13, to an urgent call from Bobby Stewart insisting that he come to a meeting that evening. The subject of the meeting, he was told, would be certain problems of Troy Post.

Ling arrived at 6:30 at the meeting place, Apartment 2114, the Athena, the bachelor home of the recently divorced Grant Fitts. Stewart was the other guest. In the language of Ling-Temco-Vought, that might be called Operation Kickoff, the first of a series of frantic meetings to be held during the rest of the week, leading to a special board meeting early on Sunday.

The relationship of these three men along with Troy Post and Sam Wyly created the motives and the means to do the job. And at a slight remove stood two other participants, Dennis Lyons of Arnold & Porter and C. Edward Acker, then executive vice president of Braniff. There are those in Dallas who speculate that the strange series of events was really instituted by Grant Fitts as far back, in at least one version, as the early 1960s. They see Fitts as nurturing a plan that involved taking over the holdings of his then employer Troy Post and later those of Ling as well—and, in a sense, he actually did. But the support for the theory that it was all part of a plan ascribes to Fitts a degree of craft and stealth, to say nothing of some high-class histrionics, that would make Renaissance Florentine plotting seem like hide-and-seek by comparison. Flattering as this idea may be to some secret part of Grant Fitts, it is most unlikely. It belongs to that peculiar school of history and journalism that sees nothing as accidental if it fits a theory, especially a devil theory. It is doubtful that Ling, even in his darkest moments, ever harbored such thoughts. And the curious ending makes it all seem like nothing but a compound of chance, greed, fear, and imperfect knowledge.

Though the participants had many business and personal financial relationships over the years, the beginning of this particular series was probably when Ling borrowed something more than $4 million from the Texas Bank & Trust Company in the mid-1960s to pay off some other personal debts. As collateral for the loan, he put up his holdings of LTV, or at least his stock in Alpha-Omega, the holding company that owned the LTV shares, then worth several times the amount of the loan. In 1968, LTV acquired Greatamerica Corporation from Troy Post and its other stockholders, paying for the company with a new $500-million issue of debentures paying 5-percent interest and due in 1988. They became known as the 5s of 88. Post himself, as the biggest Greatamerica stockholder, got the largest block of them, nearly $100 million face value, though more like $60 million at actual market value. (The balance of the value came in the form of stock warrants issued with the debentures.) Soon after he received them, Post sold part of his holdings for $15 million cash. But he remained the largest single holder of the issue at this time.

Shortly after LTV acquired Greatamerica, in the spring of 1968, Grant Fitts set up Gulf Life Holding Company, which bought from LTV the insurance companies that Greatamerica had owned. That left LTV with Braniff, a bank in California, which it sold, National Car Rental, which it also sold, and some real estate, including an unfinished hotel in Acapulco. Fitts's new company, Gulf Life Holding, also owned a big chunk of LTV securities, dating back to earlier financial dealings between LTV and Greatamerica.

These were the principal financial intertwinings among this group of participants, but by no means all of them. Even so, it is apparent that, at that point, Post's financial well-being rested largely on the value of his holding of LTV 5s of 88 and ultimately, therefore, on the health of LTV. To a much lesser degree, that was also true of Fitts and his Gulf Life Holding. Ling's own wealth also, of course, depended largely on the value of his LTV shares, now mortgaged to the Texas Bank.

A year after the Greatamerica acquisition, in June, 1969, Ling decided to buy out the two other shareholders in Alpha-Omega so that he would in effect own all of its LTV shares. To finance that deal, Ling went to Bobby Stewart at the First National, where Ling himself was now a director. He asked to borrow about $5 million. The Justice Department had filed its antitrust suit early that year, and LTV's stock had dropped to around $40. That still gave Ling's shares a market value of something more than $17 million. But Ling could not put up any of those shares as collateral for his new loan from the First, because they were already tied to the Texas Bank loan. What is more, in an act he described as being "a good Samaritan," Ling had co-signed two $5-million notes at the First National, one for the Roman Catholic University of Dallas and the other for Southern Methodist University. That meant that Ling's name already was on $10 million worth of paper at the First, with no collateral.

The prospect that the two schools or Ling might default was extremely remote. Still, Stewart demurred. For one thing, a bank must be extremely circumspect in its dealings with its officers and directors. For another, remote as the prospect might be, it could inflict grave damage on the bank and on Stewart's reputation if it ever did happen. So Stewart suggested that Ling get some sort of repayment guarantee behind the loan he was applying for.

Ling got the bolstering he needed from another director of the First, Sam Wyly. Wyly's University Computing Company owned Gulf Insurance Company, which, despite its name, is no relation whatever to Grant Fitts's Gulf Life

Holding. UCC's Gulf agreed to provide Ling with a "comfort letter," a kind of insurance policy that guaranteed that UCC's Gulf would make good on the loan if Ling couldn't. Ling paid UCC's Gulf a premium of $200,000 for that guarantee, and he got his $5-million loan. That was the origin of a crucial financial link between Ling and Wyly. Later, when LTV's shares fell further in the market, UCC's Gulf Insurance Company got a little nervous about its potential obligation to the First National Bank. To bolster its own position, it insisted that Sam Wyly and his brother Charles assume personal responsibility for the guarantee behind the Ling loan. They had no choice but to agree.

Now if LTV got into serious trouble, Ling, Post, Fitts, Stewart, Wyly, and their companies would find themselves in varying degrees of hot water, with Fitts's the most bearable, but only by comparison.

Later in 1969, Wyly and his enterprises became even more deeply involved with LTV. After Ling's attempts to sell Computer Technology, Inc., to Prudential Insurance Company aborted, he proceeded with what he had always considered to be his back-up plan and sold it to Wyly's UCC, in a complicated and controversial deal. In partial payment for the stock in Computer Tech, UCC issued to LTV's Aerospace subsidiary a short-term note for $20 million. By the time Ling arrived that evening in May at Grant Fitts's apartment in the Athena, that deal had gone awry. In the course of a great commotion stirred up by the Computer Tech deal, the stock of that company had dropped from around 15 to somewhere near 5. UCC refused to come up with the $20 million cash when its note to LTV came due, and Sam Wyly was attempting to renegotiate the terms of the deal, asserting that the Computer Tech that UCC bought was nothing like the one it had bargained for. The stock of UCC itself, the source of Wyly's own wealth, also had been falling, from a historic high of 186 to less than 20. That meant Wyly was even further enmeshed in the affairs of LTV.

These were some but not all of the panic buttons wired into the circuit. Among the giants now locked together,

Troy Post would have appeared the strongest financially. He had built his holdings in Greatamerica from nothing into a block of securities once worth $60 million and, even with the decline of LTV's securities and, therefore, his fortunes, he was still presumed to be worth many millions. But that was not the case. For, after his withdrawal from Greatamerica, he had launched into the realization of a dream. Post's reputation as a financial wizard had been based on his recognition of one crucial aspect of one business, the heretofore undiscovered value of life-insurance-company stocks. Despite the range of properties his company had acquired, including Braniff Airways and National Car Rental, his entire business life had been pinpointed in the life-insurance business. That devotion had served him well up to a point, but it had not turned him into a worldly and knowledgeable man of affairs, as many may have thought. In many ways, despite his wide contacts and his local social attainments, he remained a country boy from Haskell, Texas, trying to make it in the big city. Once he was clear of his original business interests, he began building a fantastic resort club on a piece of land on the Pacific Coast near Acapulco. It was called Tres Vidas (Three Lives) and it was to be a veritable paradise, private and exclusive. Membership would cost $10,000 plus substantial annual dues (with a $4,000 cut rate for charter members). It would offer golf, tennis, sumptuous food, a limitless range of drink, and every other desire of the best people, defined pretty much by their ability to pay. (Ling, Gus Levy, and Prince Rainier of Monaco were among the names Post featured on his club's board of directors.)

Post had originally projected an operation that would take about $5 million of his ample funds. But before he got it going, he had put up something more that $25 million, or nearly his entire worth, a good bit of it borrowed from Stewart's First National Bank and secured by his 5s of 88. The ineptitude and corruption attendant on the rise of Tres Vidas merit a chapter of their own somewhere. All that need be said here is that the splendid fantasy bombed from the start. Members to whom money meant nothing came away screaming at the prices. Thousands of local people swelled the payroll without contributing perceptibly to the efficiency of the service. It has been suggested that the gross take at the cash register may not have been enough to cover the interest charges, let alone the enormous operating costs. In time, those problems might have been solved. But Post could not wait. When the price of the 5s of 88 dropped to 27 (per $100 of face value, originally marketed at a little over 60), Post was reportedly no longer covered on the bank loans he had secured with those debentures.

Few people in Dallas, including Ling, had any notion of the extent of Post's immersion. So, of course, Ling had no sense of how Post's precarious situation could affect his own future. But it was all suddenly very simple to somebody, maybe Fitts, maybe Stewart, maybe somebody else. If Ling were ceremoniously booted down and maybe out, the market would think that LTV was about to undergo some marvelous rejuvenation, the prices of LTV securities would soar, and the First National Bank of Dallas, Troy Post, and everybody else in the chain would be on the road to recovery again. And what was not immediately cured by that process could be patched up once the new people took over at LTV.

But that was not quite the way it went at the first meeting at the Grant Fitts apartment. It started as a plea to help Troy. It seems Post had come to Fitts and sought his help, pleading that he was in serious trouble, despite his hefty financial statement. Moreover, he felt that if he went down because of Tres Vidas, Ling ought to go down for having put him in his present position by taking LTV into Jones & Laughlin.

Why Fitts responded to Post's plea is not clear. Though the two men had worked closely together for several years, they had no great love for each other and practically no contact at all after LTV acquired Greatamerica. Fitts evidenced little respect for Post as a businessman either after he took over Post's insurance companies or before, when he worked for him. He sometimes gave the impression that he considered himself the real, unrecognized brains of the empire. And Post certainly made no effort to fit him into his new social circle, though Fitts was welcome as a paying member of Tres Vidas. It may be that Fitts took Post's part just because he wanted to try his hand at giant-killing again. After all, it had been Fitts who had instigated Ling's acquisition of Greatamerica that put Post out to pasture, converted his assets into the 5s of 88, and got Fitts his very own company. It may even be that his heart was softened by Post's plea that he was too old to start over again. Or, more likely, it meshed with his own efforts, begun early in the year, to put pressure on Ling, a man whose swaggering self-confidence and persuasive powers must at times have pained Fitts, especially after his company lost LTV's insurance business.

The conversation that evening detoured quickly from the plight of Troy Post to the state of Ling-Temco-Vought. Fitts and Stewart criticized the corporation's high living and the performance of Clyde Skeen, who was not then in good health, among other issues. They raised the unassailable argument that the LTV board of directors was too big and too docile and was actually nothing but a rubber stamp. They also asserted that Ling's personal financial situation impaired his ability to manage with a clear head, though of course such pressures may often improve a man's ability. That raised the specter of Ling's obligations to Stewart's bank and the pressure that Stewart could bring to bear to force Ling to yield.

Ling responded that the whole thing was rather precipitous and that the appearance of instability could cause the corporation some serious new problems. A major reshuffling could give the federal judge in Pittsburgh a reason to hold up his approval of the antitrust decree, to say nothing of its effect on Aerospace attempts to negotiate new defense contracts, and on the corporation's plan to restructure its relationship with its meat-packing subsidiary, Wilson & Company. But Fitts and Stewart persisted.

The next day, Ling met with them again, and now they were joined by Troy Post. Gradually, it appears, Ling saw that they were determined to bring about some kind of reshuffling at headquarters, so he began to yield, particularly on the role of Clyde Skeen.

But whatever inclination Ling may have had to go along

peaceably dissolved when a letter over Troy Post's signature
and addressed to Fitts and Stewart was circulated among
several LTV directors and executives. Its author said that by
firing Skeen, it would be made to appear that Skeen was at
fault and "that Mr. Ling is really strengthening his position,
control and influence in LTV" and "would emerge stronger
than ever." Post's letter said that "the stock and its debt
securities would immediately decline in the marketplace,
and, as a result, I would be hurt further and other debt security holders would be hurt further." But Post thought he
knew how to remedy that problem: "It is absolutely impera-
tive that it appear to the public in a clear and unmistakable
way that Mr. Ling's power and influence in the Company
has been *reduced* rather than increased. . . . He must bear
the responsibility, primarily, for the condition of the Company today and its securities, which endangers my present
financial condition and all the holders of the 5s of 1988."

The Post letter demanded that Grant Fitts be made chairman of the board, that Bobby Stewart be made chairman of
a finance committee, that Eddie Acker become executive
vice president, and that Ling be reduced to president, with
nobody carrying the title of chief executive officer. "Too
much attention," he concluded, "has been given to trying
to save Mr. Ling's face and not enough to saving the security holders, and particularly the *unsecured* debt security
holders." Meaning the holders of the 5s of 88, and particularly Troy V. Post.

Ling apparently read the letter as evidence of a plot against
him rather than merely as a dispassionate attempt to shore
up the corporation, and he reversed his relatively conciliatory position. It was now war. His opponents called for a
special board meeting on the coming Sunday morning, at
which they proposed to ask several members to resign and
then reshuffle the top of the corporation. Ling met frequently during Friday and Saturday with his staff, with Sam
Wyly, and with his opponents. Out-of-town board members
began arriving Saturday afternoon. That evening, ironically,
a party was held at the Post house for the Posts' son Johnny
and the Lings' son Ricky and their teenage friends. It had

been scheduled before the spleen and the liver hit the fan.

The special board meeting was set for 9:00 Sunday morning, May 17, but Ling called an informal meeting for 7:00 A.M. The directors were polled on their willingness to resign. Theoretically, no director could be forced off the board against his will, a point made explicit several times during the meeting. Several directors were effusive in their support for Ling and vehement in their determination to retain their seats. It sounded as though the meeting would end shortly with a proclamation of faith in Ling.

But that was only the beginning. When it was Stewart's turn, he launched an attack on the management and the board and ended with the threat that if the board did not approve the proposed changes in the management, the First National Bank in Dallas would refuse to renew its credit to LTV Aerospace Corporation and other LTV subsidiaries. Even though other banks might be found which would extend credit, Stewart's action still would look bad for the corporation, and the prospect of Aerospace not having enough capital scared some of the directors.

Post in his turn denied any interest in controlling LTV, but said that he thought the public had decided that Ling was LTV's main problem and that Fitts, representing the bondholders including himself, ought to be brought in to help Ling, who, he assured the board, was his friend. Fitts then spoke, referring to a thick sheaf of papers in front of him. He reviewed the situation: the high corporate living, the hotel suites, the costly co-op apartment on Fifth Avenue in New York (bought the year before, at the peak of the New York real-estate market for $600,000), the jet fleet, the chauffeurs, Eagle Ranch, the fat payroll. He reminded the meeting that bondholders come before stockholders. He too denied any interest in controlling LTV and even made a little joke when he said he couldn't imagine who would want to control LTV. He insisted that he was an admirer of Ling but feared that Ling was too kind-hearted to do the necessary paring of overhead by himself. Unless a major change was made *that day* in LTV's image, he would demand that Ling and Skeen both be fired and their long-term employment-benefits contracts be canceled. And he said that he would institute lawsuits charging wrongdoing and mismanagement by the corporation's executives and put LTV into receivership on the grounds that it was insolvent.

The threats of Stewart and Fitts were now on the table, and it was apparent that if the two were serious, there was no way to maintain the status quo. Not only was the life of the corporation in jeopardy, but so were the personal involvements of all those in hock to Stewart's First National Bank. That also included those who owed money to the Texas Bank & Trust Company, among whom, of course, was Ling. Stewart's bank had lent the controlling shareholder of the Texas Bank the money he used to obtain that control. So if Stewart needed to, he could exercise pressure on that bank as well. None of that came out at the meeting, but it was there in the background. So too were Sam Wyly's financial relationships with Jim Ling and LTV. Though Wyly was then under great financial stresses of his own, some of them independent of his relations with Ling and LTV, he also had a kind of hold on Ling's own shares in LTV, because of his guarantee on Ling's loan. And he wanted to assert that claim, perhaps even by taking over LTV himself. That he had seriously considered such a step is likely. He had been invited to the special meeting to be elected to a seat on the new board.

The formal meeting began about 9:00 A.M. in the Control Center across the hall from the board room, with a slide presentation by Ling and members of his staff on the steps taken or in the works to cut down the overhead and sell everything that wasn't welded to the floor. William Stephens of Jones & Laughlin reported on the steel company's dismal earnings and conceded that he was considering passing J&L's second-quarter dividend, which would cut even further into LTV's vital cash flow.

After that grim news, the meeting moved out of the surreal Control Center—with its brightly colored, swiveling, tilting armchairs, remote-controlled panels and slide projection, and moon-crater textured ceiling—and back to the board room. The earlier tone was resumed as directors were asked to resign. Several still refused, until Ling intervened. He repeated Stewart's threat, which affected him as much as it did LTV, and indicated that he believed it fully. LTV's counsel, Bill Tinsley, who had come onto the board only three weeks earlier, also backed down in the face of the threat. Skeen said he would quit as president but wouldn't get off the board if his employment contract was canceled. After a brief caucus of Ling and the dissidents, a compromise was reached. Stewart would become chairman and Ling would become president; nobody would be called chief executive officer; the employment contracts of Ling, Skeen, and Roscoe Haynie would be honored; and several directors would resign, reducing the number from twenty-one to fourteen, including the newly elected Sam Wyly.

The meeting had been marked by acrimony, confusion, and even tears, though Ling didn't shed any. Despite the powerful threats, it is doubtful that the rebels could have brought off their coup in the face of firm resistance. The victors won with what might well have turned out to be bluffs. Not that Stewart and Fitts could not have made good on their threats. But on reflection, they might have discovered that the effect would have been as damaging to them as to Ling, with no apparent gains. Stewart's bank was not a major source of LTV credit or even one of the participants in its principal line of credit. The Bank of America was LTV's main bank, and its top management had indicated—to Ling at least—that they were *not* in favor of removing him. But Stewart's action would have meant that LTV had no credit at all from any of the three largest hometown banks, and that might have caused other banks in the credit line to refuse to renew LTV's subsidiaries' loans, which would have been most damaging.

If Fitts and the bondholders had publicly charged insolvency and succeeded in putting the corporation in receivership, First National almost surely would have called Ling's loan, to squeeze him even harder. That would have required him to liquidate his personal assets. But with LTV in receivership, the market for its stock and that of its subsidiaries would have fallen apart, and Ling's stock would have become nearly worthless. That would have created serious losses at both the First National and the Texas Bank, not only from Ling's stock but from loans made to others who had secured their borrowings with LTV's and its subsidiaries' securities. Pulling the plug on LTV and Ling could have made a shambles of the whole financial structure of the city of Dallas. Several other banks had millions in loans that were no longer fully covered by their collateral, as a result of the hair-raising slide in the Dow-Jones average that dropped it more than 300 points in a year and more than 160 in two months, with the bottom coming only nine days after LTV's Sunday-morning board meeting.

It is reasonable to assume that a disproportionate share of the bank-loan collateral in Dallas was securities of LTV and its subsidiaries. One local banker said that the bank examiners were well aware of the situation and generally were already willing to permit banks to carry loans if they were covered at least 80 percent by their collateral, even though that was neither sound nor legal. Major losses to the banks from the bankruptcy of LTV, then the city's largest employer, would have upset this precarious balance and probably caused the failure of a string of banks and large private investors. That, in turn, could well have produced a money panic in Dallas with grave consequences far beyond the city's borders.

Stewart, in joining Fitts's showdown game, certainly must not have considered that likelihood, unless he was only bluffing. But a major banking crisis surely would have been the result of their acting out their threats, whether they realized it or not. That Sunday morning, however, Ling did not think of such prospects. He fully believed that, aside from being wiped out himself, he also would be causing the liquidation of his corporation if he refused to give up at least the appearance of total control of his creation. Whether he was right or not is quite another matter, one of considerable tactical importance in terms of what was yet to come. Of even more importance was the strategy, if any, of the men who challenged Ling.

What did they hope to gain by toppling Ling? At best,

they may have harbored the hope that their announcement that Ling-Temco-Vought was now somehow different and better—"streamline" was the verb they used in their press release that Sunday—would cause the value of its securities to climb enough to take the heat off Post, Stewart, and everybody else involved. At worst, it has been suggested, they may have thought that if the corporation were put into receivership and ultimately liquidated, the holders of the 5s of 88 might wind up with 50 to 60 cents on the dollar, compared with a market price then only half that high. That represented a somewhat optimistic view of the value of the corporation's assets and a somewhat inaccurate view of their seniority in the debt structure. The corporation's assets probably would not have been worth enough to pay off the debt that had priority over theirs and still leave very much for the 5s of 88, let alone the stockholders that these directors had a legal obligation to serve. But there is reason to believe they did not know that at the time they made their initial move. In other words, it is conceivable that Ling's opponents attempted a dangerous coup without bothering to find out if it was *possible* to win.

That Sunday board meeting had ended in a truce that seemed to have relieved the mounting tension, even though no plan had been put forth for repairing the corporation. As the meeting ended, one of the surviving board members, Gustave Levy of Goldman, Sachs, said he thought the market would be happy with the changes. Levy, a man generally reputed to be one of the most agile traders in Wall Street, was wrong this time.

On the Street, the news of Ling's demotion and of Stewart coming in "on a non-salaried basis and for a limited time" was read as an evil portent. In New York that Monday morning, Ling's picture on page one of The New York Times and the report of a shake-up and an obscure banker in the top spot looked like trouble. If Levy bet on his prediction, he probably dropped a bundle. LTV's securities plunged. Commercial bankers in Dallas had reason to be frightened. If a loan backed by LTV common at 15 a share or the 5s of 88 at 29—their prices just before the meeting—

was shaky, consider the tremors that must have spread through Dallas the following week when the common fell to 7⅛ and the 5s nose-dived to 15. To the extent that the move against Ling was a rescue operation for Post, it failed.

The battle of the board room had established one fact: Jim Ling was no longer the omnipotent creator. Holes had been revealed in his stainless-steel resolution. He had been got at for the first time. The taste of defeat was as bitter for Ling as it would be for any man in his place. A week after the meeting, the Dallas *Times Herald*, whose publisher, Jim Chambers, was one of those who had resigned from Ling's board of directors, carried an editorial on the event. It hailed the fallen leader as a "sound citizen of Dallas," praised him for his business and charitable contributions to the city, and reflected that he "has been, is, and will continue to be a great citizen of Dallas. He deserves the community's compassion and support during this difficult period of his life." Other press mentions of the story, no matter how darkly they viewed LTV's future, seemed diffident about writing off Ling and noted that he had been up against the wall before and had come back. He might still have another shot at the title. Ling probably shared that view. But, as he himself understood well, the unthinkable had been thought, and the immovable had been moved.

There really was no reason why the move against Ling should have succeeded in solving anything, whatever the hopes of its participants. The corporation had serious short-term cash problems. And unless it was to get more than a face-lift, its short-term cash problems would soon become long-term capital problems. Some investors saw the move as a takeover by creditors, a sort of prelude to bankruptcy, and that certainly wasn't going to move the stock up. The vague way that Stewart was "positioned" in the hierarchy certainly didn't create an impression that major substantive changes were in the works. After all, his orientation to corporate finance was as a commercial banker. He had achieved a certain distinction in Dallas by having worked his way, before he was forty, to the top job in the bank, following in the footsteps of his grandfather. But his experience as a commercial banker was limited largely to assessing the risks of lending local businessmen short-term funds. It didn't take a lot of insight to figure out that Stewart's potential contribution to a financial structure as tangled as LTV's could only be a modest one. Even on a good day, as he himself recognized, he would be in over his head very quickly at LTV. That was why he agreed to take the title of chairman of the board only for a short time: his reputation would help push up the price of LTV's securities, and then he would withdraw and be replaced as chairman by Troy Post.

But if Stewart was only the front man and could not run LTV, somebody else had to. Though some people in Dallas had some idea of Fitts's role in the scheme at the time, he has never been publicly linked to it. He probably figured it could not help his own or Gulf Life Holding's image to be bracketed with a sick elephant. So he hung in the shadows, as he often prefers to do, and tried to exercise control of LTV from there. Fitts of course had been number two to Post at Greatamerica and undisputed head man at Gulf Life Holding. But both these were holding companies set up pretty much to run themselves. In neither did Fitts have anything to do with managing the operations of a large industrial corporation. But he tried. His method was to hold frequent meetings with Ling, reviewing, needling, blandishing.

During the first two weeks in June, Fitts and Ling met at least once every day that Ling was in Dallas, never in Ling's office. Ling left the city twice in those two weeks, once to go to Pittsburgh to work on the antitrust settlement, another time to Washington to assure the Pentagon that everything was going to be all right. Stewart went along on both those trips. Fitts hardly can be said to have seized the reins.

In the meantime, there was a power vacuum. Somebody had to be the boss, and that somebody turned out to be Jim Ling. To a substantial degree, he ran the company as he had before, but from a slightly lower position and without Clyde Skeen. One of the matters Ling had to handle was the removal of the last major obstacle to approval of the antitrust settlement by the federal court in Pittsburgh. Leaders of a Pittsburgh local of the United Steel Workers wanted assurance from LTV that their members would not lose jobs at Jones & Laughlin. Ling felt as strongly as ever that the key to LTV's future was the rapid recovery of J&L. The mounting suspense over the months of delay in getting the decree approved must have been great. When Ling met the union leaders in Pittsburgh at the beginning of June, accompanied by Chairman Stewart, he was anxious to get the thing over with now that it was so close to the end. In a letter to the union summing up his stand on their questions, Ling wrote: "You have my personal assurance that LTV has no plans to close the Pittsburgh works, or any other facility, or to decrease the hourly paid work force." It was a rather sweeping commitment, especially considering that the Pittsburgh works was one of J&L's chief problems and that no major effort could be made to improve the steel maker's waning earnings without cutting back, if not closing, this ancient mill.

Of course all Ling's letter really guaranteed was that the corporation had "no plans." It didn't actually say that LTV never would make such plans. And it also hung everything on Ling himself, which Stewart had encouraged. It was, after all, Ling's "personal assurance," not the corporation's, because he was no longer chief executive officer, and his word no longer was law, whatever the union people might think. By way of mitigation, Ling cites another statement in the letter: "It is my intention to obtain an independent study of ways and means by which the efficiency and viability of the entire J&L operation—including the Pittsburgh works—can be improved." That, he argues, provided LTV with an out if it did decide to cut back in Pittsburgh.

Ling's letter, however risky its commitment might have appeared, got the job done. The judge signed the agreement the following week, and LTV was finally in a position to do something about J&L. To that end, Ling had entered into negotiations with a management-consulting firm to prepare a study of the steel company's problems. The fact that he was not himself consulting sufficiently on the matter with the others apparently concerned Fitts. It was as though Ling still did not know his place.

The next step taken by Grant Fitts, while it seemed to

prepare for Ling's resumption of command, reduced even further his power on LTV's board. One morning in the second week in June, Fitts invited Ling to a meeting in his office, a typical occurrence during those weeks. When Ling arrived, he found not only Fitts but Troy Post. Fitts, it seems, had made a mistake in his efforts to repair LTV: Ling was the only one who could get the corporation out of its difficulties. Fitts then apparently suggested that, since everybody knew that Ling was still running the corporation, he would propose to the board that Ling resume the title of chief executive officer, but later, to avoid the publicity of more turmoil. Fitts also indicated that he would attempt to relieve some of Ling's personal financial burdens by proposing that the board grant Ling an option to buy 200,000 LTV shares at around 16 plus an offer of $4 million par value of an issue of a subsidiary's debentures, which the parent corporation itself owned. The offer would permit Ling to buy these debentures from LTV at market price, which was about a third of par. What is more, Ling would be allowed to pay for them with an interest-bearing note to the corporation. The net effect of this arrangement would be that Ling would wind up with an increase in his annual income of more than $160,000. What it would mean to the corporation would be an increase in its interest cost of that amount plus the fact that it would put into Ling's hands a debt obligation of $4 million and only receive a third of that amount in exchange.

Post also offered Ling a chance to buy something—about $3 million par of his own 5s of 88 at the market price, which was only about a fourth of par. He too would take Ling's note. How come, Ling wanted to know. So that Ling would also be a holder of the 5s and would identify with their interests. Ling thanked him but turned him down, noting that his own stockholdings gave him incentive enough and that, after all, the common stock was not worth much unless the debentures could be paid off.

When Ling asked Fitts how he intended to justify to the board his extremely generous offer, Fitts reportedly told Ling that he would state that he had simply acted in error against

Ling. Needless to say, Ling was pleased and even flattered at all this.

But there was more. Fitts wanted to give Ling extra help in running the corporation. The way he proposed to do that was to replace two outgoing pro-Ling directors—Dr. Vanda Davidson and LTV chairman emeritus Bob McCulloch—with choices of his own. One would be Vester Hughes, a Dallas lawyer who once had represented Ling but was now a close associate of Troy Post, and the other would be Dennis Lyons of Arnold & Porter, who was, among other things, an adviser to Fitts. The offer of financial help to Ling was made contingent upon his acceptance of a board of directors the majority of whose members would be aligned with Fitts and Post. Fitts insisted that the board needed men with the skills of Hughes and Lyons who could keep up with the speed of Ling's mind and the complexities of LTV's problems. Ling conceded that they were both able men, and he bought the package.

Instead of waiting for the next regular LTV board meeting, Fitts called a special meeting for the morning of Saturday, June 13. Hughes and Lyons were voted in as members. Roscoe Haynie, who had got the title of vice chairman at the special Sunday meeting the month before, gave it up in favor of Troy Post. And the executive committee, which had been dissolved at the same Sunday meeting, was reestablished with Post as its chairman and with Fitts, Ling, and Stewart as its members.

When the matter of the options and debentures for Ling came up, he was asked to leave the meeting room, a practice followed by many corporation boards. Fitts then noted that the board now had the membership it wanted, he denied any interest in taking over LTV, and he insisted that he never had any doubts about Ling's ability and that Ling could help in important ways to solve the corporation's problems, now that he was "restrained." He then proposed that the board help Ling out of his financial difficulties so he could devote his full attention to corporate affairs. When he outlined his aid plan for Ling, questions were raised about the legality and propriety of the proposal and whether shareholder approval would be required for the debenture deal, which would cost the corporation substantially in principal and interest. Ling himself had had some misgivings about the debenture offer, and, sometime later, while the whole proposal was being studied by the lawyers, he suggested that the debenture deal be replaced by more stock options. But nothing came of either proposal.

Some observers think the whole business of the blandishments to Ling was simply an attempt to con him into believing that he would soon resume command, in the face of continued erosion of his power. That may indeed have been the case, especially if one chose to believe in the existence of some diabolical plot. But in the face of the blunders made by Ling's opponents at critical points, it seems more likely that they didn't really understand what they were doing half the time and had only a vague notion the other half.

Nobody is suggesting that Stewart and Fitts are not able in their respective professions. But in the matter of assembling the wriggly elements of a running conspiracy, they turned out to be the rankest of amateurs. Nothing they attempted had any important effect on the general situation or on their particular problems. LTV's securities prices, after their initial drop in May, would gradually work back up to their levels of just before the May 17 meeting. What that meant was that the financial community decided maybe the bankers had not stepped in, as Stewart was trying to make everyone believe, and maybe LTV was still worth about what it had been recently. Ling still seemed to be in charge, whatever his title might be: the statement to the union in Pittsburgh indicated that. And if there was anybody who could find his way through the problems of the corporation, it had to be Ling. The belief also persisted that Troy Post might have some useful advice to give and was now in the position to give it. But the truth was that nobody outside and hardly anybody inside really had anything approaching an accurate picture of who was in charge and what was going on.

Fitts, Stewart, and Post almost certainly made their move

in the belief that it would make things better for LTV and for their respective stakes in it, at least by boosting the value of its securities. But that was not all that impelled the participants. Each had private motives as well that went beyond the profit principle and any concern they may have had for the welfare of the corporation whose direction they had tried to assume.

Troy Post was angry: Ling had made a fool of him by buying his Greatamerica with the 5s of 88 and then using Greatamerica's assets in his disastrous acquisition of Jones & Laughlin. Post might even have weathered the embarrassment of Tres Vidas or at least have been able to keep it afloat out of his own resources if Ling had not—by acquiring J&L—caused investors to lose faith in LTV. Many people knew that Post had helped Ling out of cash problems at various times, including the $750,000 loan that Post's American Life Insurance Company had made to Ling to help him complete his house in 1961. Post did not always make money from his investments with Ling, but there is no reason to think he didn't intend to. And they certainly were not in the habit of exchanging confidences. Ling seemed genuinely surprised when he heard that Post was under financial strain that evening at Grant Fitts's apartment. When the story of Tres Vidas began filtering through Dallas, people who had believed there was a certain shrewdness behind Post's bland façade were no longer so sure. And whatever hope Post may have entertained that Ling could work a quick miracle, especially if he were leaned on a little, soon dissolved. In its place, there was little more than the determination somehow to get even with Ling.

Stewart had been chairman of the First since he was thirty-eight, and now, at forty-five, he faced the beginnings of a power struggle at the bank. The collapse of Post, Ling, and LTV would mean huge losses for the bank and perhaps even cost Stewart his job. As chairman of LTV he was sticking his neck out even farther. He had given—or at least not denied—the impression that he represented other banks as well as the First when he took over as chairman of LTV. Unless something happened to save the situation, he was bound to get a lot of the blame.

Only Grant Fitts had managed to keep himself free of any public responsibility for the situation. And he stood to lose the least financially from a failure to make LTV look better. Even a total loss on all of Gulf Life Holding's 5s of 88 would have been manageable. It would have amounted to a decline of only 7 cents a share in the company's earnings and a write-off of assets of maybe $2 a share, nowhere near the ruin that others faced. Fitts also was getting $75,000 a year from an LTV employment contract and another $50,000 a year for giving up some stock options. So he would be out $125,000 a year in income, still nothing compared with the trauma faced by Stewart, Post, Ling, and Wyly, among others. But that was a lot to lose for a poor boy from Alabama who had made good in Texas. Beyond the money, Fitts was bothered by the fact that Ling still did not seem to be taking him seriously enough. The Monday after the special meeting that had put Hughes and Lyons on the board, Fitts loosed a barrage of letters, more than a dozen over the next three days, addressed to both Ling and Stewart ("Dear folks" or "Dear Bob and Jim"), mostly consisting of little pronouncements and pointed suggestions about the cutting of personnel and executive expenses ("Good hunting, men!" was one scrawled postscript) and about simplifying "our complex corporate structure" as well as others dealing with the redistribution of LTV's legal business and assignment of corporate titles, some sneering comments about lower-level executives he found personally offensive, and announcements of his vacation and business travel plans, in case anyone needed to consult with him.

After bulling the antitrust settlement to final approval, Ling now looked to Pittsburgh again as the way out. He had steeped himself in reports on the steel company's problems, and he probably knew more about that situation than anyone else in Dallas. So he began final negotiations with the consulting firm of Booz, Allen & Hamilton for a survey of steps to be taken to fix J&L. In the process, he failed to pay proper respect to the new regime. In a letter answering a Fitts complaint, Ling conceded that the executive committee might be useful in assisting him, but he also advised its members to pay more attention to what was going on.

Ling had already been back to Pittsburgh to persuade the J&L brass to go along with the Booz, Allen study and prepare for more supervision of the steel company's operations by LTV. The antitrust settlement had lifted an injunction against LTV's active participation in the management of the steel company. On June 25, Ling, Fitts, and Dennis Lyons were elected to the board of J&L. On that day, it certainly did not look as though Fitts and his people were about to move against Ling again, especially since less than two weeks earlier they had dangled the chief executive's title and all those financial goodies in front of him. It was true that he had a title a notch lower: president. And he had moved out of his huge office on the thirty-first floor of the LTV Tower, the one that had belonged to Troy Post until Greatamerica was acquired, and was now using his former office on the fifth floor. But nothing else seemed about to change. Only one more move was in the works. Stewart had stated that he would resign as chairman as soon as things got straightened out, so there was a question of who would succeed him. Post had been mentioned as the next chairman, but he had problems enough. Ling still wanted the title, of course, and had even been offered it at one point in those strange days.

But new troubles for his opponents which began surfacing at the end of the month may have made them more angry and worried and caused them to change their minds about sitting tight. For one thing, an attempt was being made by one of Post's creditors, Bernard Cornfeld's Investors Overseas Services, to foreclose on Tres Vidas because Post was overdue on a $5-million loan. Post sued IOS, claiming it had reneged on an agreement to produce long-term financing for a major expansion on the resort property, a group of apartment buildings. That would have improved Post's ability to pay. Now he was cut off from that important source of hope, because, whatever the outcome of the suit, he surely wasn't going to get any of the $38 million he and IOS had talked of, at least not right away, when he needed it. At about the same time, a lawsuit was being prepared by a Birmingham, Alabama, law firm on behalf of two Gulf Life Holding Company share-holders. It would charge that Grant Fitts, Gus Levy, and some friends, relatives, and associates profited improperly from a deal between Gulf Life and LTV. It would be some weeks before the suit reached the court in Dallas, but when it did, it might be difficult for Fitts to have anything further to do with Ling-Temco-Vought. Since he had been a director of both companies at the time of the transaction, he might appear to have had conflicting interests. Stewart certainly would not want himself and the bank to be associated with any of the unpleasantness that such a suit might cause. And since he had accomplished little in his admittedly temporary tenure as LTV's chairman, he was anxious to remove himself as far as possible from the scene of any further action. The next regularly scheduled meeting of the LTV board was to be on July 17. But as word spread from Birmingham to Washington to Dallas that the filing of the suit was imminent, the collaborators began considering action again.

One afternoon at the end of June, Bobby Stewart suddenly canceled a meeting called to discuss with Sam Wyly the University Computing Company $20-million debt to LTV Aerospace. Wyly had already arrived for the meeting when he was told Stewart couldn't make it. Stewart, it seems, had to go to New York to talk to some of LTV's top commercial bankers. When he returned, he went to Ling's office and told him that a special board meeting was being called for the next day, July 2, where he and Ling would be asked to submit their resignations. This move, following so closely on Stewart's meeting in New York, gave the impression that LTV's principal bankers wanted Ling out. That was not, it turned out, the case at all. But the Fitts people pressed for the removal of Ling and the installation of Eddie Acker—Braniff's financial man and a confidant of Post and Fitts—at or near the top of the LTV hierarchy. Ling refused to quit once he had spoken to some of LTV's bankers and was told that they did not seem to want to dump him. The special meeting took place, but Ling's opponents had decided to back off, so nothing happened. Ling had gained a short reprieve. But Fitts and his people controlled the board.

On the afternoon of Wednesday, July 8, Ling was summoned to Fitts's office. Even then, Ling attempted to hold out. Fitts was in a hurry now, so he gave a little, at Ling's insistence. Acker would not leave Braniff to become an executive of LTV; he would only get a seat on the board, Stewart's seat. And Paul Thayer, the boss of LTV Aerospace, would be named chairman (replacing Stewart), president (replacing Ling), and chief executive officer. Ling reportedly objected strongly to being removed from the LTV executive committee and from the board of J&L, but he settled for seats on the boards of LTV and Braniff and the title of vice chairman of the board (replacing Post). What is more, Fitts proposed that Ling's office be moved again, because he feared that Ling might continue to exercise control through Paul Thayer if he were conveniently located near his successor. For all his skills as an operating executive, Thayer was hardly an adept in the intricate style of LTV finance, and Fitts wanted him shielded from the old master. All this was to be implemented at another special board meeting to be held the next day.

By morning, word of the impending meeting had spread through the executive offices of LTV. People who might know something were buttonholed for some indication of what was going to happen. Everybody sensed that the outcome was not going to be happy for Ling and his people. People like Bob McCulloch, now a director emeritus who could attend meetings but not vote, passed in and out of Ling's office to get the word. At midday, Ling went up to Grant Fitts's Gulf Life Holding Company office on the nineteenth floor of the LTV Tower. He was seen again briefly in the late afternoon as he proceeded to the board room. The meeting was called for 5:00 P.M.

Eddie Acker was there to be initiated into the seat to be vacated by his cousin Bobby Stewart. An ambitious man, Acker often gave the impression he was meant for bigger things, as he did that afternoon. (He would soon rise to the presidency of Braniff.) Dennis Lyons, an ally of Fitts for some months now, seemed destined for higher horizons too. He was one of the brighter lights among the sixty-odd partners in his law firm now that Thurman Arnold was dead, Abe Fortas (whom he replaced as counsel for Braniff when Fortas went onto the Supreme Court) was out, and Paul Porter was nearing retirement. The firm had billed LTV more than $700,000 for its year of work on the antitrust case, though Lyons himself had not had much to do with it. Now he was about to gain a great deal more legal business from LTV, and some people even thought he might have an interest in an executive position in the corporation. He was a man of unquestioned ability as a lawyer. The fact that he may have been confused about some aspects of LTV's financial structure at that time reflected more on its complexity and its current problems than on his talents as a legal adviser to Fitts.

Everybody present, except Ling and Roscoe Haynie, had some reason to believe that his best interests lay with the new men and not with Ling. A new and fatter employment contract was in the works for Harding Lawrence. The prospect that Braniff might buy Tres Vidas and bail out Troy Post had also been suggested. The only problem seemed to be the effect that opening the club to the public might have on members who had already paid a lot to exclusivity. Even at the moment, however, a man close to the situation predicted that the deal would never go through, no matter how favorably it might be presented to the airline board. But it was a source of new hope for Post. Paul Thayer, ready or not, was about to step into the top LTV job, a move that Ling went along with. And Roy Edwards, head of Wilson & Company, was a man who certainly could be said to have bright prospects in the organization. Sam Wyly had yet to settle his disputed debt to LTV Aerospace, and though he was close to Ling, his interests at that moment did not rest primarily with Ling. Gus Levy and Bill Osborn would be less than prudent if they risked their substantial commissions from LTV's financial offerings because of any feelings of friendship or loyalty to Ling.

Bobby Stewart chose not to attend the meeting. Instead, each member was presented with a copy of Stewart's resignation from the chairmanship and the board. The meeting lasted a little more than two hours, and it ended with the summoning of John Johnson, LTV's public-relations vice president, who was presented by Dennis Lyons with a previously composed press release announcing all that the board had done. Johnson was not invited to alter the wooden prose that began: "In completion of the management reorganization at Ling-Temco-Vought, Inc., which was commenced in May, a spokesman for the company states . . ." Johnson carried the release up the back stairs to his office on the sixth floor, where he phoned and wired it out to the press. It was front-page news in Dallas but not in New York, where it settled onto the financial pages.

When the members of the board left the meeting, they did not smile or pause in the corridors as they had when they arrived. They disappeared quickly. While the meeting was in progress, hardly anybody among the executive staff left the floor. Men who did not generally have much contact drifted in and out of each other's offices, drinking Cokes and coffee, knowing full well what was supposed to happen but perhaps hoping the outcome might be different. One who was sure he would not survive the next cut was Francis X. Reilly, a corporate vice president.

Fran Reilly may well have triggered Fitts's first attempts to move against Ling. He was the man who—at Ling's direction—had moved LTV's employee-insurance business away from Grant Fitts's company without giving Fitts a chance to underbid and keep it. Among the dozen letters Fitts had fired at Stewart and Ling in the previous month, one specifically designated Reilly as "surplus" in Fitts's splenetic book, though not for any discernible reason reflecting on his ability or service to the corporation. In a sense, men such as Reilly are the most wounded of casualties in the corporate wars. The man who runs a boring mill at LTV Aerospace has no cause to concern himself about his job, no matter what happens at the LTV Tower, so long as his company has metal for him to mill. And at the other end, a Clyde Skeen may lose his job, but he has an employment contract that assures him a substantial income, and he is prominent enough to find something else suitable to his ability if that should become necessary. But Fran Reilly had neither anonymity nor special prominence, and he knew it.

As he waited for the meeting to end, he confronted his own situation unhappily. The year 1970 was not the best time to be looking for a high-salaried executive job. Reilly, a Dartmouth Phi Beta Kappa and a Harvard lawyer, had gone to Chicago in 1953 to work for Wilson & Company as a lawyer, negotiator, and financial administrator. At the time that LTV completed its acquisition of his employer, Reilly was Wilson's treasurer, responsible for its entire financial system. He came down to Dallas with the merger and took a financial management job at LTV headquarters. It did not seem to entail any special risks. The Wilson deal had been Ling's crowning achievement, and LTV's stock soared as Wall Street put its blessing on the man from Dallas. Reilly's savings seemed as secure in shares of LTV as they had been in Wilson stock. He would use the dividend income to educate his children. At least, that is how he had it figured. But even before the move against Ling, the future of LTV dividends had become less than promising, and the value of his stock had tumbled along with everybody else's. And now, approaching fifty-four, he faced the most harrowing work of all, looking for another job. He sipped his coffee, shaking his head, and then he brightened a little. "I can't imagine," he said, "that a man with my training, ability, and experience won't be able to find another job." It was a logical conclusion, however difficult it might be to sustain in the dreary context. But Reilly, a victim, managed the best of all. He landed on his feet, as vice president and treasurer of B. F. Goodrich.

When the meeting broke up, Reilly, along with the rest of the executive staff, was summoned to Ling's office for a personal word from the deposed leader. Drinks were served, and Ling, with considerably more emotion than his bland delivery usually carried, passed the word. When he emerged alone, Scotch in hand, from a side door, his eyes were red and he was wounded. His farewell to his officers over, he hurried upstairs to the Lancers Club at the top of the LTV Tower to drink and speculate with some friends and associates from outside the company. They expressed determination to help him in whatever he wanted to do, but he didn't know what he wanted to do. He was angry. Maybe he should consider calling a special stockholders' meeting and taking his fight to the grass roots. But somebody pointed out that he didn't control enough shares to call a special meeting on his own. A banker indicated that he could bring pressure to bear on some of the people involved in Ling's demise and that they damned well better help Ling or he would squeeze them hard. (Later these people did help Ling.) Ling wasn't sure what he might want from them at that point. Everybody had another drink and railed at the enemy. Then Ling went home.

15

THEY moved Ling and only one of his two secretaries up to a small suite of offices on the twenty-sixth floor of the Tower, the only LTV people on that floor. With only one secretary, he sometimes had to answer his own phone, something he hadn't had to do in years. But, as Ling had told Fitts months before, he was still a long way from the legendary $2,000 stake of 1946, and he was tough enough to give up the perquisites without suffering too big a blow to his ego.

However badly he had fared, a lot of people in Dallas still figured he was in good shape as long as he held onto his fabulous house. According to a Texas law that originated back in the days of the Texas Republic, a man cannot be forced to give up his homestead, his horse, or his plow even in bankruptcy. In fact, once a man has paid off the mortgage, he cannot get another one on that house. This law helps protect from indigence women whose husbands might not be able to resist hocking the old homestead to take yet another flyer on something like an oil well. It even makes a sale contingent on the knowledge and approval of the wife. There was considerable speculation in Dallas that Ling's splendid house, the well-situated land, and the costly furnishings including his Camille Pissarro painting would remain his, as long as he made the mortgage and tax payments. In fact, some even figured that he had put so much money in the house in the first place to provide himself with a kind of reserve against bankruptcy. But those people did not know Ling and did not realize that the prospect of personal failure almost never figured in his plans. By this time, however, the house was not even his. He had pledged it to Sam Wyly and UCC as partial collateral for his loans and was living in it as a tenant.

Ling continued to attend directors' meetings and keep in touch with LTV's financial problems. His own economic future—that is, his prospects for getting out from under his bank debts—still depended largely on the value of his LTV shares and, therefore, on LTV's chances for recovery. He offered suggestions for refinancing the debt and recombining the units of the conglomerate to produce tax advantages and unlock encumbered assets. And he played a lot of golf and thought about his future.

The stock market still seemed unsure of what had happened in Dallas and what was likely to come of it. LTV's stock hung in a range about where it had been before the move against Ling. Neither Ling nor his opponents nor his successors said much for publication, and, judging from the absence of "inside dope" stories, they apparently weren't saying much off the record either. There really wasn't much to be said. The problems were all still there. The new management was doing nothing more hopeful than cutting more overhead, increasing the reserves for losses, eliminating dividends on various securities, and scurrying around trying to figure out where to lay hands on enough cash to pay interest and loans as they came due. J&L made a valiant attempt to create hope by turning in a "profit" for the second quarter of 1970 of $101,000, all of it from tax credits. But the figure had no effect on the market because it sounded as though someone—having decided that any six-figure profit (plus $1,000) would persuade somebody that things were better—simply made that figure happen. There is enough latitude in accounting practices, particularly covering quarterly figures (which need not be certified by the auditors), to "create" at least that much "profit" in a big corporation, no matter how scrupulous its bookkeeping. So J&L—which had lost money in the second half of 1969 and the first quarter of 1970—squeaked into the black, for a few minutes.

All in all, the total effect of the agonizing reshuffling was to cut the staff, shatter the morale, and get rid of Jim Ling. If there were other objectives, they came to nothing. Within a few weeks, Troy Post resigned from the board. But if Ling's ouster had been designed to get Post a better price for his LTV debentures, it failed. The price of the 5s recovered somewhat, reflecting falling interest rates and some speculative interest. After all, when those debentures had dropped, after Ling's demotion, to $15 a hundred, their $5-per-year interest was yielding a return equal to 33⅓ percent, and even at $25 they yielded 20 percent, a good return for even so shaky an investment.

In a matter of months, Dennis Lyons of Arnold & Porter, then Grant Fitts and Vester Hughes, Post's lawyer, resigned from the board. Stewart was already off, of course. And in the new year, Sam Wyly resigned too, but by then he and Ling had gone into a new business together. That venture would relieve Ling of his immediate financial burdens and give him another chance. But it would require him to bet everything he owned.

The strange withdrawal of the contestants from the field was barely noticed and hardly mentioned in print. Yet, in a way, it was as important as their arrival in May, even more so. When they came, they could rely on the empty rhetoric of business to substitute for explanation of their purpose. They could "announce a major restructuring of the corporation in a move designed to streamline the company's operations." Their press release could talk about "confidence in the future of LTV," "turnaround for LTV," "best interests of both company and stockholders," "be more effective and closer to operations," and similar meaningless statements. When they left, they tried to do the same thing. "Mr. Post stated that he was resigning his offices to devote his full time to his personal investments." When Lyons quit, "personal reasons prompted his resignation." And when Fitts and Hughes followed him, the press release reported that Thayer said, "Both men have made a fine contribution to the company, but their business affairs and commitments forced them to relinquish their role as LTV directors." That is the bulk of the public record covering one of the strangest events in recent business history. As epilogue, there came an announcement a few months later that Troy Post had sold a large share of his real-estate holdings, including a chunk of Tres Vidas, for "an undisclosed amount of cash."

Nothing was said about the months of virtually fruitless infighting that had begun that evening in May when Ling was invited to Grant Fitts's apartment to discuss ways of helping Troy Post out of his troubles. It was as though none of it had happened. The fourteenth largest industrial corporation in the United States was shaken to its foundations for months with almost no apparent effect, and then the whole chain of events ended with no other record than those canned statements of hope, regret, and good wishes and some rehashing of the clippings and the legends.

The strange departure of the conspirators against Ling before they had accomplished any of their presumed objectives leads to the conclusion that they simply gave up once they discovered the difficulties they had taken on. One LTV executive says they left when they concluded that LTV could not meet its obligations and would have to declare bankruptcy. Another suggests that they ran away in fear of legal action by shareholders. Still another says, "It was all spite against Jim. Once Fitts got him out, he didn't care much about anything else." Or some of all three.

Whatever their reasons, they left the huge burden of LTV to Paul Thayer, the onetime war ace and test pilot, and George Griffin, Ling's master financial technician. Both had enjoyed close personal relationships with Ling in the past, but neither wanted to turn to him now for help. After all, they were the leaders and ought to be able to work things out themselves. Ling had been fond of the term "game plan," but Thayer now referred to the need for a "battle plan" to emphasize the enormity of the situation. And they tried hard not to pay too much attention to the master plans, concepts, game plans, financial profiles, and all the other ideas that Ling continued to formulate and dispatch to

Thayer (and which provided the basis for many of their actions to keep the company afloat). Ling was still a director and vice chairman of the board, and he felt a strong obligation to help, though he knew that they didn't want to seem to be listening to him. Occasionally, they found Ling useful as an emissary and negotiator with their creditors, and Ling even got to pilot an LTV Falcon jet once in a while on company business. But mostly they wanted to avoid anything that would give support to rumors around Dallas that Ling either was still running LTV from the background or that he might take over again, which certainly crossed his mind.

It may be difficult to imagine how he could get started again with the bulk of his assets tied up as inadequate collateral for bank loans. But Ling still had friends, allies, and awed fans, and that combination—plus his loan guarantors at UCC—would help to bail him out and give him a way to start a new enterprise. There were plenty of offers of jobs and deals. A major New York investment-banking firm offered him a partnership. He got calls and letters from all over the country wishing him well and offering him deals. Ben Hogan invited him to play golf one day just to make him feel better, it seemed. Ling needed a vacation, but he knew it would not be much fun until he could get the burden of his debts off his back for a while. Ling and Sam Wyly worked out an arrangement for extending Wyly's and UCC's guarantee on Ling's loan at Stewart's First National, for which Ling gave Wyly the voting rights and an option on his LTV stock. Ling's other assets included an option to buy 100,000 additional shares of LTV stocks at 12⅝ a share. That option was then worth about $500,000. Ling also had an employment contract with LTV worth about $300,000 a year for ten years. While he was working out his new plan, Ling received a bid for his house from Lamar Hunt, son of H. L. Hunt and owner of the Kansas City Chiefs football team and most of the professional tennis players in the world. In a handwritten letter, Hunt offered about half what the place was worth. Ling turned him down.

When Ling worked out his loan agreement with Wyly, the

two also established a plan for a new corporation. Ling would put his employment contract and his stock option into the deal, and Wyly's University Computing Company would put into it two small companies it owned, in exchange for stock. The new venture would be called Omega-Alpha, the reverse of the Greek letters with which Ling had named the personal holding company through which he held his LTV stock.

At one point, Wyly and Ling talked of a plan for buying from Fitts's insurance companies their holdings in Ling-Temco-Vought and putting them into Omega-Alpha. That would probably have given the new company enough LTV securities and options to take over control of LTV again. Ling always felt that he knew how to set his original creation right again. But the parties couldn't come to terms, so the prospect of retaking LTV finally eluded Ling. Meanwhile, he and Wyly continued shaping their new corporation into what they hoped would become, in Wyly's words, "a wealth-producing vehicle." Ling stayed on in his homestead for a time. But without his LTV salary, which had run to $375,000 a year with bonuses, he was hard pressed to meet its high operating expenses. He shopped around for something more modest and wound up with another house in the neighborhood that cost him less than $300,000 to buy and a lot less to operate than the celebrated château. Lamar Hunt finally did manage to buy the big one from UCC, but he paid about $1.5 million for it.

In November, 1970, to replace his employment contract, a new agreement was drawn up that would still provide Ling, or rather his new Omega-Alpha, with about $160,000 a year, instead of $300,000. Ling also surrendered his 100,000-share option to buy more LTV stock, and he became a consultant to LTV rather than an employee, though for the time he remained on the board, with the title of vice chairman.

Ling had a special regard for the Okonite Company, despite its relatively poor recent performance. When he was still running LTV, he once remarked that if LTV couldn't find a suitable buyer for the maker of cable and floor covering, he might put together a syndicate of investors and buy it himself—he liked it that much. He gave sound business reasons for his interest, and they no doubt existed. But his interest also seems somehow connected with his memories of his days in the Navy stringing Okonite cable in the Philippines. He had so often described Okonite as "the Cadillac of the industry" that his associates frequently echoed his phrase, as they surrounded him at meetings. After all, who among them knew its products from actually working with them?

With his new LTV contract, he no longer had the option that might have helped him move back into LTV. But he was free to consider buying Okonite. That would take a lot of new money. So, meanwhile, Omega-Alpha bought a smaller company, Harbor Boat Building Company, from Tyler Corporation, a medium-sized Dallas conglomerate. So much had happened to Ling and LTV in the interim that few outsiders recalled that Tyler Corporation had itself been an LTV creation known as Saturn Industries, which Ling had set up in 1966 to help his former associate Joe McKinney, and that in those days Harbor Boat had belonged to LTV until it was acquired by Saturn. One feature of the Harbor Boat deal was that Tyler would guarantee to reimburse Omega-Alpha for the difference if the boat company earned less than $1 million before taxes in 1971. That assured the new enterprise of enough cash to operate, no matter how the other subsidiaries it got from UCC—a construction-equipment leasing company and an installer of special equipment for the oil-refining and petrochemical industries—fared during the year.

But the big prize in Ling's book was Okonite, which also owned General Felt Industries, a major floor-covering manufacturer. LTV had had several offers for Okonite or parts of it, but none materialized. Ling had made his interest known when his contract was rewritten, and he set about trying to find the $40 million or so that the acquisition would require. Omega-Alpha took on as its investment bankers the recently expanded New York firm of CBWL-Hayden Stone, and the search for money was on. Plenty of bigtime investors were interested in being associated with Ling in his new venture, in some cases, it seemed, as much for the magic that still clung to him as for the numbers in the deal.

But there were obstacles to his acquiring Okonite. One was an anonymous letter written to the stock exchanges and to government regulating agencies accusing Ling and his new enterprise of all sorts of dubious practices. The charges appeared baseless, but the letter did apparently cause the SEC to delay the effective date of an LTV security registration statement, and it caused temporary apprehension on all sides. Then just before LTV's board, with Ling absent, approved his acquisition of Okonite, a higher offer came in. The bidder, it transpired, had no money, but his offer nevertheless caused some painful breath-holding by Ling and his associates. Omega-Alpha had offered $40.5 million for Okonite, and this new bid was for $45 million. It appeared that maybe somebody was trying to infect the proceedings with the notion that LTV was giving Ling special consideration by selling Okonite to Omega-Alpha too cheap. Neither the source of the letter nor the motive for the counter-offer ever became clear, but one possibility was that it came from a high Okonite executive who feared he might lose his job in any housecleaning that followed the sale.

There is always legitimate concern about self-dealing and conflict of interest in any transaction among principals with the complex relationships of LTV, UCC, Omega-Alpha, Jim Ling, and Sam Wyly. That was one reason why Wyly resigned from the LTV board before it considered the Okonite sale. It was why Ling had nothing to do with the vote either, even though he remained on the LTV board. Despite the strange, fluid, convoluted deals in which Ling has been involved, he has managed to emerge with his reputation intact (though some LTV shareholders filed suits attempting to undo the Okonite sale). The nearest thing to a blot on his shield was the SEC action against him and his associates in Electro-Science Investors back in 1964. It is natural, of course, that financial conservatives should look down their noses at Jim Ling's free-wheeling ways. But the difference is more a matter of personal taste and style than ethics or principles. When Ling began working his Omega-

Alpha machine, a New York investment banker asked an executive of LTV if Ling were a crook. The LTV man, familiar with Ling and his methods for a decade, was astonished at the question, but finally replied, "Jim Ling is the most honest man I know." And he was serious.

Ling's mind can get to places inaccessible to others until after he has shown the way. He has an awesome instinct for his special brand of finance. But he has also demonstrated curious naïveté and insensitivity to the feelings and motives of others. He seldom stops to find out if others are keeping up with him, and he is occasionally impatient when they are not or when they disagree. But it is not disdain that shapes these feelings so much as his apparent disbelief that Jim Ling, drop-out, really can be so far ahead of his audience. This failure to communicate his soaring plans as he unfolds them has left people who should have been kept informed ignorant of where he was taking them, and it has created dangerous antagonisms.

This time, Ling was determined to avoid his past errors. His new investment-banking firm, CBWL-Hayden Stone, itself a very flashy young operation, helped him get the new enterprise into shape. That was quite a job, since its principal asset, aside from the buy-out of his LTV employment contract and his house, had been his debt-laden LTV shares, deeply connected with the Wylys and University Computing. But Ling finally managed to get federal court approval of his purchase of Okonite from LTV, after some unpleasant moments in the court in Pittsburgh. Because of the pending Okonite deal, Ling resigned from the LTV board and CBWL set about the job of selling his LTV shares. For once, after a long interval, his timing was good. Jones & Laughlin, in the first quarter of 1971, seemed to be turning around after a couple of disastrous years. It earned enough to resume paying dividends. That meant LTV would have a little more cash income, and its stock price zoomed up, actually passing 27 briefly. By the time CBWL was able to put Ling's shares into the market (there was a last minute foul-up while the SEC was deciding whether Ling could sell them, since he might still be considered a "controlling person" under the law, a thought that amused and annoyed Ling, who had been thrown out of the company he supposedly might still be controlling), the price had fallen back a little. But he still managed to net about $9 million from the disposal, enough to get him out of his major debts.

LTV's stock then fell back sharply when the corporation announced it was getting out of Braniff by selling some of its shares and trading others, along with additional LTV common shares, for what turned out to be about $200 million of the 5s of 88. And LTV lost money again in 1971 and had to postpone repayment of bank debt.

So Ling was out of LTV and into Omega-Alpha, and LTV was out of both Okonite and Braniff, as it had to be under the terms of its settlement with the Justice Department. Ling began his Omega-Alpha operations with only sophisticated professionals as his investors. Soon, though, he had an SEC registration, which gave him public shareholders and a market. In fact, when Omega-Alpha offered its shares to the public in late August, 1971, at 5½, they were oversubscribed and rose briefly to 6¼. There are still a lot of people who are betting their money with him. But they will probably go with him as much from faith in the old magic as from understanding of his complex new vehicle. If so, there may be a new company on which he can put his name.

Meanwhile, the old one had been considering dropping his name, at the suggestion of, among others, Ling himself. As part of its efforts to pull out of its doldrums and solve some of its cash problems, it was considering merging itself into Jones & Laughlin and giving the new company a new name which, in the words of one of Ling's last memos to his successors, "would eliminate the public relations stigma attached to LTV and partially eliminate the drabness associated with any company principally involved in the steel industry."

The corporation did change its name from Ling-Temco-Vought, Inc., in the spring of 1972, though the new one, while it eliminated Ling's name, was hardly an inspiration. It is now officially LTV Corporation. About the only thing left with Ling's name is a $2.50 1/48-scale, all-plastic assembly kit of the "Ling-Temco-Vought A-7D Corsair II," still on sale in a lot of toy stores. (Its real-life prototype had, of course, been a major source of LTV sales and profits during the good years.)

Needless to say, Ling's Omega-Alpha was moving, if not exactly flying. He had reshuffled Okonite's management and was attempting to solve its excess-capacity problems, in the hope that the company—now wholly owned by the parent Omega-Alpha—could be put back onto the stock market as a redeployed subsidiary, along with Okonite's former subsidiary, General Felt. In fact, Ling took his Project Redeployment concept along with him when he left LTV. (The very expression must certainly be taboo in the shrunken executive headquarters of LTV.)

Late in 1971, Omega-Alpha began the process of acquiring a corporation listed on the New York Stock Exchange that offered Ling a way to resume the pursuit of his redeployment method. That corporation, Transcontinental Investing Corporation, a real-estate development company that had branched out into finance and phonograph-record distribution, needed shaking up. What is more, it offered Ling's Omega-Alpha access to some assets that could be converted readily into cash, plus at least one subsidiary that seemed a likely candidate for redeployment to the public, once it was reorganized. That is Transcontinental Music Corporation, the third largest record rack-jobber.

Even before the shareholders of Omega-Alpha and Transcontinental Investing had approved the acquisition, Ling was preparing his next moves, since he would become chairman, chief executive officer, and biggest stockholder of the merged enterprise. When it was finally put together, the merged company expected to have sales of somewhere between $300 million and $400 million—not bad for a beginning, and big enough to afford a used Falcon jet for its leader, but still only about 10 percent of what LTV had been at its biggest and shakiest.

In the process of working himself out of his crushing financial problems and into the saddle of this new company, Ling also seems to have had the opportunity to look carefully at what went wrong the last time. This time, he seems determined to avoid high debt and, especially, high interest rates. And his new redeployment plan involves an old financial device for getting shares of Omega-Alpha's subsidiaries into the hands of the public. He plans to spin them off in a variation of a more or less classic device by offering the right to buy these subsidiary securities to Omega-Alpha's shareholders first, rather than to the general investing public.

Just past his forty-ninth birthday, Ling looked as fit and sounded as enthusiastic as he did back in 1964 when he was spinning out the details of his first Project Redeployment offerings. He still talks fast and easily, using complex financial terms and unfamiliar abbreviations and acronyms for the subsidiaries he is readying for the market. It appears that Ling is more aware of the operating problems and the need for good managers and controls than he was in his last and most expansive days at LTV. He no longer seems driven to build an enterprise of the scale of his old one, though he does seem to enjoy as much as ever designing financial machinery and making it work. The Ling towers may not reach their former heights, but they may well be even more dazzling. The prospectuses will be long and complicated. But the prospects these days seem brighter. In any event, here comes Jim Ling again.

Meanwhile, the questions of why he paid $425 million cash for Jones & Laughlin and why a broker advised his customers then to buy LTV at 120 fade into the past. The stories are now saying that Ling is up to his old tricks again, whatever that means. And one—an article in *Forbes* magazine—even parodied a future business-school class in which Omega-Alpha was the case study. The article ended with the following conversation: The professor, watching some students leave the class, asked, "Where are you guys going?" One answered, "To my broker. I'm buying Omega-Alpha stock." Another said, "I'm going to mine, too. But I'm selling short." The third said, "I'm quitting business school to work for Ling."

EPILOGUE

———◆———

LING-TEMCO-VOUGHT is still around, of course—as LTV. But nobody in Washington or anywhere else considers it any longer a threat to American civilization. It is left with a group of not very interesting companies—in steel, in meat packing, in aerospace, among others—and with a lot of debt to pay off, costing interest in the meantime. Whatever else its managers will confront in their continuing efforts to keep it afloat while they try to turn its operating units around, they are not likely to produce another remarkable stock-market phenomenon.

Ling himself is happily building another vehicle, and his new one may turn out to be a more stable means for him to work his various theories. He is less likely to get hung up in ponderous businesses like Jones & Laughlin—certainly not without knowing more about their nature and their problems than he did that day in the Cleveland hotel room when he agreed to pay an inflated book value for a company that had never sold in the market for the price he paid. If he focuses on comprehensible companies that are not overburdened by unalterable tradition and intractable managements, he may even get back into the billion-dollar club some day soon. And his redeployment idea may well prove to be an effective way to solve the enormous problems of managing large-scale enterprises, if each of Omega-Alpha's publicly held subsidiaries is permitted enough autonomy so that they do not have to bail each other or their parent out of financial difficulties when that is not in their own best operating interests.

Ling's nemesis, Richard W. McLaren, is out of the Justice Department. He is a federal district judge in Chicago. Whether that was a promotion or not is a matter of debate, as are his accomplishments during his three years as head of the antitrust division. The suit against LTV's acquisition of Jones & Laughlin, however damaging it was to LTV's stock-market performance, was not what brought Ling down or thwarted the corporation's growth. The suit had nothing to do with the fact that the $40 million or more that Ling still expected his companies to earn as late as the fall of 1969 turned out at year end to be only a little more than $2 million. That terrible surprise had to be the result of his subsidiary managers either lying to him or not knowing how poorly they were doing, or both. Project Redeployment had failed to provide headquarters with information it had to have. It is inconceivable that Chevrolet could approach the close of a disastrous year without General Motors' headquarters management knowing what was happening. But that is what happened at LTV. McLaren had nothing to do with that.

The curious settlement terms of the lawsuit in effect indicated that the Justice Department concluded that it had no valid case and had caused LTV to suffer enough for its unseemly behavior. Neither the suit nor the settlement established any significant guides or deterrents to conglomerates, acquisitions, or economic concentration. The Justice Department filed a similar suit against ITT's acquisition of the Hartford Fire Insurance Company and then agreed in 1971 to a similar settlement, permitting ITT to keep Hartford if it divested itself of some of its other acquisitions. Again, the only principle that seemed to issue from the consent decree was that if you are going to take over some venerable American corporation, the Justice Department is going to make you suffer in some way to be agreed upon in court. (Since then, Ralph Nader, another free-form Big Business fighter, has sought to undo the ITT-Hartford deal in a court action filed in Connecticut. Meanwhile, questions of

the merits of the antitrust action and the justice of the settlement have been obscured by the recent controversy over
ITT's relations with the Administration.)

Late in 1971, the House Judiciary Committee's antitrust
subcommittee finally came out with its staff report, a 703-
page document with three-and-a-half pages of "Conclusions
and Recommendations." Congressman Celler's "Investigation of Conglomerate Corporations" had previously taken
several thousand pages of testimony and exhibits, published
in seven fat volumes. This material will certainly provide
students of recent American business history with more than
enough reading matter, a lot of it of great value and interest.
The investigation failed, however, to provide answers to any
of the basic questions about conglomerates, such as whether
they are more or less efficient than other kinds of corporate
organization; whether their growth has been dangerous to
business, to stockholders, or to the undefined public interest;
or how the public interest ought to be safeguarded and by
and against whom.

The report, largely a summary of the subcommittee's
gleanings, included such statements as this: "Some observers
foresee a situation where the American economy will be dom-
inated by a few hundred business suzerainties and under
whose influence a multitude of small, weak, quasi-independ-
ent corporations will be permitted a subordinate and sup-
plemental role." The subcommittee's staff can be excused for
such banalities on the grounds that its task was a virtually
impossible one. It can also be excused for recommending
as its major legislative proposal an old hat from Emanuel
Celler's rack, that an Office of Industrial Organization be
set up in the Executive Office of the President "for control
and supervision of major corporate structures in the economy." They surely could not have meant that as The Way
to deal with conglomerates, Big Business, mergers, or anything else.

The report's failure—an inevitable one—is that it does
not recognize, let alone come to terms with, the inchoate,
irrational nature of business, business management, and businessmen. In its section on ITT, the report discusses the

efforts of ITT's Avis car-rental subsidiary to get a garage in Paris that had been owned by Chrysler, a major supplier of cars to Avis. On the stand, ITT's chairman, Harold Geneen, had shrugged the matter off as local and French and of minor importance. But, the report noted, it was important enough to be mentioned by Winston Morrow, boss of Avis, in his Manager's Monthly Letter. "Certainly," the report observes, "men of the importance in ITT's organization as Mr. Morrow and Mr. Geneen would not concern themselves with details that they thought were not important."

That statement pretty much sums up the failure of the report and, for that matter, of many observers, critics, and analysts of business. There simply isn't any way of saying with certainty what "men of the importance" of Geneen would or should concern themselves with.

The information and the documents gathered by the subcommittee might well provide the basis for an examination of the efficiency of conglomerates and of large-scale enterprise in general. But, even then, it would be impossible to draw any abstract conclusions that would be valid throughout business. General Motors used to be the model of corporate efficiency, but lately it seems to be less so. A lot of conglomerates have done poorly. But others have done well, including ITT and Loew's Corporation, among others. Success has stemmed from acquisitions in some instances and in spite of them in others, and even that is not a consistent circumstance in any specific corporation. Success or failure, as revealed at the systems-ridden Litton Industries, too often can be seen only after the fact, though not invariably then.

But if a congressional subcommittee, with its skilled staff people and its ability to subpoena witnesses and documents costing millions in man-hours to produce, cannot provide the bases for determining and protecting the public interest, who can?

The securities industry cannot be expected to do the job. After all, its interest is in selling securities to public and institutional investors. The Donaldson, Lufkin & Jenrette recommendation to buy LTV in 1968 at 120—however well-intentioned and supported by intellectual reasons—was not a sound judgment. Nor was it atypical of the enthusiasm of the securities industry for its products. The recent history of the so-called performance funds amply demonstrates the ability of intelligent men to deceive themselves as well as their customers. Mutual funds used to be nice things for widows and orphans to invest in; they weren't supposed to be hot stocks, just safe ones. Then along came people like Gerald Tsai, and the funds were performing like uranium stocks in the good old days. But when it appeared that there was nothing much holding many of them up except zeal, they collapsed, along with the market, or ahead of it, in some cases.

The wages of greed, obviously, is not wages; it is either big winnings or big losses or both. There are plenty of answers, of course. Things like: investigate before you invest. But how? The prospectuses are supposed to provide investors with all the relevant information about companies and their securities, and maybe they do. But few ordinary people can wade through them and work out their crazy dynamics. So they turn to their brokers and their brokers' security analysts, who are looking to sell them securities.

The SEC wants corporations to disclose *more* information about their operations in their prospectuses. That probably won't hurt. But who is it going to help, except the printers of prospectuses?

Perhaps more to the point are proposals that accounting principles ought to require disclosure, in simple ways, of the realities of earnings and assets rather than the fantasies of imaginative corporate builders. But what, after all, is simple to an ordinary investor or even a securities analyst?

Ralph Nader may be expected to have some answers. His recent court action against the ITT-Hartford merger indicates yet another kind of tactic against Big Business. But his efforts to get public members onto corporate boards of directors seem somehow irrelevant to the fundamental and still largely unfathomable problems of the motives of corporate managers and investors and the effects of growth and size on business efficiency. Even Nader's relentless passion and his remarkable ability to make news are unlikely to produce public directors who will know much about business and the public interest, however that is defined.

Neither Naderism nor its populist and trustbusting predecessors seem to offer much in the way of enlightenment or solutions. Surely no one can imagine that the American economy could function without Big Business in some form. Whatever the social advantages of building automobiles in back-alley garages, the economic costs would far outweigh them. And it is certainly a lot easier to watch a few hundred publicly held giant corporations than thousands of private and closely held small ones. Whether it was regulation or stupidity that destroyed the nation's railroads is immaterial. Competition would probably have been just as useless. Consumers certainly didn't benefit in the days before the Interstate Commerce Commission was established to protect the public or—as the revisionists would have us believe—the railroads.

Would the public interest have been better served if the Standard Oil Trust had been regulated instead of broken up? After all, it could have been argued at the time that Rockefeller didn't create the petroleum in the ground, that it was part of the national patrimony, and that it ought to belong to The People.

But that has little to do with the problems of scale that unquestionably affect the functioning of corporations and of the economy. Lately, it is being argued that small units, even within big companies, are the most effective means of protecting everybody's interests. Teams, tribes, families, whatever you want to call them, may well provide more manageable ways to organize industry than the units that are presently used. Prehistoric business organizations seem to have been based on how many people a man's voice could reach or how many people it took to stalk, kill, and carry home a mammoth. Business units today probably ought to be based on other criteria.

Whatever its flaws, Ling's Project Redeployment envisioned something like that. Other corporations have recently attempted the same method, more often for the financial rather than the organizational results. Armour & Company created a separate corporation for its Dial soap operation. Studebaker-Worthington Corporation has created several such redeployed corporations, most renowned of which is Andy Granatelli's STP Corporation. And Warner Communications, Inc., got out of the building-maintenance business that way too.

Whether smaller units will prevent the tragicomedies of a Penn Central collapse may not be as important as whether they will make corporate life more fulfilling and more productive for its participants. In fact, that may be the most crucial issue of all.

Social Insurance commission, for Mr. Dist was employed...
Manchester-Amsterdam Corporation, has erected a...
such telegraph corporations, First removed of ...
... to satisfy all Governors. And Walter Cannon,
... ... saddle horses
therein of.

Which ... ... with ... ... also of
... ... selected
... ... and your own
... ... July but may be the most
...

Index

Stanley H. Brown

Stanley H. Brown has observed business and finance as a reporter and as a participant. His articles have appeared in *Fortune, Esquire, Life, New York,* and *Business Week,* among many other publications.